GRANDMOTHERS OF THE LIGHT

GRANDMOTHERS OF THE LIGHT

A MEDICINE WOMAN'S SOURCEBOOK

PAULA GUNN ALLEN

BEACON PRESS · BOSTON

BEACON PRESS
25 Beacon Street
Boston, Massachusetts 02108

Beacon Press books
are published under the auspices of
the Unitarian Universalist Association of Congregations.

98 97 96 95 94 93 92 91   8 7 6 5 4 3 2 1

Text design by Christine Leonard Raquepaw
Illustrations by Patricia Amlin

Library of Congress Cataloging-in-Publication Data

Allen, Paula Gunn.
  Grandmothers of the light: a medicine woman's sourcebook / Paula Gunn
Allen.
    p. cm.
  Includes bibliographical references (p.).
  ISBN 0-8070-8102-7
  1. Indians of North America—Women. 2. Indians of North America—
Religion and mythology. 3. Indians of North America—Legends.
4. Goddess religion—North America. I. Title.
E98.W8A439 1991
398.2'08997—dc20   91-11367

TO MY FATHER

WHO TAUGHT ME TO LOVE TO TELL STORIES,

AND TO MY MOTHER

WHO TAUGHT ME TO LOVE THE EARTH

MAYA DAWN PRAYER

LOOK AT US, HEAR US!

HEART OF HEAVEN, HEART OF EARTH!

GIVE US OUR DESCENDANTS, OUR SUCCESSION,
AS LONG AS THE SUN SHALL MOVE!

MAY THE PEOPLE HAVE PEACE,
MAY THEY BE HAPPY!

GIVE US GOOD LIFE,
GRANDMOTHER OF THE SUN, GRANDMOTHER OF THE LIGHT,
LET THERE BE DAWN, LET THE LIGHT COME!

CONTENTS

ACKNOWLEDGMENTS

Writing is indeed a sullen art, and writing this book would have been much more difficult without the kind offices of many people. I owe thanks first to my parents, at whose home in Albuquerque I wrote some of this book, and whose cooking, company, interest, advice, spelling help, and inspiration were as always invaluable. My son Sulieman's interest, wise advice, and cheerfulness were welcome additions to this process—and on a couple of occasions at least were sorely needed. I am grateful to Mary Churchill for her valuable research assistance, Patricia Amlin for her wonderful illustrations and, with Sandy Boucher, for lively conversation and super motivation. Gabrielle Welford did my typing, Carolyn Dunn provided lasering and other important help. I thank also the folks at Beacon Press. To all of them, and the many people who have given me stories over the years, bless you.

PREFACE

The stories in this collection are gleaned from the vast oral tradition of Native America. I have collected only twenty-one, those that have served as my guides and as my sourcebook as I navigate the perilous journey along the path that marks the boundary between the mundane world and the world of spirit. Each of the stories in this collection contains information central to a woman's spiritual tradition. Garnered from each of the four directions and the seven directions, they span North America from the Yucatán to Washington State, from Arizona to New York State. Among them, stories about the Great Goddess in a variety of guises—Xmucané, Sky Woman, Six Killer (Sutalidihi), Thinking Woman, Changing Woman, White Shell Woman, Tonan, Scomalt, Selu, Iyatiku, Ic'sts'ity, and Nau'ts'ity—tell how the cosmos was formed and the ways of magic. These goddesses, possessed of creative power, bring forth through supernatural ritual a variety of beings that include the galaxy, the solar system, the planet with all of its resources and denizens, language, social systems, architecture, science, agriculture, hunting, and laws of action and interaction that secure harmony, balance, and propriety. Each of the accounts as I have rendered them are drawn from a variety of ethnographic and literary sources, from the oral tradition, and from direct communication from my own spirit guides.

I have divided the stories into three sections. The first is titled "Cosmogyny," a word you won't find in your dictionary yet. I built it by changing "cosmogony," which is defined as "a theory or story of the genesis and development of the universe, of the solar system, or of the earth-moon system, from the Greek *kosmogonía,* the creation of the world," to "cosmogyny" (Greek *gyné,* "woman"). For my purposes, "cosmogyny" is more accurate. It connotes an ordered universe arranged in harmony with gynocratic principles. As I have written elsewhere (see *The Sacred Hoop: Recovering the Feminine in American Indian Traditions*), many of the tribes of the western hemisphere were organized along gynocractic lines prior to contact with European patriarchies in the fifteenth century. In gynocratic tribal systems, egalitarianism, personal autonomy, and communal harmony were highly valued, rendering the good of the individual and the good of the society mutually reinforcing rather than divisive.

Tribal societies found a way to institutionalize both values, providing a coherent, harmonized, supportive social system that nurtured and protected, and was enriched by, individual life and creativity. It is from this long-disparaged social system that "man" has so recently "evolved," or so we are all too often told.

In concert with this complementariness of individual enterprise and social benefit, gynocratic social systems are defined by their bipolar structures. Institutions such as inside chief and outside chief, white district and red district, domestic and foreign bailiwicks of control and organization, systems where half the populace are born into one group while the rest are born into the other and where marriage is allowed only between persons who belong to different moieties all support and maintain a social balance that reflects the harmony desired within itself and between the mortal and supernatural realms. These structures also demonstrate tribal understanding of polarity as completion rather than adversariness or opposition.

Gynocentric communities tend to value peace, tolerance, sharing, relationship, balance, harmony, and just distribution of goods. A cosmogyny, then, is a spiritual system that is arranged in harmony with gynocratic values. To my mind the myths in the first section of this book show those values or principles as they operate in a sacred cosmogyny.

The first section, like the others, contains myths, not necessarily as recorded or told, but as I understand them. Rendering works from the tribal ritual tradition aims to enable readers unfamiliar with those traditions to comprehend implicit as well as explicit meanings of the myth. To facilitate this process, I wrote the narratives with as much an eye to the meaning implicit in the social, environmental, and ritual contexts in which the myths are embedded as to their purely metaphysical content. Short of glossing virtually every word—and even that wouldn't be particularly efficacious—rendering the myths in this larger context seemed the wisest course. There is still some glossing, of course, but I've tried to keep it to a minimum, putting En- glish "equivalents" after a local word, entering alternate possibilities in parentheses, or stringing several alternate words after the first.

A story must remain a story though, and such apparatus as glossaries, cultural notes, and alternate texts can become so cumbersome that readers may well find themselves lost in an intellectual wilderness, unable to discover the central point. In this book, the central issue is metaphysical. The stories, when used as ritual maps or guides, enable women to recover our path to the gynocosmos that is our spiritual home.

The stories contained in the section "Ritual Magic and Aspects of the Goddess," tell how supernaturals of long ago lived and worked, and tell also how certain rituals are performed and how and why they are suffused with power from the worlds of Great Mystery. In the stories contained in this section, the "long ago" dates anywhere from three hundred to fifteen hundred years ago (mundane time bearing only slight approximation to medicine time).

The Yellow Woman stories relate how ritual power is transmitted from the world of the supernaturals to that of the humans by way of the clan matron cum irriaku (sacred ear of corn), stolen from her place and, after marriage with the wind or sun, returned. "A Hot Time" recounts, in humorous tones suitable to its presentation as a modern story, how tiny, aged Grandmother Spider brought fire and light to her people. It is, among other things, a commentary on the supposed infirmities of old age. The story of Qiyo Kepe, the extraordinary medicine woman of the Lagunas, is a creation story in some of its particulars; it also speaks to the magical power of woman and water, and it contains a prophecy that, sadly, came all too true. White Buffalo Woman brought the religion of the Sacred Pipe to the Lakota people centuries ago, while Older Sister and Younger Sister, and Oshkikwe and Matchikwewis, wielded medicine power wisely if erratically among their respective peoples, defining in their lives and ways the particular energies that inform the Navajo and the anishinabeg. Clear Sky and Fair Maiden's story testifies to the great power women have possessed, and how that power when exercised within the life circumstances common to women everywhere can reshape (terraform) the earth. Each story in its own way demonstrates the uses of ritual magic for good and ill. Each contains warning for the apprentice shaman, and each illustrates complications and consequences attendant on the use of such power.

The stories gathered together in "Myth, Magic, and Medicine in the Modern World" testify to the pertinence today of the ways of power. They indicate that relations between human women and supernaturals are as viable and powerful in the present time as in days gone by.

Tonantzin, an aspect or guise of the goddess Tonan, appeared to Juan Diego on Tepeyac Hill shortly after the fall of Mexico to the conquistadors. The story of the pikiawish woman (a priestess) is quite recent, probably nineteenth century. The story of Shimana and the giantess, one my great-grandmother told me, must have taken place in the long ago, judging from the rocks that are the petrified remains of the giantess, but magic doesn't follow the laws of geology, so who knows? As I understand the story, it might have taken place no later than the eighteenth century. Historically, the pueblo of Laguna, near which the petrified remains rest, was founded (rather, refounded) in the mid eighteenth century by a group of largely Keres-speaking refugees of the earlier Spanish invasion and ensuing Pueblo war against the Spanish. That action (referred to by historians as the Pueblo Revolt) resulted in the eviction, for a time, of the Spaniard from Pueblo lands. Shimana must have had her adventure after the pueblo's refounding, which, for a people whose tenancy in this country dates back thousands of years, is recent indeed.

The last two stories, "Deer Woman" and "Someday Soon," are very recent. Indeed, they are present time, in whatever year you are reading this collection. Deer Woman is a contemporary part of native life in Oklahoma—and perhaps in the old homelands of the South as well—and Crystal Woman, in her communication device and intelligence-holding implement the crystal skull, continues to reside with her English-born keeper. Perhaps she can return to her ancient homelands in Belize someday soon, when wars and threats of war have become a thing of the past and her safety is assured.

These two stories focus on female supernaturals, demonstrating their continuing power. "Someday Soon" indicates the ongoing presence of the sons of the Goddesses in worldly and sacred affairs. These stories, along with the story of Xmucané in "Cosmogyny," are about very recent events and are told in such a way as to underscore both that fact and the actual "ordinariness" of events moved by medicine power. Many tribal people see the connection between this world and the other one as an actuality, even in the midst of modern environmental disaster and materialistic secularism. These stories bear witness to their ancient faith and let us know that the spirits, the supernaturals, goddesses, gods, and holy people still have a hand in human affairs.

THE LIVING REALITY OF THE MEDICINE WORLD

MYSTERIOUS BUT REAL POWER DWELLS
IN NATURE—IN MOUNTAINS, RIVERS, ROCKS,
EVEN PEBBLES. WHITE PEOPLE MAY
CONSIDER THEM INANIMATE OBJECTS, BUT TO
THE INDIAN, THEY ARE ENMESHED IN
THE WEB OF THE UNIVERSE, PULSATING WITH
LIFE AND POTENT WITH MEDICINE.

—ALFONSO ORTIZ AND RICHARD ERDOES
INTRODUCTION TO *AMERICAN INDIAN MYTHS*
AND LEGENDS

Stories connect us to the universe of medicine—of paranormal or sacred power. This universe of power referred to by the old people of some of the tribes as the Great Mystery is the universe that medicine people inhabit. Many of the stories contained in the oral tradition concern that universe, detailing its features: its terrain, the physical and psychical laws by which it operates, the orders and kinds of beings who dwell there, their ethos, ethics, and politics.

Thousands of stories collected from hundreds of tribes have been published in the United States. A sampling of them reveals a wealth of information about the universe of power. An apprentice medicine person becomes familiar with a number of these stories because they act as general guides to that special universe. They enable practitioners of the sacred to recognize where they are and how to function, the entities they might encounter, their names, personalities, and likely disposition toward them, the kinds of instruction they might gain from them, and how to explore the universe of power to gain greater paranormal knowledge and ability.

Every medicine path has its attendant stories, and medicine people, also known as shamans, wise women, conjurors, adepts, mages, practitioners, or masters, teach apprentices through story. Walking the path of power is not the same as therapy, university studies, or activities such as drumming, chanting, dancing, or pointing magic wands. To walk the medicine path is to live and think in ways that are almost but not quite entirely unlike our usual ways of living and thinking, and the stories show the right and wrong ways to proceed.

In *Pretty Shield: Medicine Woman of the Crows,* the ethnologist Frank Linderman recounts a story that Pretty Shield, the elderly Crow medicine woman he interviewed in the late 1920s, told him about chickadees. The story was prompted when he entered the house where their interviews were held whistling the chickadee's spring song. Pretty Shield asked him if he knew the chickadee well, and he said he did, though he soon discovered that he didn't know they had several tongues that grew or shortened by season, shaping the different songs they sang at different times in the year. Upon investigation, Linderman ascertained that Pretty Shield's anatomical information about the birds was accurate. In Pretty Shield's mind, anatomy was not the whole extent of Linderman's ignorance of chickadees—or of reality.

She told him about an occasion when she was very small. She and her grandmother were out together, and they came upon some chickadees. Because she knew that the birds had been stealing fat from the meat the women were drying on racks in the village, the child threw dry buffalo chips at them, causing them to scatter. Admonishing the child, the grandmother picked her up and carried her to a nearby bush where the chickadees had landed. Apologizing, the woman promised the birds that her granddaughter would never throw anything at them again. She asked the birds to forgive Pretty Shield because she didn't know any better.

Turning her attention to the child, she told her about her own grandmother, Seven-stars, and her encounter with the chickadees. Seven-stars' medicine was the chickadee, and the story was meant to educate Pretty Shield to the way of the nonphysical world, and to help her in her own future role as wise woman.

Seven-stars and her friend Buffalo-that-walks were tanning robes. A chickadee flew to a bush near Buffalo-that-walks and greeted her, saying that summer was near. Buffalo-that-walks, a short-tempered woman, became annoyed with the bird and ordered him away because she didn't want to be bothered by him. She got more irritated at his continued greeting and threw a stick at him. Dodging the stick adroitly, the bird addressed Buffalo-that-walks. He agreed that he was bothering her, but he added that he had news of something even more bothersome. Buffalo-that-walks would die that very night and be wrapped in the robe she and Seven-stars were softening. He had come to warn her, he said, only to be thanked by having a stick thrown at him.

The chickadee next flew to a bush near Seven-stars and greeted her in turn. Afraid of the bird's possible anger at having been abusively treated, Seven-stars picked up her little daughter and started toward her home, assuring the bird she meant it no harm.

Her friend tried to convince her to stay, but Seven-stars retreated into her lodge. Later Seven-stars brought some fat to a likely bush, and soon the chickadee came to pick at the food she had brought. He told her not to worry, his warning had been only for Buffalo-that-walks.

Buffalo-that-walks died that night and they wrapped her
body in the robe the women had finished that afternoon.

The following spring another chickadee came to Seven-stars
and told her to meet her at the creek. After purifying herself in
the sweatlodge and making herself ready to speak to the chickadee, Seven-stars met her. The chickadee told Seven-stars her
future and the importance of every creature tending to its own
work everyday, and then the chickadee flew higher and higher
into the air,

> Straight up it went, growing larger and larger and larger,
> until it was as large as a war-eagle. . . . "See," it called
> down, . . . "there is great power in little things." . . .
> The bird held a buffalo calf in each of its taloned feet. "I
> am a woman, as you are. Like you I have to work, and
> make the best of this life, . . . I am your friend, and yet
> to help you I must first hurt you. You will have three
> sons, but will lose two of them. One will live to be a
> good man. You must never eat eggs, never. Have you
> listened?" asked the bird, settling down again and grow-
> ing small.   (Linderman 1972, 155–60)

In medicine stories as in medicine life, it is always difficult to
discern where the mundane merges with the arcane. Their
boundaries are not sharp and distinct but barely discernible
and, for long stretches, invisible, like faint trails in the grass and
forests left by small creatures. So in all stories from the oral tradition, some of the details are from the world we know while
other details refer to the supernatural or nonphysical universe.
Many times the stories weave back and forth between the everyday and the supernatural without explanation, confusing the
logical mind and compelling linear thought processes to chase
their own tails, which of course is a major spiritual purpose behind the tradition's narrative form.

For those raised in the rationalist world where the linear
mind reigns supreme, distinctions are mighty. In it there is no
possibility—other than the imaginary or "psychological"—of
being seated amidst the rainbow. To rationalists, giants, like the
"little people" (and like their contemporary counterparts, the
extraterrestrials), are clearly figments of overactive imagina-
tions and "mass hysteria." Yet traditional people insist that con-

versations with animals and supernaturals—little people, giants, immortals or holy people—are actual. They tell many stories about women or men being changed into bears, about Antelope Spirit girls playing with a human girl, about Ogre Women— huge and terrifying—abducting children, about meetings with Thunderbirds, Dlanua, katsinas, goddesses, and gods.

Many native people both young and old admit to seeing what are referred to in some circles as extraterrestrials. White Bear Fredericks (who was the primary source of Frank Water's *The Book of the Hopi*) insists that the kachinas (katsinas) are extraterrestrials. Reservation people from all over the continent contend that they are often visited by the space ships or magical disks, tubes, ovals, and beings similar to those described in modern (white) UFO literature and news accounts around the world.

Are those who make such assertions pulling our collective leg? Are they caught in the sort of projective neurosis that some psychologists claim for writers and investigators of contemporary paranormal experiences with strange beings who do not obey this reality's physical laws? If so, there still remains the peculiar fact that their accounts often predate those of modern white Americans and are to be found in oral accounts deeply embedded in the community's ritual tradition.

Presumably, shamans are describing what they have seen, what they have experienced, or what they know to be the case even if they themselves have not experienced it, much as a San Franciscan who has never been to London speaks of it as though it really exists. True shamans live in a world that is alive with what is to rationalist sight unseen, a world pulsing with intelligence. To them the world Pretty Shield describes is the ordinary, the real world.

Interchanges with the supernaturals are the bedrock of native spirituality. What are called "myths" in the white world, and thought of as primitive spiritual stories that articulate psychological realities, are in the native world the accounts of actual interchanges. Pretty Shield is not indirectly articulating hidden and disowned psychological drives. She is telling about actual conversations with some chickadees. Accordingly the stories in this collection are not to be taken primarily as metaphors for instinctual patterns deeply embedded in the human psyche as Jung would have it, or as meta models of the structure of the

human mind as Lévi-Strauss claimed. Though they function on
a number of levels of significance, as is the nature of all literature, they are factual accounts. They inform consciousness and
direct awareness within as well as without, and they connect
with deep levels of being, not because the figures they tell
about are immaterial denizens of the shadowy world of the unconscious, but because the supernaturals live within the same
environs that humans occupy, and interchanges with them are
necessarily part of the fabric of human experience. The myths
detail those interchanges, as well as the lives and times of
supernaturals.

THE RITUAL TRADITION

Ideas about "*myth,*" as medicine stories are called, abound. The
word has not been used synonymously with irrational belief
until recently. Earlier it was synonymous with fable, from the
Greek, where it had the connotation of moral story. The Greek
terms it is derived from mean "one who is initiated" and "a
mystery, secret, a thing muttered," and are based on the Indo-
Germanic root *MU.* A related Greek term, "a sound of muttering," and its Latin forms, *muttum* or *mutum,* meaning "a slight
sound," both signify muttering and muteness. Thus, while the
Greek (*uú, uû*) has been translated as "fable," it is more accurately defined as "ritual verbalization," that is, a language construct that wields the power to transform something (or someone) from one state or condition to another.

In its action myth reflects implied belief, at least on the magician's part, else why would she or he be engaged in the process?
At base myth is a vehicle, a means of transmitting, of shaping
paranormal power and using it to effect desired ends.

Muttering, in which magicians frequently indulge, is an activity presently ascribed to the mad, the elderly, the female, and
the powerless. Muttering is a word that once signified whatever
mothering signified at the time the original root word was current—several thousand years ago. Even today, the German word
for "mother" is *mutter.* Myth and mother—both discredited in
the modern world—are nevertheless essential to the modern
world's existence. Certainly Jungians would argue that myth is

mother of life. Through it we contemplate the meaning of our existence and the significance of all our relationships, not only with human beings but with all varieties of people, animals, spirits or immortals, and divinities. Through it we capture intimations of the vastness that lies beyond linear understanding, ungraspable unless mother myth informs it with life.

Myth and ritual are wings of the bird of spirit, two tiers in the four-layered headdress of American Goddesses. The one contains knowledge of language while the other embodies that knowledge in action. Myth, you might say, is noun, while ritual is verb. Myth is weft, ritual is woof. The true shaman weaves them together in harmony with all that is to create a tapestry that furthers wholeness and enriches life for all beings. Myth and ritual are twin beings; together they function to aid the practitioner in entering and using the life-generating forces contained in and by the Great Mystery.

The ritual tradition is nothing new. It is at least as ancient as humankind, reaching back into the distances of human tenancy on the planet hundreds of thousands of years. The ritual tradition is the great body of articulated experiential knowledge that deals with the features of the universe of power. It is the point of entry into that universe, and it contains both stories (myth) and practice (ritual). Myths can be seen as reports or recipes for ritual practice, and rituals can be seen as enactments of myth. But either seen separately from the other is seen falsely.

In the ritual tradition, wholeness is the rule; in it chronology ceases to function, though both temporality and duration play a fundamental role. Ritual affirms an order of reality that secular materialists, logical positivists, and deconstructionist postmodernists believe to be false, imaginary, primitive, or impossible. Yet within the workings of ritual, the impossible becomes the very probable, the imaginary becomes the factual, the primitive becomes the sophisticated, and the false becomes the actuality. Within the ritual universe the entire matter of true/false is turned on its head, and the dancers bring down the rain. The ritual dancer with the power to transform dry air into rain-bearing clouds is similar to the card called "the World" in the Tarot deck, to Shiva of the Hindu Way, to the Dancer of the African mysteries. Rain Dancer is a key, a point of entry into the mystery, the myth-matter-mother of arcane reality.

The ritual tradition is of ancient and worldwide standing, a

living tradition even now, despite the horsemen of the Apocalypse who thunder through its environs attempting by war,
plague, famine, and pestilence to destroy it. Why is it that the
United States armed forces have a bombing range on a Hawai-
ian island once filled with temples and sacred sites? Do they seriously believe that bombs can destroy the gods? I hope they
will soon recognize that what destroys can only destroy itself;
what nurtures and nourishes can only flourish. Over time, out
of time, the law of balance will always function. Even bombs
can't weaken the power of the ritual tradition because its
strength is in its truth. It has failed only where it has given way
to destructiveness and deceit. The oral tradition, wedded inextricably to the ritual tradition, records even these lapses, main-
taining its life by adherence to veracity.

In this time, pagan ritual reemerges more beautiful, more
whole, and more powerful than before. The sacred tradition is
the changing fourfold form of the Goddess: Maiden, Mother,
Crone, and Mystery. In past ages we have cycled through each
of these over and over. In this age we turn again to recognize
her heart as our own.

There are many Ways we can walk to greet our returning Beloved, many ways but all are the same Way. The Tao, the Sufi
Path, the Way of the Madonna, the Quest for the Grail, the
Good Red Road. All lead into the Heart of the Great Mystery,
the Heart of Heaven that is at one and the same time the Heart
of Earth. Spiritual discipline is the hallmark of any ritual path.
The discipline required of those who would walk the medicine
path is referred to in the oral tradition, some of it lodged in one
story, some in another. As one becomes familiar with the oral
tradition and the ways of the People, one learns how to "walk
in a sacred manner" as the Lakota put it, "walk in beauty" as
the Diné say, or "walk in balance" as the Keres term it. One
learns to make of spiritual discipline a Way of life.

THE SEVEN WAYS OF THE MEDICINE WOMAN

Once upon a time (and even yet), the Mothers and the Grandmothers formed a vital and immediate part of the lives of Americans. In the old times, every inhabitant of this Turtle Island, as
some Native Americans refer to North America, knew about

supernaturals who were female in gender, varied in temperament and potency, and who lived among and near humankind.

The disciplines of the medicine woman's way include the ways of all women as well as those of advanced practitioners or specialists in the medicine path. These ways include the way of the daughter, the way of the householder, the way of the mother, the way of the gatherer, the way of the ritualist, the way of the teacher, and the way of the wise woman. These are disciplines that accord with the age of the aspirant and her duties within the sacred wheel of life and lead one to ever more specialized, more advanced modes of the work. They involve a commitment to one's family and community that is the primary requisite for success along the medicine path. These seven ways give the true shaman the force, connectedness, and discipline she needs to channel the power of the Mysterious without harm to herself or others. They help her master humility, orderliness, respect, dignity, and caring, and give her a strong sense of herself in her inner and outer aspects.

The Way of the Daughter: The way of the daughter covers the period from birth to young womanhood. In that passage the prime task is learning, and all her time is spent preparing to gather experience. She is learning to live in the normal world, to understand its workings and those of her physical self. Unawakened mentally and emotionally, as well as physically dependent, she simply takes in what stimuli impinge on her. If those influences are structured, reasoned, emotionally balanced, physically and psychically appropriate and demanding, she will develop the skills, balance, respect, dignity, and self-reliance she will need to walk the path of life in harmony with all that is.

A traditional woman receives her first welcome into women's mysteries with menarche. But this time is one of limitation and a great deal of psychic discomfort because, while she is instructed in her duties as a grown woman, she is mostly kept ignorant of the arcane matters that govern the new rules she must follow.

The Way of the Householder: The way of the householder concerns the years when a young woman develops self-reliance, learning to manage a life independent of adult command. In this period she learns through experience and develops inde-

pendent thinking and emotional, self-supporting, and relationship skills. She takes charge of her personal environment and
social life and begins to acquire her own spirituality and explore
her sexuality. She learns who she is as she uses the training she
acquired during the way of the daughter. In the modern world,
this period covers roughly the years from age seventeen or eigh-
teen to the late twenties and may overlap with the way of the
mother. In earlier times, it ran from around age twelve or thirteen to the late teens (as it still does for many women in modern America).

The Way of the Mother: From a medicine point of view, the
most important event in a woman's life is the birth of a child,
because that birth allows a woman to enter fully into the woman's spiritual community. Heretofore she could participate in
various ceremonies in various capacities, but she was largely
excluded from women's secrets, most of which refer to the
woman's medicine way. Having traversed the borderland between life and death in childbirth, she is welcomed into the
community of matrons and her true instruction in the woman's
way begins. In this period she learns the discipline of sacrifice:
her body, her time, her nutrients, her psyche, her knowledge,
her skills, her social life, her economic capacities, her relationships, and her spiritual knowledge and values all are called into
the service of her children. This passage, ambivalent at best,
pushes her to reach far beyond whatever limits she thought she
labored within, making her stronger and more able to follow
the rigors of the path of a shaman when the proper time for that
specialization arises.

During these years, she learns to manage her world. She
must master a complex network of skills, meet competing and
conflicting demands, and she must do this while contributing
to her community through her labor and her participation,
learning as she does so what her limits, needs, and proclivities
are and how to harmonize them with the external demands
placed upon her, achieving the powerful balance between inner
and outer reality that sacred ritual depends on.

At this time, her spiritual life takes root and flowers. She
continues to walk the way of the daughter and the way of the
householder while increasing her involvement in the way of the
gatherer and becoming proficient in the way of ritual.

The Way of the Gatherer and the Way of the Ritualist: The way of the gatherer, like the way of the ritualist, is as ancient as the human race. Women have walked both paths over generations. Gathering is a discipline that requires respect on a primary spiritual level. It develops refined powers of observation and discernment in the ritualist and extensive knowledge of seasons, weather, astronomy, and healing, conferring on its devotee a degree of mental sophistication that rivals that of physicians, scientists, computer experts, or metaphysicians.

Armed only with a digging stick (which is the mother of tools), knowledge, intuition (inner knowledge), and prayer, the shaman goes forth to harvest a multitude of plant and animal substances for use in healing, magic, cooking, hygiene, and cosmetics. The gatherer must know where to find what she needs and when, the proper methods of culling, harvesting, preserving, and preparing the substances, the variety of ways to use them and all the conditions under which their use may be efficacious or harmful. Native healers don't apply the same medication or process to the same physical symptoms in different patients because they treat entire entities, whole persons, not symptoms. Doing medicine this way entails knowing not only the uses of a host of substances preserved and prepared in a number of ways, but also the patients, their families, their spiritual, mental, social, emotional, environmental, and physical condition, and how they will combine in the healing process. Healers also must know the spiritual causes of diseases, the spiritual condition of patients, and the spirit that informs each plant and animal entity they use in treatment. Each of these entities must be addressed and given a fair exchange for the gift they are giving to the healer so that their approval and satisfaction will aid in the healing. Similar considerations apply to other uses of plants and other entities, including some mineral forms such as clay for pottery, cosmetic, and medicinal use, rock, sand, crystals, and stones used in ritual ways.

This portion of a medicine woman's work is fraught with spiritual tension, but not more intensely than her childbearing, particularly the first pregnancy and labor; her moons, especially those before the first birth; and her householding responsibilities, especially as they concern respect for self and others, human and nonhuman alike, and the proper treatment and use of fire, water, earth, plants used for clothing and decoration, wood, stone, and food substances. In all of these areas, as much careful attention must be paid to the spiritual or psychic level as to the social, physiological, or psychological because in them one is especially close to the realm of Great Mysterious. A medicine woman's failure to remain in a balanced, responsive, aware condition can spell disaster not only to herself but to many members of her community, for the power of woman is great, and the more discipline and devotion she renders, the greater her power grows.

But power is not necessarily pleasurable to her; quite the contrary, in most cases. Those who essay to walk the medicine path hoping for a more pleasurable existence are bound to be disappointed. Each increment of power one gains along the path of power requires sacrifice and exacts its toll of suffering and pain. In the universe of power everything has its price. If the practitioner is unable or unwilling to make a conscious sacrifice of ego, time, personal inclination, or the fancies dearest to her heart, the powers she seeks will turn on her and on her family and community. She has to be willing to forego pleasures when necessary and put herself in whatever danger and inconvenience her spirit guides require of her. She must be disciplined and committed enough to follow the requirements of her path regardless of the pain it causes her.

It is not uncommon for medicine women to suffer frequent periods of illness or social isolation. Many traditional medicine women are prohibited by their guides or the spiritual tradition they follow from eating certain foods or engaging in certain activities. As often as not, medicine women find themselves taking jobs for which they feel unequipped or have little affinity—or even that they actively dislike—because their medicine guides have instructed them to do so. Being a medicine woman means doing many things one would rather not do because one's path goes that way and not some other way that might be personally preferable.

Women who walk the path of the gatherer and the path of the ritualist cannot afford to be passive; they must of necessity be inwardly secure, deeply caring of planetary spiritual life at all levels, committed to their work and their community's greater good, and always willing to follow the dictates of their guides.

The basic spiritual law women on the medicine path learn is that the would-be shaman gives and gives long before she takes even a small bit, and what she takes she uses, through hard work and real drudgery, to further and nurture life.

The Way of the Teacher: Learning, experiencing, nurturing, working, apprenticing—the developing shaman in time reaches the age where she becomes a transmitter of spiritual and social wisdom. At this stage she becomes a teacher, sharing the stories, the skills, and the wisdom she has gained over the years. By now menopausal, she has ripened and deepened like fruit, like forests. If she has walked the path in balance over the preceding decades, she will not become unbalanced as more and more Great Mysterious is revealed to her. She will enter the realm of the sacred as a mature, fully participating member of the cosmic community, a right she has earned through sacrifice, pain, labor, and devotion.

At this point in her journey, she may choose seclusion, even isolation, should her guides indicate to her that this is the proper way for her. Performing rituals, teaching the mysteries, healing, meditating, spending most of her time with plants, nonhuman creatures of all orders, bringing rain, tending the wilderness, gardening, gathering, muttering, mumbling, and myth-making, she might become what the white world recognizes as a medicine woman—though there are other, less obvious modes of being one.

She might choose politics, public service, or a profession as her arena of practice. Becoming a leader, she will advocate a spiritually sane way of practicing whatever profession she follows. Or she might be a grandmother, continuing to raise her grandchildren, nieces, nephews, great-grandchildren, or other children who would otherwise not have a home.

How the practicing medicine woman chooses to focus her paranormal awareness and ability will depend on the nature of the spiritual work she has been guided to do. Much of the teaching she does during this stage is through example, regardless of her more obvious occupation: she will serve as a model for younger women on the path, and her presence, her essence, will enter into the life of her community to enrich and revitalize it.

The Way of the Wise Woman: At last, having reached the fullness of her age, the shaman will enter her period of mastery, having developed true wisdom through gathering information

and experience and applying them in every area of her life. By this time the sense of balance that characterizes the universe is deeply a part of her. Likely, her sense of humor is at its peak, and her ability to discern patterns underlying human and natural activities is so complete she may seem almost simpleminded or "primitive." Walking the way of the wise woman, she has fully entered her power in the heart of Great Mysterious and taken up her share of the great work of furthering planetary and cosmological well-being. She is in direct contact with supernatural and natural entities, able to accept their instruction, follow their directives, generate and coordinate inter- and intra-species events. The sphere of her work has broadened far beyond that of her personal, private self and of her familiar group; her community extends to the stars. In terms of the medicine dance of the anishinabeg, she is *manido,* more of the realm of mystery than of mortal flesh. She is *wakan* (Lakota), filled with and able to manipulate *orenda* (Haudinashone), *iyañi* (Keres), the spirit-force of the cosmos, the true—that is, the sacred—universe. She has become a sacred being, something on the order of Crystal Woman before crystallization, or White Buffalo Woman, for she has transcended the limits of the mundane world and walks in the ways of beauty (*hózhó,* Navajo), balance (*iyañi,* Keres), and spiritual power (*orenda,* Haudinashone). She has walked the Sacred Hoop, the medicine wheel of spiritual life, and she is more than complete.

THE UNIVERSE OF POWER

The basic nature of the universe of power is magic: the name given to the practice of a mage. *Ma* (the *m*-syllable again) comes in variants: *ma, mo, mu, mi,* and *me.* All are versions of the same morpheme (syllable with meaning) and refer one way or another to the Great Mother or Great Goddess of the Indo-Germanic tradition. The Goddess, named variously Ma, Maa, or Maat, was in time demoted and even changed gender over the ages, but she is known even today in her identity as Tiamat, Aphrodite, Ishtar, Astarte, and Isis. She can be discerned in words such as mother, mom, mammary, mutter, *immic, om* (a cognate of *mo*) and related concepts such as *mer, mal,* and *mar,* which refer respectively to the sea (modern French), evil or disorder (modern Spanish and English as a prefix), and light or nobility (modern Arabic, meaning "lord"). *Ma* is the essential female syllable, *om* being its masculine variant, and at its root designates mystery, mother, and myth, all feminine forces or powers.

Ge, another interesting fragment, one from which words such as geology, geomancy, geas, geometry, geophysics, and geopolitical derive, is part of the name of Gea or Gaia—pronounced *gay-ah,* as it is presently spelled in English (does spelling something enchant it?)—and refers to those of the Great Goddesses' powers that emanate from her planetary body. Thus a mage (ma-ge) is one who utilizes the paranormal or supernatural powers of MA in both her spiritual—that is, rarefied and light (not dense)—and planetary *Ge* bodies. A mage is a shaman or medicine person who specializes in the control and application of the two aspects of the multitudinous Great Goddess(es). Magic refers to the ritual activities of a mage, who in later times is referred to as a "magician," or one who practices magic. A shaman (the word comes from the Turkish) is a person who exercises power within the rubric of the universe of power, engaging in ritual actions that result in transformations. These include weather changes (rain bringing, for instance), physiological changes in both humans and animals (healing), bodily changes (metamorphosis or change from one physical body to another, practiced by nefarious rather than beneficial practitioners), soul keeping, bi-location (being in two physical places at one time), second sight (various kinds and degrees of clairvoyance, clairsentience, and clairaudience), telekinesis (transporting objects by nonphysical means), teleportation (transporting oneself by nonphysical means), earth renewal, terraforming (making mountains, rivers, drainage plains, and other geological features), and other activities too numerous to mention here.

At this level, practitioners function by thought, using language, movement, sound, painting, drawing, mimetics, gestures, dress, laughter, shock, herbs, minerals, and repetitive devices as foci for that thought. Most of all, they use their ability to deal adeptly in supernatural realms to achieve their objectives, depending on long training, familiarity with Great Mysterious and its (their) ways, and contacts among the supernaturals. The

ability to dance, drum, chant dramatically, or alter consciousness so that one can see amazing things are of little use without
the aid and protection of some helpers from the other side.

The universe of power where shamans spend most of their
time bears slight resemblance to the mundane world. There

time works quite differently. Synchronism and achronism are
the rule, and much chronological time can pass in the ordinary
world while only moments or hours pass in the universe of
power. Conversely, much time can pass there with only moments or hours passing here. Subjective time seems approximately the same in both worlds, largely because we take ourselves—our basic sense of how things go—with us wherever
we are. Any sense of time distortion we might experience there
(or here) is temporary, a function of suddenly increased or de-
creased energy in our system and of disorientation in a different
reality from the one we've adjusted to.

The plasticity of time in the universe of power is related to
the laws of movement and the relative impermeability and per-
meability of matter. In the ordinary world, we get from one
place to another by walking, running, riding on animals, or
riding or flying in machines. We are presently able to move signals through the air or subspace by way of microwaves, radio
waves, or light waves, but we cannot transport objects in ways
other than those we use to transport ourselves. But in the universe of power we, our signals, and our objects can traverse
great or small distances with the speed at which a message can
presently be sent over a fax machine. Objects and subjects alike
can be transported through solid matter—windows, walls,
stone buttresses, or mountains—and they are as independent of
gravity as of other physical constraints. And while in some circumstances solid matter becomes as thin and as penetrable as
air, on other occasions it becomes so dense a projectile cannot
pierce it. Thus the Lakota medicine warrior Crazy Horse could
not be killed by bullets. They simply couldn't pierce his body.
Unfortunately, the same was not true for blades, and Crazy
Horse was killed when treachery combined with knives.

The medicine or "sacred" states of fragility and impermeability are evidenced in other ways: geological structures such as
hills, rivers, mountains, deserts, and plains have a disconcerting
impermanence, forming or dissolving without warning in an

instant's time. Humans, beasts, and plants are equally liable to sudden transformation in appearance or age and can undergo rapid shifts in density, location, visibility, and speed of movement, as do weather and astrophysical phenomena.

Travel and distance in the realm of Great Mysterious are peculiar as well. Moving from one place to another is as much a matter of changing one's psychological (or psychical) space as of changing one's physical place, and the traversing of long distances instantaneously is no less commonplace. However, a great deal of self-discipline is required to alter internal states of consciousness before one can travel without the assistance of the supernaturals, and a certain amount of spiritual preparation is necessary in any case.

There are a number of physical locations on the earth we usually inhabit that serve as crossing points between the mundane and supernatural planes of existence. Somewhere in the lands of the Pueblos, for example, there is a path that leads right next to Spider Woman's nest. On occasion, initiates take that path to her dwelling to gain her assistance. Anyone who enters her province becomes absolutely subject to her and if untrained, that is, if unfamiliar with the laws that govern her realm as well as with her ways, is not likely to return to the mortal realm. However, an initiate can gain great benefits from her, including the help of her grandson Spider or her other grandsons, the Little War Twins. Among those benefits is the ability to travel rapidly from one place to another, especially from the mundane world to the world of the supernaturals. Sometimes she arranges transport by way of "magic arrows," sometimes by agency of the white material that spiders excrete for wrapping their catch.

A shaman may travel to other worlds and other dimensions in locations that are to all appearances local, albeit distant, such as a mountaintop, deep in a canyon, far up- or downriver, and so on. But as the oral tradition assures us over and over, these various familiar locations are the same only in the metaphysical sense where, in essence, all geological and natural phenomena permanently dwell. It is this world of essence, this essential place, that myth and ritual refer to and connect us with. The universe of power is the universe of essence, and while its laws underpin the mundane world modern people inhabit, the ability to use those laws in modern reality depends on the strength of one's connection to the fundament. It is not that the laws of the universe of power do not function in ordinary life but rather that they only function for those who are reared in a ritual sys- tem and trained to utilize its processes and procedures. Travel to and in the universe of power thus is more a matter of psychic travel than of physical movement. "Dialing" different gestalts or clusters of awareness results in becoming conscious in another world.

I use the word "dialing" advisedly; the procedure is quite analogous to selecting a radio station or television channel, or using a rotary telephone. Although such a modern term may seem out of place in the context of the sacred, the apparent dissonance is more a function of our stereotypes or conditioning than of shamanism itself. Modern shamans use modern methods, as did those of the past, but what was current or modern three centuries ago is of course different from the "modern" of today.

Thus a contemporary shaman can go from sitting in her living room watching a sit-com on television to walking along a rocky road in a far and unfamiliar terrain instantaneously, simply by dialing another sense of being—a complex confluence that includes sense of self, environment, expectations, beliefs, perceptions, emotions, ideals, ideas, and subvocalizations, a gestalt that conforms to the alternate circumstances.

Some contemporary medicine people can bi-locate, that is, be in two places at once, be in one place one moment and at another quite distant a moment later, make brooms dance to their tune for the entertainment of grandchildren, or transport an object like a saddle or a stick from some distance. Some medicine people can walk under the sea by lifting it as though it were a blanket and walking under it, go to the moon and bring back moonrocks, visit other planets such as Mars or Saturn and make detailed reports on their features that are, years later, validated by scientific explorations.

States of awareness are key in shamanic practice. Learning the possible states of awareness forms a large part of shamanic training, while learning how to achieve specific states chosen for the completion of a specific task makes up much of the rest. Neither is easy, though familiarity with a ritual tradition helps greatly. It happens that much of the published lore presently concerning shamanic practice is derived from male traditions, though sometimes pronouns are changed to suggest—incorrectly—that gender is not at issue in the practice. The practice for women differs in many particulars from that for men, partly because of the historical differences between women's and men's life circumstances, but more because of the differences in male and female psychic structures. The psychic differences are reflected in hormonal and other physiological variances, though it is important to recognize that the physical only reflects the essential. Thus, as psychic states are central to shamanic practice, the procedures for feminine psyches necessarily differ from those devoted to training and facilitating masculine psyches in magical work.

There are numerous kinds of beings who regularly inhabit the universe of power. Many have been depicted on rock drawings scattered about the Americas. Some possess a human form; others look more like geometric figures. There are beings with wings, beaks, horns, tails, three fingers, snouts, scales, feathers, talons, claws, lots of eyes, no eyes, many arms, more than two legs—in short, beings of greater variety than we ordinarily imagine. Some are what in the mundane sphere are thought of as inanimate forces, such as thunder, rain, blizzards, hurricanes, tornadoes, while still others are what appear ordinarily as mountains, rivers, lakes, trees, rocks, plants, animals, and even buildings.

Many are reasonably friendly or neutral toward humans who venture among them, but many are unfriendly indeed. Much ritual is devoted to courting the one and avoiding or protecting against the other. Still others are so vast that humans come no more to their attention than microscopic creatures come to ours, and with about as much opportunity to communicate with or influence them.

FEMALE SUPERNATURALS

Women are far more likely to encounter supernaturals of the female persuasion, an occurrence that demands familiarity with the women's shamanic tradition. Happily, the oral tradition is

replete with narratives and rituals that concern themselves with
female supernaturals of various kinds, and girls raised in tribal
traditions become acquainted with these from an early age. It is
to an investigation of myths from the women's shamanic tradition that this volume is devoted, and a number of female entities are introduced in these stories. The orders of being they
occupy range from goddess to medicine woman. All are denizens of the universe of power. All live and function in the realm
of the Great Mystery. And all possess a certain level of compe-
tency in that functioning. However, they are of different orders
of being, you might say of different species, or even different
kingdoms in the biological sense.

While this brief discussion cannot provide an exhaustive tax-
onomy of supernatural beings, suffice it to say that among the
orders of being who make up the universe of power, goddesses
possess powers far beyond those of shamans, while supernaturals are an order of being somewhere between shamans and
gods. For the most part, supernaturals, also referred to as holy
people, persons, "katsinas" (or kachinas), manido, or spirits,
are seldom human in origin, though some, like Oshkikwe and
Matchikwewis are half human. Occasionally humans are transformed into supernaturals, at which time they cease to be human, of course.

Supernaturals are widely thought to have been created by the
Goddesses in their creation ritual. Exactly how supernaturals
and humans procreate, being of different "species," is not spelled
out—even the laws of reproduction and genetics take on a peculiar cast in the other reality. Interbreeding is not terrifically
common between the realms, but it is not unheard of, as worldwide mythologies attest.

Medicine people are truly citizens of two worlds, and those
who continue to walk the path of medicine power learn to keep
their balance in both the ordinary and the non-ordinary worlds,
giving to each what is necessary and sufficient. Great medicine
people perform their tasks in each elegantly.

Much of the oral tradition is concerned with the universe of
power and the interface between that universe and the world of
mortals. Cautionary, prescriptive, descriptive, metaphysical,
and mythic narratives tell us how we must behave as individuals and as societies in the face of the Great Mysterious that sur-

rounds and fills all that is. The fact that tribal civilizations live in constant awareness of their relation to the Vast Mysterious (the *nagual,* or shadow world) accounts for most of their institutions, mores, customs, and attitudes.

The oral tradition of all tribal people—whether Native American, Hindu, Greek, Celtic, Norse, Samois, Roman, or Papuan— is best seen as psychic literature. It cannot adequately be comprehended except in terms of the universe of power, for it speaks to the relationships among humans, animals of all kingdoms, supernaturals, and deities in a landscape that is subject to influences of thought, intention, will, emotion, and choice under the kinds of conditions described above. It is realism of a kind that refers, not to the psychological, political, economic, or historical world of modern literature, but to the world of the sacred or the paranormal. It is the literature of vision, not in the sense of "unreal" or "hoped-for," but in the sense of known directly, "apperceived" in ways other than by the physical senses. It narrates events in the plane of the super-real or the meta-real, the plane that is the source of the psychological, political, economic, and historical. Its reality is social, as is the reality mainstream literature depicts, but the social system to which mainstream literature refers is sociological. In that sense, the reality articulated by mythic literature is spiritual, but it is no less true than any other reality for that. Nor is spiritual meant in the same sense as religious, for the plane of spirit may or may not be touched by religious activity.

Tribal thought is essentially mystical and psychic. Its distinguishing characteristic is a kind of magicalness—not the childish sort imagined by collectors of tribal "lore," as they are pleased to call it, but rather an enduring sense of the fluidity and malleability, the fragility and plasticity of the creative universe in which we live and dwell and have our being.

Tribal people perceive things as alive, intelligent, and self-aware; they know that living things are subject to processes of growth and change necessary to their aliveness. Since all that exists is alive and must change as a basic law of existence, all existence can be manipulated under certain conditions and according to certain laws. The particular conditions and laws that govern these controlled changes are contained in sacred myths, that is, myths that derive from and inherently connect with

Great Mysterious. A medicine person must therefore be cog-
nizant of those sacred myths that relate to her specific practice
so that she can know the laws and conditions under which her
sacred work proceeds.

The symbolism contained in tribal ceremonial literature is
not symbolic in the Western literary or psychoanalytic sense;
"corn" is not shorthand for dinner; "lake" does not allude to
economic prosperity via fishing industries; "red" as used by the
Lakota in reference to ceremonialism doesn't stand for "sacred"
or "earth," but is the quality of a being the color of whom
when perceived in a sacred manner is red. Red in this context is
a psychic rather than a physical condition. Sacred red is not a
consequence of light refraction and excitation of special or-
acular cells. It is a condition inherent in certain beings who are
of a certain order and possessed of a specific kind of power.

As the Western metaphysician Madam H. P. Blavatsky com-
mented, the physical is not a principle. Or as the Lakota shaman Lame Deer phrased it in his memoir *Lame Deer: Seeker of
Visions* (1972), the physical aspect of existence is only represen-
tative of what is real. Both are suggesting that what modern
people call material or physical reality is a symbol or reflection
of the real. The tribal philosopher and metaphysician Plato said
approximately the same thing. Lame Deer goes on:

> We Sioux spend a lot of time thinking about everyday
> things which in our mind are mixed up with the spiri-
> tual. We see in the world around us many symbols that
> teach us the meaning of life. . . . We Indians live in a
> world of symbols and images where the spiritual and
> the commonplace are one. To us [symbols] are part of
> nature, part of ourselves, even little insects like ants and
> grasshoppers. We try to understand them not with the
> head but with the heart, and we need no more than a
> hint to give us the meaning.   (Lame Deer 1972, 109)

What to the uninitiated might seem like a symbol, that is, of a
way of not talking directly about something, is to the knowl-
edgeable a way of denoting a sacred phenomenon or fact. Sacred facts are verifiable, replicable, and for that matter quantifi-
able, and the manipulation of certain sacred symbols results in

particular, predictable transformations much as the manipulation of certain physical phenomena results in the predictable transformation of roast beef or corn soup.

This brings me to the matter of the relation of ritual magic to women's lives and especially to the women's tradition: magic, as the word itself implies (ma-ge[c]), is primarily a womanly enterprise. Its closest kin are the domestic arts, and its chosen implements and procedures most closely resemble those developed by women to facilitate their tasks. It should surprise no one that the modern age, from its beginnings in the Renaissance to the present, has become more and more intensely patriarchal over the world and thus more and more thoroughly separated from womanity, from ritual magic, from tribal social systems, and from harmony with the earth. The four have ever danced together: woman, magic, tribes, and earth, and the dance goes on, even yet. Indeed, as the last stories in this collection demonstrate, the dance grows strong again.

COSMOGYNY: THE GODDESSES

The Great Goddess has for one reason and another (all of them *tri*vial, if feminine spiritualists will excuse the pun) endured a cultural and perhaps metaphysical absence of some years. The period of time during which she has been hidden (like the moon during one phase) varies. In some planetary regions the duration of her disappearance is as long as four thousand years, while in others, such as the Zuñi, Hopi, and Keres Pueblo tribes of the American Southwest, her dark phase is very recent, perhaps twenty or fewer years. There are even traditions where she has recently reemerged very powerfully.

It may be that the Navajo, given their peculiar history, have been the earliest to signal the Goddess's return, for they entered the world of the Pueblo around the twelfth century as Christians tell time, and in the eight hundred years since they began arriving in her country they seem to have gained a growing sense of her centrality to true spiritual life. Perhaps while much of the world was turning to a patriarchal (or, in the Americas, an avuncular) paradigm, the Diné had already passed through it. Maybe that is why they left the far north (Alaska) and moved south—to claim the Goddess as she claimed them.

The goddesses the Navajo have claimed are the multiple goddesses of the Pueblo—the Anasazi as they are called, the elders. These supernaturals include Thinking Woman, also known as Spider Woman; Nau'ts'ity and Ic'sts'ity, or Iyatiku; and the Little War Twins, Masewe and Oyoyowe. In the Navajo pantheon these beings become Spider Woman, goddess of weaving at which the Diné excel, and Changing Woman and White Shell Woman, along with their sons Monster Slayer and Child of Water. Nor is this pantheon of goddesses and supernatural brothers unique to the Southwest. They form the center and foundations of the gynocentric universe throughout the Americas. In this section you will read stories that reveal this ancient ritual matrix.

Thinking Woman (S'ts'tsi'naku as nearly as I can render it, or Susisstinaku, Tse-che-nako, Ts'its'naku, as it is spelled in various sources) is the Great Goddess of the Keres Indians, of whom my tribe, the Laguna Pueblo Tribe, is one. Usually referred to as Spider Woman or Grandmother Spider, she is, as my own great-grandmother told me, a being "like a fairy" who is possessed of magical power. I used to imagine her as Queen Mab because of Grandma Gunn's characterization, but small and wrinkled, with white hair and deep dark eyes that were filled with fathomless wisdom. Perhaps she somewhat resembled my grandmother, who was in her eighties when I was very small, but as I recall the image I had in my mind and compare it to Grandma Gunn's picture, the resemblance is of the generic sort; in particulars, such as shape of eye, posture, coloring, and length of hair, they are no more alike than any two women of advanced years might be. I knew as a child that she lived in the night sky and was somehow present in the vast, deep brilliance of the stars that shone in full dusty beauty over my rural New Mexican backyard. It was more that she was the night sky, and I felt safe and watched over as the great stars wheeled overhead as I slept. I don't know that anyone human told me that about her, but perhaps when I was very small indeed someone did.

Grandmother Spider, Thought Woman, thought the earth, the sky, the galaxy, and all that is into being, and as she thinks, so we are. She sang the divine sisters Nau'ts'ity and Ic'sts'ity (or Naotsete and Uretsete, or various other spellings and pronunciations, depending on the Keres tribal dialect and transcription being used) into being out of her medicine pouch or bundle, and they in turn sang from their bundles the firmament, the land, the seas, the people, the katsina, the gods, the plants, animals, minerals, language, writing, mathematics, architecture, the Pueblo social system, and every other thing you can imagine in this our world. The Keres story is of interest not only because it is my familial story of origin on the Indian side, but because it bears uncanny resemblance to my familial stories of origin on the Scots and Lebanese sides (yes, I have three sides, or actually four, but the last is a mystery).

She shows up among most of the Pueblos, existing in the ceremonial life of the Zuñi and the Hopi, and she is also present in the godly society of the Navajo, who take much of their spiritual intelligence from the Pueblo, their near neighbors. The borrowing is probably due to their proximity, centuries of intermarriage, and most important, their tenancy on the land that is her earthly center in the Americas. Her sister-creatrixes, Nau'ts'ity and Ic'sts'ity, become in the Navajo pantheon Changing Woman and White Shell Woman, who like their prototypes give birth to the sacred twins (who are a kind of cousin among the Navajo

while they are siblings among the Pueblo). The twins, Masewe
and Oyoyowe among the Keres, are known as Monster Slayer
and Child of Water among the Diné. Their analogs, Older
Sister and Younger Sister, bring the major ceremonials to the
people. Other traditions included in this collection also name the
sacred twins: they are female among the anishinabeg (Ojibwa,
Chippewa), sisters named Oshkikwe and Matchikwewis. The
Cherokee know them as Wild Boy (or Clotted Blood Boy) and
his half-brother, who is Selu's and her consort Kanati's son; and
to the Haudinoshone, the Cherokee's northern cousins, they
are Sapling and Bud (or Flint, depending on the Haudinoshone
group naming them). We find them also among the Maya, and
the likelihood is that it is from the Maya that the entire spiritual
system descends. (It is said the same system came to the Maya
from the Toltec, who may have gotten it from the Olmec before
them; one cannot be sure about that claim as it is more scholarly speculation than proven "scientific" fact.) Metaphysically,
it is probable that the system, wherever it "originated" among
human groups, actually emerged in the realm of the Great Mystery, and it is only in that land that the source of the system and
its variant forms might be ascertained.

Somewhere I was told that originally the sacred twins were
female, and certainly the prototypes of the Little War Twins,
Nau'ts'ity and Ic'sts'ity, seem to bear this out, as does the sisterhood Oshkikwe and Matchikwewis. One thing is reasonably
certain: where the sacred twins occur, there lies magic, and
there meanders the woman's medicine path.

Xmucané (pronounced, approximately, SHMOO-ca-nay), or
Grandmother of the Light, is the Maya goddess who creates human beings. She and her consort Xpiyacoc (SHPEE-ya-cock),
Grandmother (or Grandfather) of the Sun, presided over four
creations, during one of which Xmucané's grandsons, the third
set of sacred twins (the first two sets being her sons), enter the
underworld by playing handball in the sacred ball court. They
best the Lords of Xilbalba, and their adventures in this ritual
process are paralleled by those of Wild Boy and his brother. In a
sense they slay the alien monsters as the sons of Changing
Woman and White Shell Woman do, and they restore order to
the upper world much as the Little War Twins, Spider Woman's
grandsons, do in the Pueblo world.

Xmucané creates human beings out of both corn and light,

and it is said that she eventually presides over the passing of the matriarchy (more correctly, the gynocracy) when she transfers much of her power to her grandsons.

There is little trace of the twins among the Aztecs, Lakota, and Northwest Indians, but perhaps their absence is a function of my lack of personal relationship to those traditions or of the historical dislocations that in these regions were far more brutal, recent, and far-reaching than for the others for whom the tradition remains a viable part of ritual life. Among the Aztecs there are hints of the existence of the twins. Smoking Mirror/Blue Hummingbird and the Plumed Serpent Quetzalcoatl seem to me to be some sort of refraction of the twins, and the disconcerting tendency with which each god/goddess in their pantheon transforms into an analog (a fairly typical pattern in tribal pantheons), along with their undeniable borrowing from Maya spiritual traditions, leads me to suppose that the twins are there but not readily found. I think the institutions of the tlatoani, or great speaker, and the cihuacoatl, the high priest, are theocratic simulations of the principle of the sacred twins. Perhaps the Aztecs—superb politicians but less accomplished magicians and metaphysicians—recognizing the validity of the principle but not its psychic and sacred factualness, institutionalized it in a social structure found widely among tribal communities that feature the twins as a prominent part of their pantheon but neglected to keep the lines of communication between themselves and sacred twins open.

By the time the Karok, a Hokan people from Mexico, get into northern California, the sisters have been transformed—or the stories told to story collectors leave out one or two of them—so the tradition of three goddesses, two portrayed as sisters with twin sons or brothers, has changed to one goddess with her one son.

One can only wonder if this shift reflects Christianization, with the goddess Scomalt becoming something of an analog of Mary, and her son analogous to Jesus, Mary's son. How heavily the Karok might have been influenced by Christian presence by the time of the stories I've based the Scomalt tale on (the early twentieth century) or whether direct influence rather than indirect influences might have brought sufficient pressure to cause a dwindling in the pantheon is not clear to me. However, it seems unlikely that a tribal society would be monotheistic; and in one

where the preponderance (if not all) of the doctors, as the Karok call medicine people or shamans, are women, monotheism seems even less likely. For the most part, patriarchy and monotheism go hand in hand—usually accompanied by a class system, a trinity of a sort, one might say. My own references to the Goddess or the Great Goddess imply monotheistic spiritual organization, and it is an implication I dislike. It falsifies both the tribal traditions I write out of and about, and I sincerely believe it falsifies worldwide gynocentric societies of the near and distant past.

However, modern women's attempts to discuss Goddess spirituality are of necessity influenced by the patriarchal monotheistic religious systems we live under, and in much the same way native informants and storytellers are affected by the assumptions of those they report to. Then again, the white collectors of Indian myths and ritual stories are also subject to patriarchal assumptions. Perhaps the questions scholarly investigators ask as well as the fact that it is they who ask the questions about a particular tribe's spiritual teachings influence the responses they receive. Yet in spite of the multitude of obfuscations that plague the whole subject of tribal life and belief, certain patterns reveal themselves when a number of myths from a wide variety of tribes are studied together.

Far to the east, among the Iroquois, for example, the two goddesses are mother and daughter. They appear as mother, daughter, and allied but separate goddesses among the Cherokee; and as a mother (Grandmother Earth) and her three daughters, two of whom figure largely in women's mystical traditions, among the Algonquians (anishinabeg being one subgroup of a vastly larger whole that extends over southern Canadian and northern American areas from the northern and mid-Atlantic coast to the Great Plains). Xmucané and Xpiyacoc and the grandsons One Hunter and Seven Hunter become Grandmother, Oshkikwe, and Matchikwewis; Six Killer and Red Bird; Selu and her sons; Spider, her grandsons, and Nau'ts'ity and Ic'sts'ity/ Iyatiku; Sky Woman, her daughter, and her grandsons; Spider Changing Woman and White Shell Woman; or Scomalt and her sons.

The figures of their relationships are not as clear-cut or

straightforward as even this somewhat complex ordering makes them seem. Truly, polytheism is complicated and multifarious. Trying to frame it in any structure as linear as a book does it disservice, makes it less itself (or should it be "themselves"?) and more what it/they is/are not. But I think a careful reader will notice the complexity of the weave of goddesses in these stories.

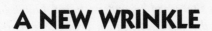

A NEW WRINKLE

In Schat-Chen, *his small book about the Keres (Queres) of Laguna and Acoma, John Gunn writes:*

> "Their theory [concerning Thinking Woman] is that reason (personified) is the supreme power, a master mind that has always existed, which they call Stich-tche-na-ko. This is the feminine form for thought or reason. She had one sister, Shro-tu-na-ko, memory or instinct [nako means woman]. Their belief is that Stich-tche-na-ko is the creator of all, and to her they offer their most devout prayers" (Gunn 1971, 89). Hamilton A. Tyler remarks, in reference to Gunn's comment, "However lofty a conception this goddess may be, it seems that when she has a form it is that of a spider, and in the popular mind she is often equated with Spider Grandmother" (Tyler 1964, 91).

Spider Grandmother, the major deity of the Keres, is weaver and thinker: she thinks, therefore we are. Though she is "supreme"—the thought sounds wrong put in those terms and read from a Western perspective where "supreme" means king or pope or dictator—she is not alone. There isn't an "only," just as there isn't a beginning as such. Surely, the Western mind inquires, something comes before her, something made her. Surely the universe has a beginning, and an end. But like their stories, which go on and on, Indians seem to believe that life itself does not have endings. And, if that is so, then what use is there of beginnings?

I have depicted Spider Grandmother as a Great Goddess whose medicine power is so vast (or whose own being is so complete and focused) that she brings thoughts or ideas into being. In my sense of her, she is akin to Wind. Indeed it is said she is Wind's Grandmother. That is because she makes movement, and from movement all else derives.

She is, like her Maya counterpart Xmucané, a weaver of life. She is also humble and small, a trait highly valued by the modest and un-affected people of Laguna and Acoma, among whom Gunn gathered his stories and sharpened his understanding. I think his stories about her approach the Keres conception because he married my grand-mother, Mita Atseye Gunn, who I am sure told him about Old Spider Woman from her woman's perspective. Perhaps what he rendered as "memory or instinct" might better be termed "collective unconscious" despite the perils involved in using that term, because the wisdom con-tained in the being of her sister Shro-to-nako is the wisdom embedded in the bones and cells of her people. But her intelligence goes beyond human beings; it permeates the land—the mountains and clouds, the rains and lightning, the corn and deer. The reference to Spider Woman's sister Shro-tu-nako reminds us that the Goddess is multiple, that sister-hood extends to the farthest reaches of the universe, and that soroates were viable social systems that thrived for centuries—not merely as a wish or theory, but as factually as the Keres themselves.

Thinking Woman (S'ts'tsi'naku, Tse-che-nako, Sussistinako, Stich-tche-nako, Ts'its'nako) and her cohorts Nau'ts'ity (Nautset, Naotsete, Nautsete) and Ic'sts'ity (Ic'ts'ity, Icsity, Utset, Iyatiku) create and re-create the cosmos giving shape, form, and meaning to all that is. As she thinks, so we are. Spider lives everywhere and presides in Shipap, the underground source of life of the people, where she sits on Iyatiku's shoulder and advises her.

Ooma-oo, long ago. The Spider was in the place where only she was. There was no light or dark, there was no warm wind, no rain or thunder. There was no cold, no ice or snow. There was only the Spider. She was a great wise woman, whose pow-ers are beyond imagining. No medicine person, no conjurer or shaman, no witch or sorcerer, no scientist or inventor can imag-ine how great her power is. Her power is complete and total. It is pure, and cleaner than the void. It is the power of thought, we say, but not the kind of thought people do all the time. It's like the power of dream, but more pure. Like the spirit of vision, but more clear. It has no shape or movement, because it just is. It is the power that creates all that is, and it is the power of all that is.

In that place where she was alone and complete with her power, she thought about her power, how it sang to her, how

she dreamed from it, how she wished to have someone to share
the songdream with her. Not because she was lonely, but because the power's song was so complete, she wished for there
to be others who could also know it. She knew this was the
power's wish just as it was hers. For she and her power were
together and of one mind. They were two, but they were the
same thing.

So she thought to the power once and knew a rippling, a
wrinkling within. Then she knew she was old, and wrinkled,
and that the power's first song was a song of great age. The
wrinkling became tighter, more spidery, stronger. It became in
one place. She named that place Northwest. She knew the
wrinkling had folded up on itself, enfolded on itself. She knew
much of the universe, the great power, was contained within.
Later the earth would be ripples and wrinkles, spidery lines of
power folded and enfolded into a tight moving shape, and it
would also hold the great power within, like a mother holds
new life. Others would also imitate this time: walnuts and
acorns, apples and pineapples, cactuses and mountains, even
the oceans would be like that. And humans, five-fingered beings, would grow wrinkled in their skin and brains, in honor of
this time when she and the power made a song to form new
life, new beings.

She was so happy with what she knew, so full of awe at the
beauty of the song, that she thought again. And again she knew
the rippling, the wrinkling, the running of spidery lines along
the edges of the forming pouch of the power's song, the folding
and enfolding into a shape that held some of the power of all
that is within. She knew that the place of that pouch, that bundle
of her thought, her song, was in the Northeast. So humming
and singing, she shaped them. Humming and singing, she placed
them where they belonged. That was how the directions came
into being. How the seasons came to be.

She thought in her power to each of the bundles and continued singing. She sang and sang. She sang the power that was
her heart, the movement that is the multiverse and its dancing.
The power that is everywhere and that has no name or body,
but that is just the power, the mystery. She sang, and the bundles
began to move. They began to sing, to echo her song, to join it.
They sang their heart's song, that was the same as Spider's heart

song, that was the heart song of great mystery, the power that moves. The song seemed to deepen as she heard other hearts singing. The song seemed more free, it seemed stronger. The two who rose up from the bundles with their singing each had a bundle of her own. And in each bundle the life of the universe rested, waiting until it was sung into life.

Spider named each of the beings; one she named Ic'sts'ity and the other she named Nau'ts'ity. They were not human beings, but supernatural beings. They did not have physical bodies because they were much vaster than even a planet, even a star. A star couldn't contain all they were and knew, all they thought.

Spider told each of them that they were to make more beings, so that the song could go on and on, so that she and the power could share the beauty with more and more beings. She told them that they would take from their pouches a part of the song and would sing it into fullness, into ripeness. They would need to sing the mystery in the way of thought to bring the lives in their bundles into being. They understood her directions because they were the song and the mystery. All of it and only a small piece of it. It was much vaster than they, and yet they could sing it into different shapes of being, different ways of singing, different parts of the great being song.

Ic'sts'ity began to sing a new chant: way-a-hiyo, way-a-hiyo, way-a-hiyo, way-a way-ay-o. She sang and sang, thinking to her bundle, and around them as she sang swirling, whirling globes of light began to form. They began pushing outward in a great whirling spiral, a great wheeling multitude of stars, all singing as they circled and wheeled like great geese upon the void. As they spiraled outward, they grew larger and brighter. Around and around the still, invisible center where Spider, Ic'sts'ity and Nau'ts'ity sang. They whirled, the outer ones flinging themselves farther and farther from the center, great arms forming in the spiral dance, following the lines of the song, the lines of the power, reaching out farther and farther into the mystery, carrying the song in their light, in their fingers, making both the darkness and the light as they danced, finding the power coming to them from the darkness, flinging it out from them in the light. The power danced in the void, in the light, in the midnight reaches of the gleaming dark. It sang.

Then Nau'ts'ity began to sing her thought to her bundle.

Aam-i-humm, humm, humm, aam-i-humm, humm, humm, aam-i-o, o, o, o, aam-i-o, o, o, o, aam-i-o. The song changed again as Spider and Ic'sts'ity joined her song, and from the brilliant globes of light new shapes spun out, dancing around and around the lights, giving shape and solidity to the darkness, carrying the spin of the song into new places, more solid, more full. The planets sang, new beings awakening, joining their minds and hearts to the huge chorus, singing their parts of the heart song. The power shaped and dipped, wheeled and danced, and over vast reaches it took on forms it hadn't known.

Satisfied with their work, Spider turned to her granddaughters and smiled as she chanted. In their begetting they would make many worlds, and upon some of them human beings would sing in the same way as she and her granddaughter-sisters sang. On those same worlds, feathered beings would swoop and wheel as the great fires around her did. And on them, life would press its way from the place of the Spider singing into the place of individual songs. And that would be far away from the place where the three stood. It would be right among them as they stood and sang in the void, surrounded by the wheeling lights and the great swooping dark.

OUT OF THE BLUE

"The most splendid tree had grown in the sky," says the old man. "It had four big white roots, which extended in four directions. From this tree all things were born . . ." The old man relates that one day wind completely uprooted the tree. Through the hole that opened in the sky fell the wife of the great chief, carrying a handful of seeds. A tortoise brought her soil on its shell so that she could plant the seeds, and thus sprouted the first plants that gave us food. Later that woman had a daughter who grew and became the wife of the west wind. (The story of Sky Woman as told by Eduardo Galeano in Memory of Fire: Genesis *[1985, 235])*

Stories change, and the teller, the audience, the occasion, the time all combine to create a man's story from a woman's story and (infrequently) vice versa. Galeano cites Joseph Bruchac's Stone Giants and Flying Heads as the source of his retelling. Bruchac has, of course, retold an old story in his turn.

The story I tell here is a combination of versions authorized by the Haudinashone, one of which was published in Akwesasne Notes in the 1970s. It is a different tale indeed, and while in many ways its telling is reminiscent of human ways, in others it clearly delineates the doings of nonhumans, prehumans, of beings very unlike us and never to be confused with us. True, Sky Woman was the wife of a great chief, but her stature did not depend upon his; true, the tree of life was central to the spiritual story, and it is the same tree that figures prominently in tribal religions all over the world—Odin's tree, from which he compelled the gods to reveal the runes of power to him; the Mayas' tree, which they still climb ritually; Sun Dance tree, which presides over the dance and takes the sacrifice to the sun; the tree of knowledge planted in the Garden of Eden; the tree of life, with which one who wishes to enter the Way is joined among tribespeople in southeastern Asia; the Kaballa, the abstract Tree, from whence all knowledge comes.

What changes I have made were made in order to render the thought I find in the originals clearly for the modern reader. What errors I have thus fallen into are my fall. Perhaps somewhere the Great Waterfowl will catch me as I plummet through the void.

39

OUT OF THE BLUE

When Sky Woman was a maiden, she was told by her dead father to go and marry a stranger. Being a strange woman, she did as he said, not taking her mother's counsel in the matter as she should have done. She journeyed to the place where the dead father had directed her to go, and there she found the man she was to marry.

Now this man was a renowned magician, a sorcerer. He heard her proposal that they marry skeptically. He said to himself, "This woman is but a girl. It would be more fitting for her to ask to be my apprentice than my wife." But he only listened silently to her, then he said, "It is well. If you can meet my tests, we will see if I will make you my wife."

He took her into his lodge and said, "Now you must grind corn." She took the corn and boiled it slightly, using wood he brought her for the fire. When the kernels were softened, she began to grind them on the grinding stone. And though there were mounds and mounds of stuff to be ground, still she was done with the task in a very short time. Seeing this, the sorcerer was amazed, but he kept silent. Instead he ordered her to remove all her clothing. When she was naked, he told her to cook the corn in the huge pot that hung over the fire. This she did, though the hot corn popped and spattered scalding clinging mush all over her. But she did not flinch, enduring the burns with calm.

When the mush was done, the woman told the sorcerer it was ready. "Good," he said, "now you will feed my servants." He noted that her body was covered with cornmush. Opening the door, he called in several huge beasts who ran to the woman and began to lick the mush from her body with their razor sharp tongues, leaving deep gashes where their tongues sliced her flesh. Still she did not recoil but endured the torment, not letting her face lose its look of calm composure.

Seeing this, the sorcerer let the beasts back out, then said she and he would be married, and so they were. After four nights that they spent sleeping opposite each other with the soles of their feet touching, he sent her back to her village with gifts of meat for the people. He commanded her to divide the meat evenly among all the people and, further, to see to it that every lodge had its roof removed that night, as he was going to send a white corn rain among them. She did as she was told, and after the village had received its gifts, the meat and the white corn rain, she returned to her husband's lodge.

Outside his lodge there grew a tree that was always filled with blossoms so bright they gave light to his whole land. The woman loved the tree, loved to sit under it and converse with the spirits and her dead father, whom she held dear in her heart. She so loved the light tree that once, when everyone was sleeping, she lay down under it and opened her legs and her body to it. A blossom fell on her vagina then, touching her with sweetness and a certain joy. And soon she knew she was pregnant.

About that same time, her husband became weak and ill. His medicine people could not heal him, but told him that his sickness was caused by his wife. He was certain they were right, for he had never met anyone so powerful as she. He feared that her power was greater than his own, for hadn't she been able to withstand his most difficult tests? "What should I do?" he asked his advisors. They did not advise him to divorce her, because that kind of separation was unknown to them. The only death that had occurred was of the woman's father, and they did not understand what had happened to him.

After deliberating on the matter for four days, the advisors told the sorcerer that he should uproot the tree of light. Then, lying beside it, he should call his wife to come and sit with him. He should by some ruse get her to fall over the edge of the hole the uprooted tree would leave, and she would fall into the void. When she had fallen, they said, he was to replace the tree and then he would recover his health and his power.

That afternoon he went outside his lodge and pulled up the tree. He peered over the edge of the hole it left, and he could see another world below. He called his wife to come and see it. When she had come, he said, "Lean over the edge. You can see another world below." She knelt beside the hole and leaning over the edge, looked down. She saw emptiness, and a long way below, she thought that she saw blue, a shining blue that

seemed filled with promise and delight. She looked at her husband and smiled, eyes dancing with pleasure. "It looks like a
beautiful place there," she said. "Who would have thought that
the tree of light would be growing over such a place!"

"Yes," her husband agreed. "It surely seems beautiful there."
He regarded her for a moment carefully, then he said, "I wonder
what it is like there. Maybe somebody could go down there and
find out."

Astonished, the woman looked at her husband. "But how
would someone do that?"

"Jump," the husband said.

"Jump?" she asked, looking down through the opening, trying to calculate the distance. "But it is very far."

"Someone of your power could do it," he said. "You could
jump. Become the wind or a petal from this tree." He indicated
the tree lying fallen next to them. "A petal could fall, gently. On
the wind it would be carried. You could be a petal in the wind.
You could be a butterfly, a downgliding brightbird."

She gazed for a long time at the shining emptiness below her.
"I could jump like that. I could float downward. I could fall into
the shining blue world below us."

"Yes," he said. "So you could."

For another long moment she knelt gazing downward, then
taking a deep breath she stood, and flexing her knees and raising her arms high over her head she leaned into the opening
and dove through.

For some time the sorcerer watched her body as it fell downward through the dark, toward the blue. "She jumped," he finally said to the council as they made their way slowly toward
him. "She's gone." And they raised the tree and placed it back
firmly in its place, covering the opening to the other world with
its roots.

She fell. She fell so long she no longer remembered where she
had come from or why she had jumped. She forgot the name of
her clan and the transparent box her dead father had lain in. She
forgot she had once long ago climbed up its side to sit and take
his counsel, or that she had been a wise woman of such power
that she had bested the most powerful of shamans in all the galaxy. She forgot the place of her home, the place of her origins.
All she knew was falling. It filled her mind and it filled all the

space around her until it became all that existed in creation. She forgot coming and going. She no longer remembered time or circumstance. She forgot what it was to begin, what it was to end.

There were consciousnesses, awarenesses, intelligent beings, who lived in the emptiness she fell through. None were beings such as she, but they had their own meanings, their own forms. There was a certain quality to each of them, a quality the stories have recorded as Waterfowl, Beaver, and Turtle. These beings became aware of the woman falling through the void. They watched her with their awareness for a long time, wondering. They thought about what to do, if they should do anything.

After taking thought together, contemplating, they decided to slow her endless fall. There was a task she needed to complete, a part she was playing in the great order of the universe, and her falling was only one portion of her task. They grew aware that they also had a part to play in the great dance, the unfolding that was before them now. Seven Waterfowl moved through the emptiness and came together, forming a firm nexus of energy, a tidal whorl, a security. So arranged, they moved their thought-wings, their intelligence-net beneath her, and her fall came to rest in their arms. Not that her motion ended; they all moved together in harmony. The directionless movement, the endless drift through the nothing she had entered when the other world ended and she fell beneath the tree of light took on a coherence, a form, that connected her within the order of all that is. They stopped her fall.

For another endless time she swam with them through the waters of night. She slept then. She dreamed. In time they again took thought of their task, and of hers. They became aware of the next opening, the next coiling or uncoiling in the flow of being that is the universe as it moved toward what it moved toward.

They knew as they contemplated a time that she should enter another kind of motion, one that spun slowly, slowly, one as ordered and serene as the dancing of human women as it would arise out of the same pattern, the same knowing in another loop of the endless coil of creation. Beaver said, "Let me move through the reaches of space until I can find that which she needs. Somewhere there is a being that moves just so, as she will move, as we will see."

Long, long Beaver searched, using intelligence he did not know he possessed. Long, long they called, sending over great reaches of the formless sea of endlessness a sweet, haunting call like that issuing from the throats of waterfowl on earth to recall that time, that timeless place.

When the call was complete, when the search was fulfilled, an ancient being such as they but distinct in her form, her essence, as Beaver and the Waterfowl were distinct, came swimming through the void. "Lay her upon my back," she said, "as it suits the endless motion in this timeless place."

Infinitely gentle, they placed their burden upon the broad firm plane. Infinitely wondrous, they withdrew within themselves. Infinitely sensible, they made their thought complete. Beaver again: "I will seek and find that which will take its shape from her thought. I will seek that which will give her significance in her essence. I will recover that which forms the next loop in the coil of endless unfolding."

Alone with her dreaming burden, Turtle swam deeply and wide. Calmly she waited, as was the purpose of her being. After an endless place of sea change, Beaver swam within her awareness clutching a substance that was shapely in its potential, nurturing in its possibility, loving in its being. "This is the pattern of the substance she will use to make and shape the possibilities that will become her earth," he said. And so saying, he blew outward in his awareness the pattern he had remembered, and it fell about her like fur and down, like beads of rain and early light, like clear crystal notes sung in a high, cold place. Then he swam endlessly away.

The woman who fell still dreamed. She dreamed she was awash on an endless sea, adrift upon an endless sky where neither memory nor anticipation had ever dwelt. She dreamed she was held safe on a course whose purpose she did not know but whose fittingness she did not question. She sighed and sank at last into a dreamless sleep. Is it any wonder she awoke at last and saw about her endless dark and felt beneath her naked form the deep pull of Turtle's muscles pulling, pulling in a slow inexorable flow?

When she was fully awake, when her knowledge of herself and what had gone before revealed themselves whole in her awareness, she sat and gazed within.

Slowly, slowly, with infinite care, she stretched out her hands and felt the pattern Beaver had blown around her. She began to sing, a long slow song, a chant that flowed through her being in ordered variousness, in cycles of multiplicity. And as she sang, the pattern entered her thought as her being entered its being, and together they sang. As they sang, Turtle's circular swimming slowed and slowed. They entered the galaxy of stars and night. They found their way to the outer reaches of the spiral whorl, the path that life would follow after, from Turtle's back, to night, to the spiraling void, to the tree of light.

After the primordial patterns were fixed in place, Sky Woman recognized her incompleteness. Again she began to chant and sing. This time she danced—a certain hopping step, almost birdlike in its execution, weaving methodically to and fro as she stepped. She danced and chanted a very long time. Turtle moved a full three circuits before Sky Woman stopped. She paused. She listened. At last she sighed. Then she began again. Hopping and chanting, meandering this way and that, she danced on and on. Old Turtle pulled through the darkness steadily until four full circuits were fulfilled. Sky Woman paused. She stood in utter stillness. No thought moved within her. No memory, no dream stirred. In that absolute calm, she waited, perfectly still.

Then she crouched down, her legs spread wide. She placed the fingers of her left hand within the folds of her darkness between her legs and slowly withdrew a long slender stalk. She pulled and pulled and the stalk lengthened as it uncoiled at her fingers' urging. At last she straightened the slender stalk. It was very long. She breathed upon it until it dried, then she waited a certain interval. Finally she took its closer end and tamped it firmly into the substance that covered Turtle's back like an ever-moving cloak of darkness. When it was thus firmly planted, Sky Woman began again to sing, and as she sang the farther end of the stalk began to rise until it pointed straight up from Turtle's back. She sang again and the pole thickened and branches formed. She sang again and it grew more layers, and more branches formed. Changing her song slightly, she chanted once more and balls of light began to glimmer here and there upon the most slender boughs.

When the tree of light she had carried within her from her husband's far home had blossomed anew in this strange place,

Sky Woman lay beneath it and fell asleep. She awakened slowly from her dream, or into her dream, to see her daughter emerge into the tree's sweet light. Now, thought Sky Woman, I am complete.

Sky Woman and her daughter lived comfortably on their island. Sometimes Sky Woman wondered what had become of the shimmering blue she had seen far below just before she jumped into the well of darkness so long before. Sometimes she dreamed of the song of the Waterfowl, their sweet song moving her heart nearly to tears. Sometimes she was lonely. But there was much to do to ready this sphere of intelligence into energies that would suit it to unfold through its destined cycles. She raised her daughter and taught her the ways of women beings. She taught her the ways of the sorceries she had learned long ago. She told her of her origins and cautioned her never to forget what she was taught or the stories she was told.

When she was grown, Sky Woman's daughter was wise and wondrous. Her active intelligence led her to seek in dreams—for what, she did not know. It made her dreaming restless, filled her belly with stirrings she did not recognize and could neither shape nor name. So in a kind of desperation, she left her mother's lodge and took to wandering. She would wander for days, seeking, musing, calling within her being, groping for a shape, a substance, she couldn't fathom.

One time, after many cycles of Turtle's turnings and spins, she came to rest beneath the shining tree. She lay in the same spot where her mother had lain eons before. And there she fell asleep. When she awoke, she became slowly aware of a large being standing before her, softly luminous, enticing in the tree's sweet light. Her thought began to dance within her and she smiled. "Ah," she said within, "you're here."

"Yes," the large luminous shadow replied. "I'm here."

They moved then into each other, dancing the dream she had sung into life, the dream she had made unknowingly, the dream that had rustled within her sending her forth to call from the darkness where Turtle swam. After they had danced and sung beneath the tree of light, the tree of life, for what seemed an endless span of time, the huge one faded from her being, faded ever so slowly until he became so faint he all but disappeared, leaving within her being only the tiniest fragment of his thought.

When their dance thus ended, Sky Woman's daughter returned to her mother's lodge and they resumed their earlier rhythms, the quiet order of their lives.

After a span of time, Sky Woman's daughter again went out. She went to the place of her dreaming and crouched against the tree of light. She breathed the fullness of her thought, the entirety of the dancing into ripeness, and felt her consciousness oddly slip into two parts. As she contemplated the sensation, which seemed to make two separate awarenesses within her—or was it four separate awarenesses?—she heard two voices speaking in the center of her being where earlier she had placed the fullness of her thought. One said, "This is how I will emerge," and she knew he was her son, and he would do it wrong. "No," the other said. "It is this way we should enter the sacred ground." And he emerged from her folds of darkness, from the place of origin and formless being into the place of shape and knowing that he was.

The other, anxious to emerge, longing to arise and become what he could not be, struggled his way from the being of his mother, nearer to her heart, tearing her asunder as he fled her cradling in sly rage. "See," he crooned, "I made it out the better way." But his mother had become another kind of being, and his elder brother could only weep.

Sky Woman, Grandmother, had become aware that something had transpired. She came to the place where the two new beings sat at the base of the tree of life near their mother's body. "Eh, what's this?" She gazed in consternation at the two small beings. Bud, the one who had emerged from his mother's being where no egress was said quickly, "He did that to our mother. He wouldn't emerge from her being as is proper but insisted on going another way. I tried to prevent him, but I was still too weak and he would not heed me." At this he burst into tears.

The sly one's brother said nothing. He was wrapped in his grief and did not speak. He was wrapped in drawing from his mother's quiet form all her knowledge and power, matching the energy patterns of her skill to his own which were as yet unformed.

"Come with me," the Old One said to her sly grandson. And taking Bud up in her arms she set off for her lodge, leaving Sapling to mourn beside the body of his mother beneath the tree of life.

Later, when the Ancient One returned, he was gone. She
didn't search for him. She had no intention of taking him in—in
fact, she would have been relieved if he had simply disappeared.
She believed he was responsible for her daughter's death.

But as things in those times were as they were, for this was
long before the world we humans would inhabit had come into
being, neither Sapling nor his mother could really die. Sapling
lived in the wilderness far from his grandmother and his half-
formed brother. He sang to the darkness and learned the ways
of creation, for creating the world the human beings would live
on would be his task.

So the Old One came to the tree of life, the light tree she had
brought from her world far away, and mourning and singing she
raised the body of her daughter and set it in a high branch of the
tree. As it touched the branch, it began to give forth a soft,
lovely light. It was the light of the night, the light by which
plants and many creatures would find their way and being, and
its seasons would set the seasons of human women in the way
of their mother, the daughter of the woman god who fell from
the sky.

Singing yet, the Ancient One lifted the head of her daughter
and sent it spinning upward until it reached the top branch of
the tree. It settled there and began to shine, its radiance growing ever more brilliant as she sang. And as she sang, she became
aware that her daughter's task had reached its time of ripeness,
and her purpose had been realized. Her daughter had not died;
she had only been transformed. As the realization claimed the
mind of Sky Woman, she began to dance, her chanting increased
in volume, and its rhythm took on the imperturbable cadence
of surety. She realized that the new time had begun, and that
with the coming of her grandsons the work of readying the
earth—the back of the Turtle which the four of them rode
through the darkness—for its myriad creatures and features had
moved to a new plane. She danced and sang beneath her
daughter's softly gleaming body and bright shining head. She
gave thanks.

THIS WAS NOT EDEN

This story reminds me of the Keres story Uncle John Gunn recounts about the sinking of Shipap, a tradition called " 'Shipop, stchemo,' the exodus from Shipop," as Gunn translates it (Gunn 1977, 67). Ella E. Clark records a remarkably similar Okanogan fragment, "The Beginning and the End of the Okanogan World," in Indian Legends of the Pacific Northwest *(1953). Her brief account tells us about the far away island ruled by a white woman of huge proportions—the giantess Scomalt. Scomalt hurls her island into the ocean, setting it adrift. In a separate volume,* Indian Legends from the Northern Rockies, *Clark records a Flathead story she titles "In the Beginning," which was sent to George Gibbs by Father Gregory Mengarini in the mid nineteenth century. At the time, it seems, the obscuration of the Goddess had not progressed so far as it since has. The name Skomeltem is recorded in that account, which also says that the goddess is Amotken's mother and that she, like Changing Woman and Selu, "lives alone on one of those worlds beyond the waters" (Clark 1966, 67). I have combined the two accounts into one in order to reconstruct more of Scomalt's story. I am intrigued that Scomalt, attended only by her son Smotken (Amotken), lives on an island alone as does Iyatiku, earth mother in the Keres pantheon, attended by the male head of the Oak Clan. I surmise that the original goddess to whom these myths refer lived in mesoamerica, as the Karok originated there. Maybe she moved northeast, or her sister did, and lived in Keres country, while the Karok went northwest, seeking her. Or maybe they all came from somewhere else, somewhere where she lived. Maybe she lives there still, on an island east of the moon and west of the sun.*

In the earliest time, before there were Indians living in this part of the world, before the sun was as warm and close to us as it is today, there was a great race of very large people who lived on a

large island. It was called White Man's Island, and the people
who inhabited it were giants compared to us.

Their leader was a great woman who had vast magical powers which enabled her to create whatever she wanted. Her name was Scomalt, and she was wise and strong, as well as powerful.

Through much of their history, the white giant people had lived peacefully enough, and they continued in this way for much of Scomalt's tenure as their leader. But for reasons that are lost to us, they began to quarrel, and their quarreling grew into fighting, and their fighting grew into wars.

Still, Scomalt kept hoping the fighting would end. She thought of peace and worked for peace. She consulted endless hours with leaders of the quarreling factions. She made decrees and promulgated them. She used all of her magical arts to restore harmony. But the situation continued to degenerate, until at last Scomalt realized that she could not end the fighting and that she had to put a stop to it lest it spread far beyond their lands and destroy all the earth.

She realized at last what she had to do, but it grieved her greatly. She spent long hours praying and meditating, consulting her powers, trying to find another way. But eventually she had to admit she could see no other course. She determined to drive the quarreling parties onto one edge of the large island, there to confine them. "I will separate the wicked ones from those of my people who long for peace," she vowed. "I will set them adrift and let them find more pressing outlets for their energies."

Accordingly, Scomalt put a great spell on the wicked doers, and through its power she herded them to one end of White Man's Island. Then she caused that end of the island to split off from the rest and to move rapidly out to sea. The turmoil that ensued caused the deaths of many of the hapless giants, and their continued warring killed many more. For a long time the island drifted at the mercy of brutal tides and winds that Scomalt's magic had set in motion. In a short time all were dead but three, a man and two women, sisters who had protected each other and taken refuge from the fighting and weather and somehow survived.

Alone on the shrinking, precariously balanced island, the

three drifted many days. The sun beat down upon them, and the rains tore at them. The island was treeless because the woods had been uprooted in Scomalt's original blast. Finally the man managed to land a whale, and they had blubber for heat and food.

Several months they drifted while large chunks of the island loosened and fell off into the sea. Seeing their danger, they made a canoe out of sun-dried logs and taking as much blubber as they could, the three set off in an easterly direction. They headed toward the sunrise for some time, at length coming to some islands. They landed occasionally for water and what provisions they could find, but kept traveling east. After a long time, they came to the mainland, which was not as large as it is now. The poor travelers trekked for a long time through the wilderness until they came to an area they found to their liking. Something about it seemed like White Man's Island, though they couldn't exactly say what. Perhaps it was the cast of light in the long afternoons, perhaps it was the color of the soil. But they settled in there at last.

On their journey their skin had been burned by sun and salt, and it had completely lost its whiteness, turning a reddish brown that took the sun's rays well and enabled them to live safely under its radiance. It is said that all the Indians are the children of those three.

But Scomalt's plan to end the fighting brought peace only for a time. Although years passed in peacefulness, inevitably people began to quarrel and soon the quarrels grew in strength and fury, drawing more and more onlookers into the fray.

Scomalt lived largely alone on a small island secluded from the main island. Her island was large enough to feature a tall mountain, on whose peak she spent much of her time, planting seeds and seedlings, studying and seeing to the needs of her people. She left the day-to-day administration to her son, Amotken, who had his hands full trying to restore harmony among his quarrelsome subjects.

He disliked consulting his mother, but wearily, from time to time, he would visit her in her seclusion and ask her advice. Together they worried over their best course, but all their harmonizing efforts failed in time. Grieved, Amotken decided to punish the recalcitrant giants severely. He devised a spell that caused a dreadful firestorm. Fire fell from the sky in great incandescent balls, igniting all it came near. And from the ashes of the dreadful destruction new life did form, a peaceful and gentle race of people even larger than their predecessors.

But in time they proved even more aggressive than the first giants, and the fighting that they indulged in wreaked devastation upon the land and upon many creatures caught in its midst. In a state, raging one moment, weeping the next, Amotken made his way to his mother's mountain retreat. "I will destroy them all," he swore. "They do not deserve to live."

But his mother Scomalt reminded him what had come about the last time, and how terrible the burning had been for innocent creatures caught in its fury. She told him about her own attempt to put the fighting to an end, and in time he agreed that destruction would not resolve the quarreling, nor would punishment alter the basic nature of his people.

"Let us work on transforming them," his mother proposed. "Perhaps it is their great size or the lightness of their skin that makes them so quarrelsome. The poor ones I cast into the sea, those who survived, developed warm brown skin and became a much more harmonious race."

Her son thought about her words for a time. The longer he thought, the more her words contained wisdom. "Perhaps it is the darkness that makes them quarrel," he mused. "Perhaps if they are cooked under the sun's rays until they become more ripe they will become more peaceful within themselves."

"Yes," Scomalt agreed, "but don't fry them the way you did the last time. Instead, why don't you bring that bright star you see in the east closer to us, or move us within its range of warmth. Then perhaps all will remain harmonious."

So with his mother's aid, Amotken moved the island and the land masses that circled in a like path with it closer to the large eastern star. As he did so, he arranged the energies around them so that the giants' skins slowly darkened. Many died in the transformation, but most survived to wake to that first morning's brilliant light and find themselves changed.

GRANDMOTHER OF THE LIGHT

The Popul Vuh, the Book of the Quiché of the highland region of the old Maya country, has seen a number of translations and commentaries. It is a problematic source of information about the classic Maya, but it can be a vital and living source of knowledge for Maya people, among whom today are many day keepers. Day keepers are people who can tell future events with some certainty with the help of a set of beans like the ones used by Xmucané and Xpiyacoc in creating human beings. The Maya have a tale that says that one of their sacred books was a Council Book: The Light That Came from across the Sea, *so called according to one (non-Mayan) writer because they had to cross a causeway to secure it. But I wonder. Perhaps it means more than that. Perhaps it came to them from beyond the waters that are said to separate a number of goddesses from humankind. Maybe it came from outer space, or from Shipap below the Earth's crust. The Maya, like Indians further north, "read" words for their cosmic import, interpreting them by recalling stories that illuminate the word rather than referring to dictionaries that "define" it. This being the case, no easy translation of anything Mayan, or for that matter, of any Native American text, can be had.*

That makes things difficult for American collectors and readers, but it suggests its own solution. The more stories you know, the more words you know. That is, any word leads to its particular string or chain of stories, all of which define and fulfill it. One word might contain scores of stories, like one metaphor in a Western-language poem contains a number of stories in its implications. Sylvanus G. Morley and Delia Goetz, who translated Adrian Recinos's Spanish translation of the Quiché Popul Vuh (see Morley and Goetz 1950), note that the Maya word for "corn" and "dawn" is the same. An entire worldview opens for contemplation when we reflect upon the stories of the relation of the one to the other in the Indian world.

To begin to comprehend the relation between words such as "sa-

cred" and "goddess," the stories must be told. Not only as they were
(and how can anyone know that?), but also and especially as they are.
This story, like a few others in this collection, is placed largely in the
present, because even contemporary humans live in the presence of the
old goddesses and gods, and exist only by their sufferance.

"**W**ho is the most important Maya goddess, or a Maya goddess I
could put in my book?" I asked a friend who has been steeped
in Maya lore and practice for a number of years. We were having
coffee at the Med Cafe in Berkeley, a few blocks from her home
and the U.C. Berkeley campus where I used to teach.

It was a fine August day in the late 1980s, and we had met to
gossip and get away for a bit from the usual hectic pace of our
East Bay lives in the fast lane: two professionals—mothers, art-
ists, and general all-around menopausal ladies—sipping ma-
chiado and bianco and trading stories.

I wanted a Maya story to round out my collection, and Patricia was the lady to talk to about it, I thought. I had one Maya
story I wanted to write, but I thought two would be better, one
from the mythic past, one from the mythic present.

"Write about Xmucané," she said. "Grandmother of the Sun,
Grandmother of the Light. You know, the Maya prayer you used
to have us say at the gynosophic gatherings? That's Xmucané."
She pronounced it "Shmoo-cah-nay," with the accent on the
first syllable. "She's the one who's the grandmother of the twins,
Hunahpú and Xbalanque, Xquic's twin sons."

I remembered, because I had read the Popul Vuh in English.
Besides I had seen Patricia's animated film version of it. "Oh,
yeah," I nodded, making an ethnocentric connection. "The
Little War Twins."

"You could write about Xquic, Little Blood. Or maybe Blood
Woman. The X means small, or woman," she added helpfully,
"and her glyph has reference to the moon." Ah, I thought, Men-
struation Woman. How neat. Woman on her Moon.

"She's the one the tree drops a shining drop of semen on and
so she conceives, right?" I ask.

"That's right," Patricia says, looking at me with a funny expression on her face. I wonder if she imagined a semen drop
when she drew that part for the film. Her drawing sure looked
like that to me. Huh. Maybe not. Then again, I think, taking

another look at her face, which now looks slightly conspiratorial, maybe so.

I looked up the names of the twins later and discovered that Hunahpú means Blowgunner, but as *hun* means one, the One is implicit in his name, so he's usually thought of as One Blowgunner. Xbalanque is a more interesting case. The X in his name has the same meaning as the X in Xmucané's, woman or small. So the younger twin brother they mention in the translations is a sister? I bet so.

But at the Med I was remembering the vivid scenes from Patricia's film, and the image of Xmucané—a skinny woman with quite a nose and wonderfully wild hair. She is angry that Blood Woman, Xquic, comes to her pregnant, claiming to be carrying Xmucané's son's child. Xmucané is not impressed because she knows both her sons were lost to the Lords of the Underworld, Xilbalba, a frightening place, long before.

Xmucané tells Blood Woman that she must go out and harvest a huge amount of corn, and the young woman accepts the challenge. But in the field she finds only one scraggly plant, and she is desolate. Xmucané is equally cruel to her grandsons when they are born, just as Sky Woman is cruel to Sapling, and Wild Boy complains Selu is to him.

In the Popul Vuh, Xmucané has a mate, Xpiyacoc, and they are referred to as "the grandparents," a nice, nonsexist, inclusive noun, right? Except that Xpiyacoc is referred to as "he," even though his name begins with the telltale X, and "he" and Xmucané together are called Grandmother of the Sun, Grandmother of the Light, I forget which is which, but I recall that they're both grandmothers. Now, I ask you, does this make sense?

Of course it does. You see, there was a bishop by the name of Diego de Landa who was convinced that he couldn't make much headway with his charges unless their books were burned, probably because they trusted their books to tell them what was what, and his book not only told a different story but was something that Catholic bishops thought only educated people like themselves should read.

So he burned them. All of them. He also was very interested in saving souls by torturing bodies, going so far in his zeal that he was recalled to Spain and reprimanded. After some years, he returned to New Spain, as the Spaniards called it, and decided

to have some of the old knowledge written down, and he got
some Maya nobles to do it from memory. Now the men who
did the writing had a censor, the bishop, and they must have
known by then that he wanted to hear as little as possible
about women of power, or about grandmothers who were
mates and partners. Treasuring their skins, and I mean that liter-
ally, you can bet that the scribes took pains to make him believe
that a grandfather and a grandmother make a divine couple, not
a grandmother and a grandmother!

Xmucané and Xpiyacoc, Grandmother of the Light and Grandmother of the Sun, I think—or is it Grandmother of the Sun and
Grandmother of the Light? Anyway, they are the oldest gods,
except that they seem to coexist with Hurricane and Beautiful
Green, who are also called Huracán and Quetzal, and they gave
birth to One and Seven Hunahpú, usually referred to as One
Hunter and Seven Hunter by Americans.

It seems to me that since Xmucané and Xpiyacoc are the
original measurers of time, or day keepers, it isn't likely that
sexual reproduction is what is happening here. Oh, no. It's their
magic, their creativity in the pure sense of the word. Besides,
One Hunter and Seven Hunter aren't exactly human beings.
None of the beings in that part of the Popul Vuh are. They are
gods and immortals. They are the people who come before the
humans, who create us or get things ready for us.

Patricia and I get to talking about the place of humor in tribal
life, and whether funny stories should be part of our work. I'm
in favor of some fun, personally. After all, humor and ritual go
together in some cases, and Indian people tend to laugh a lot.
It's a survival mechanism.

"It's in the Popul Vuh," Patricia says. "What could be fun-
nier than Xmucané's attempts to create beings that satisfy the
other gods?"

When she makes the first ones, the gods decide they will be
the animals because when Grandmother of the Light says, "Talk
to us. Praise us," the animals just stand, or lie, or slither, or fly,
or creep. Grandmother of the Day, which is what I call her
sometimes, says, "Okay," or words to that effect, "then just
stalk or lie or sit or slither or fly," and tries again.

This time she makes the bodies of earth and mud. It's all lop-
sided, all mushy. Besides, the mix isn't right, and it crumbles.

"We'll let this one just be a thought," Grandmothers Xpiyacoc and Xmucané say. You don't suppose this is a sly dig at Bishop Landa's version of how people are made, do you?

Anyway, the next batch of people made out of wood can walk, but they can't think. They are empty-headed, like Pinocchios who failed. Aggravated, the gods destroy them. Rain pelts them, Hail beats them, Rocks fling themselves from the mountains and flay them, Lightning shocks them, Fire burns them, and Sea drowns them. Sounds like the Atlanteans, at least in some stories I've heard, doesn't it? Or Noah's doomed people. Did you know there's stories about a great flood all over the world? Almost all ancient traditions tell the story of a deluge that sweeps all life away so that the world can be made anew. Makes you wonder.

Persevering, Xpiyacoc and Xmucané set about the task a third time, and this time they're so determined to get beings who have some sense, they overdo it, and the amazing four they create can stand in one place, open their eyes, and know everything. Everything.

That doesn't please the gods. After all, they didn't want competitors, they wanted worshipers! So they just call on Xpiyacoc and Xmucané to try again, and the pair get some corn. Xmucané grinds the corn into nine bushels each of white and yellow corn. She mixes it with water, and it becomes the flesh and fat of human bodies. Then they are "born," the human beings, the people of the surface of the earth, and they can learn and grow. They can praise the gods, and they can become day keepers, as their grandparents, Grandmother of the Light and Grandmother of the Dawn are. They can learn the laws of the universe and take their proper place within it.

It is said that Xmucané herself presided over the destruction of the gynocracy. That's because when her grandsons—actually, her grandson and granddaughter—triumph over the Lords of Death, the Lords of the Underworld (who are, after all, their grandparents too, since Blood Woman was a citizen of Xibalba and daughter of one of the lords), they jump into the fire and disappear. I should mention that Xibalba's X doesn't mean little or woman for some reason that linguists probably understand. It means frightening place, maybe. It does if the root is *xibah,* which means frightening, and the last part, *ba,* is from *bal,*

which means place of. These things are hard to know for sure.
Maybe burned books make everything more difficult.

Anyway, after her grandchildren are gone, Xmucané is crying
beside the corn plants her grandchildren had planted. She had
seen the plants wither and die, so she offered some copal, a
kind of incense, in front of the dead plants in memory of the
twins. The plants are restored with her sacrifice, and so are the
twins. She has saved them with her act of protection, just like
Grandmother Spider saved Shimana, or the people. While she's
at it, Xmucané creates an efficacious ceremony, the honoring of
corn, that the human beings will be able to make good use of in
times to come.

How her restoring the corn ends the gynocracy is beyond me.
It seems to me that making corn the central sacred being of
the Maya, and eventually of the world for thousands of miles
around, would fix the power of woman in place.

It's also a great mystery to me how the scholars can make
women's stories into such a mish-mash wherever they go. It's
far more of a puzzle to me than any of the spiritual practices of
the pre-Christians. The Maya tradition seems so simple. The
Grandmother of the Dawn is also Corn Grandmother, because
corn and dawn probably come from the same word in Quiché,
or so Morley and Goetz, who translated Recinos's version of the
Popul Vuh said.

When Xmucané and her sister goddess Xpiyacoc are ready
for the fourth creation, the dawn is fully upon them. That is,
the corn, the spirit or soul that will animate humans and make
them exactly what the gods ordered, is abroad in the land. As
they say, the time's ripe for the coming of earth-surface people,
and corn, sweet corn, is the connective tissue between the human and the divine, a link that is created and made to move by
the twin, or dual, Grandmother power of Dawn (Corn) and
Light (Day).

It's so simple. The stories are told over and over. There were
some women—sometimes two, sometimes three, sometimes
more—and they did it.

They were great sorceresses, divine shamans. They brought
life to the planet, they became the planet. They are the light
and the shapers. They are the corn. They are the dawn. One
guy says that Xmucané and Xpiyacoc probably represent the

left side and the right side of the same body, the spirit side and the flesh side—like the Pueblo women who wear mantas with the left arm and shoulder bare. The dress fastens over the right shoulder. My grandmother told me not to put it on the other way, because the left side was the death side. Or was it the other way around? I always get mixed up. Being left-handed, I get confused about things a lot.

Anyway, some Indians say this is the time of the fifth creation; some say it's the sixth. Let the day come, as the line goes in the Maya prayer I used to lead at the gynosophic gatherings I pastured at a women's coffeehouse in Oakland. I was the *pasture* because pastor comes from the word, and it means nurture or nourish, as in grazing, or maybe as in eating corn.

You know the prayer I mean. It goes, Grandmother of the Sun, Grandmother of the Light. Let it dawn. Let the day come.

▼▼
▼▼

BE THAT WAY THEN

▼▼
▼▼

Nau'ts'ity and Ic'sts'ity, the sisters Grandmother Spider, Thinking Woman, ritually sang into life a major part of Keres spiritual lore. Their images are inscribed in rock near La Cienega, New Mexico, once a Keres pueblo that was abandoned when its inhabitants fled to Enchantment Rock near Acoma sometime during or after the Pueblo Revolt (ca. 1680), and the inscription tells a ritual story, one version of which I have recounted here.

Naiya, our dear mother, Iyatiku, Beautiful Corn, is the beloved mother goddess of the Keres. She lives in Shipap, Sipapapu, the underworld where the four rivers join, from whence she governs the traditional spiritual life of the people and to which the dead go to dwell, coming at times as rain to their villages. Her helpers, the outside or countryside leader (hochin) and the mother chief (ya-ya) or cacique (after the Spanish word for the office) together govern in her stead and with her authority. They seem to me to be reflections of the Little Twins whose office is to mediate between the five-fingered beings, the humans, and the immortals or holy people (katsinas or kachinas). It also seems to me that perhaps Iyatiku is the major being whose reflection, Yellow Woman, she empowered and put among the people.

A long time after their awakening from the bundles, the goddesses began to be unhappy with each other. Ic'sts'ity, who was now called Iyatiku, Corn Woman, saw that Nau'ts'ity was always trying to get the better of her. She noticed that Nau'ts'ity would go off and spend long times alone, avoiding her company. She saw that they were not as happy as they had been. Iyatiku would go to Nau'ts'ity and would try to comfort her. She would ask Nau'ts'ity why she had changed.

Iyatiku and Nau'ts'ity had awakened at the same time, but

Iyatiku liked to believe that she was the elder. Once Nau'ts'ity complained that Iyatiku had gotten to bring more of the things in her bundle to life than she had. She wanted a chance to use her bundle more often. But Iyatiku argued. She said, "No, I am oldest. That's why I use the things in my basket more."

"That's not true," Nau'ts'ity had said. "We were sung to life at the same time, long ago, when they called you by another name. Don't you remember that?"

But Iyatiku was adamant. She enjoyed singing the things in her bundle into life and instructing them in their proper ways. She didn't enjoy it as much when Nau'ts'ity did the instructing. Because of this, she would not admit that they were the same age.

Nau'ts'ity said, "Let us have a test to see which one of us is right. Tomorrow, when the sun rises, let's see who it shines upon first. I say it will strike us both at the same time, for we were created equally."

Iyatiku agreed to this. But she worried that Nau'ts'ity was going to trick her somehow and make the sun strike her first. To outwit her sister, she went to the magpie and instructed it to fly far to the east, not stopping for any reason, and to spread its wings over the rising sun in such a fashion that it would shadow Nau'ts'ity from the sun's rays. The magpie agreed. But on its flight, it stopped for food at a place where a puma had killed a deer. And in its haste to eat, it got the deer's blood on its back, wings, and tail, but it did not notice. It flew on as instructed, arriving at the sun's house. There it made a shadow that would shield Nau'ts'ity from the sun's rays. So the sun shone on Iyatiku first, and triumphant, she claimed to be the elder. When the magpie returned, Iyatiku punished it for stopping to eat, contrary to her instructions. "From now on," she scolded, "you will not know how to kill your own meat. You will have to eat only what others have killed, and much of the time that meat will be rotted. And you will carry forever the blood stains that are splattered all over you now."

So the unhappiness between the sisters grew. Nau'ts'ity spent more and more time alone, roaming the hills and the plains, even staying away for weeks. Once in her wanderings when she felt very lonely, she lay on a rock to watch the sun as it rose over the desert floor. It moved toward her, streams of light. In rosebright joy and power it grew toward the mesa on which she lay. Slowly, the sun, Utset, sometimes called Ic'sts'ity, came. Filled with longing, Nau'ts'ity lay, legs opened to the light. She raised her hips so that her vulva was open, exposed to the rosebright rays as they came toward her. She held the lips of her vulva wide as the sun fell upon her thighs. She let it enter her womb. She lay there, open to the bright, warm splendor of the sun until it was gone, passing over her head on its way. After it was gone, she lay for a long time, waiting.

In the proper time, Nau'ts'ity gave birth to twin sons. Iyatiku was with her and helped her in her labor. She helped Nau'ts'ity with rearing them. But the Spider came to them, angry that the twins had been born; the sisters had been instructed to avoid pregnancy. Indeed, they had no need of children at that time, for they had much work to do. The Spider, She Who Dreams, told them that since they had chosen to follow their own inclinations instead of her instructions, they would be on their own from that time. "I will not help you in your work anymore since you have seen fit to take things into your own hands," she said. This did not distress Iyatiku and Nau'ts'ity, who indeed were glad to be left to their own decisions. So the women lived happily enough while the boys grew up. Nau'ts'ity gave one of them to Iyatiku as her own son, and for some time the tasks of caring for and instructing them took the women's attention, and they were content with their lives and with one another.

But the trouble between them had not been completely banished, and after some time they became unhappy with each other again. At last, after thinking long about their trouble, Nau'ts'ity, Sun Woman, said to Iyatiku, "We aren't happy together. I think we should share whatever we still have in our bundles and then separate. I have many things left in my bundle. Look," she said, "here are domestic animals. I will share them with you, but remember that they will take much caring for."

Iyatiku refused the animals, saying, "No, I don't think I want them. It will be too much trouble to care for them, and my children won't need them," she said.

Nau'ts'ity looked again into her bundle and found some seeds that had not yet been planted. They were seeds of wheat and certain vegetables and fruit trees. She said, "Here are some seeds we have not yet planted. These too take much care, but I will share them with you."

Iyatiku again refused the offer. She did not want them, and she thought that those plants she had already planted would be fine for her children. "See," she said, "I will not need those plants. I have corn and squash, beans and pumpkins already. I have tobacco and other foods as well. It will be enough," she said.

In Nau'ts'ity's bundle were many metals, and these she offered to Iyatiku saying, "I will share these metals with you, but remember that the use of them will entail much work." Iyatiku, Mother of the Indians, again refused these, thinking that she and her children had all they needed from her own bundle, and that Nau'ts'ity's offers might be tricks.

When Nau'ts'ity had looked very deeply into her bundle, she found something with writing on it. She offered this to Iyatiku, but again Iyatiku refused. Nau'ts'ity said, "There are many things that are good for food in my bundle, but I know that all of them will require much caring for. Why is it, sister, that you are not thankful? Why do you refuse to take any of what I have offered? I am going to leave you. We both realize that we will give life to a great many of our own kind, and in a long time from now we shall meet again, and even though much will have changed with us we will still be sisters. If you take none of the things I have offered you, I will have the best of you in that later time, and again we will be troubled in our hearts with one another. I don't want it to be like that when that time comes."

But Iyatiku persisted in her refusal, saying that she did not want any of the trouble that Nau'ts'ity's gifts would entail.

So, taking the child she loved with her, Nau'ts'ity went away to the east. Iyatiku stayed on where they had always been, and she was sorrowful and lonely for a long, long time. But she comforted herself as best she might, saying often to her son, who Nau'ts'ity had left with her, "Let us live here with all that the Spider has given us." Thus they lived alone for a long time, until the boy grew up. When he was grown, he became Iyatiku's husband, and she named him Ti'a'muni. Then she bore many children, and the first, a girl, she named for Nau'ts'ity's clan, the Sun Clan.

Now Iyatiku came fully into her power. She did all her work
in the ways she had been instructed: she took the babies when
they were four days old and held them up to the sun as she had
been taught when she came into the light, and she put pollen
and cornmeal that she had empowered with her own breath into
each infant's hand. She taught this to every child she bore. And
the brothers and the sisters all lived together, marrying one another and having children of their own. Iyatiku was the Mother
and ruled.

And whenever a girl was born to Iyatiku, she gave it the
name of a clan, teaching each the ways of the people as the
Spider had instructed her so long before.

Later, maybe eons later, after the village of Kush Katret was
established and the rules and customs were set down, Naiya
Iyatiku lived on an island in the center of the lake. Tired of
people and their quarrels, she closed her house to everyone.
Only the outside cacique, the mother chief, was allowed to see
her. He took her instructions and gave them to the people and
the katsina, the immortals, as she commanded.

The people lived around the lake, near her. But she was seldom seen by them from the time she had ordered the villages
and the caciques, named the clans, and instructed the people in
all of the rituals. She put her power into the sacred ears of corn,
so that they might use that power when they had need. Only
the priest, cheani, and the outside cacique would use it in the
power ways. She left each sacred ear in the permanent keeping
of the proper clan mothers, who "lent" them to the men, priest
or chief, at appropriate times.

When she made the corn maiden, Iyatiku told the outside
cacique to guard her house. No one was to come near. The path
to her door was made of white abalone shell. It lay, soft and
pale, tinged with pink, open to the sun and rain, open to the
moon. Only Iyatiku walked upon it. Only she watched it, and
only she knew what it meant. When she made the corn maiden,
she took the power that was in the pale, glistening shell and
placed it within the hollowed ear. She placed honey in the hollow, to bathe the shell in, to keep its light. She breathed her
breath into the hollow. She made the opening secure. When she

did this, she remembered Nau'ts'ity, who was gone to the east, to the place of the sun's brightness. Remembering her sister, she breathed, and she sealed the corn maiden. She gave it to the outside cacique. She told him that its power was love. It was the bond of honey and of golden morning light.

She instructed the people in the last days of her tenure in their world. She taught them dances and prayers. She taught them the proper use of the corn maiden. She gave them dances for their pleasure. She gave them toys for their entertainment, and taught them games to play with them. This was after the people had moved to the beautiful white village she had designed and helped them build. She had told them to move there where they could raise their growing children in peace, where there was sufficient land and good pasture, where there would be sufficient rain, as long as they remained peaceful and respected her and her creations.

But good living affected them. After they learned to dance for pleasure, after they mastered the games, the young men among them got the idea that they could make up a game of their own. They made up a game that they could play in the kiva. It was a gambling game. They became so interested in this gambling that they forgot to go to the ceremonies. They neglected to pray. They forgot to plant the prayer sticks. They stayed in the kiva sometimes during the dances.

And while they gambled, they began to make up songs about the women, songs ridiculing the aunties and the clan mothers. Iyatiku was angry. And some of the old men were angry too. But the young men continued to sing their songs of ridicule and dishonor. They kept playing the gambling game. They got worse and worse, finally making songs that ridiculed Iyatiku, and when the outside cacique heard about it, he scolded them. He told them they must stop. Stop the gambling. Stop the songs.

They did not gamble or sing the shameful songs while he was in the kiva, but when he would leave they would resume. They even said that playing the game was more likely to result in gain to the players than the ceremonies of Iyatiku ever could.

Hearing this, Iyatiku was angry. She said, "Then, if this is the way you are thinking, I will leave you to yourselves. Then you may see if it is not because of my teachings and my rules that you have prospered and have all that you will ever need." She told them she would disappear from their lives and remain silent. They would not hear from her again. And when she had spoken, Naiya Iyatiku disappeared.

But she told the outside cacique to keep watch over the people, "For they are my children, and I am always their Naiya Iyatiku. I will wait for them at Shipap, there in the center place, and I will greet them when their life is over."

This was the first time death was mentioned among them.

RIVER, BLOOD, AND CORN

Agawela (Old Woman or Crone), or Selu (Corn Woman), is perhaps the most familiar goddess to the Cherokee. Her name is the most often mentioned when talk about female deities comes up among us women, offered by whatever Cherokee might be present at the gab.

Through these loving and familiar references, I have come to feel very close to Selu. She is a form of Iyatiku to my mind, Iyatiku, Beautiful Corn, the Earth Goddess (if you go in for such easy categorizations of female gods) of the Keres.

Interestingly, corn and gynocracy seem almost inevitably to occur together, which suggests that horticultural societies depend heavily on female energies. It does not suggest, however, that social systems that feature hunting and fishing are patriarchal, or even male dominated.

Probably patriarchy is only one form of male-centeredness possible. I think that had many of the tribes gone the way they seemed to be going prior to white contact, a kind of avuncularchy, an uncle-centered system, would have developed. There were strong indications that something like this was occurring after the fall of the classic Maya and Pueblo civilizations, around the twelfth century. Uncles are the important males in gynocentric communities such as the Keres. Perhaps the shift toward uncle-ism itself brought on the fall, or perhaps the decline set in as one of a number of reactions to a changing social order. Maybe avuncularity was "what time it was" then, and even perhaps now. After all, we refer to the U.S. government as "Uncle Sam."

Long ago Selu, Corn, and her husband Kanati, the Lucky Hunter, lived happily together. They had plenty to eat because whenever they needed meat Kanati went into the forest or up in the hills and readily secured some meat for their meal. Selu could just as readily shake or rub corn and beans from her body,

which she prepared in a variety of ways into meal, fresh vegetables, and grits.

One day, while Kanati was off somewhere and Selu was on
her way to visit with Long Man at the river below their townhouse, she noticed a small pool of blood under her as she took a
step. She reached down and gathered it up, knowing it had
fallen from her womb to the path. As she touched it, it almost
leapt into her open palm. Then it curled upon itself until it resembled a small worm. She took it to Long Man, and they
agreed it should be mixed with water and covered. So she took
some of Long Man's essence and covered the wormlike mass of
blood with it, placing the mixture carefully in a hollow stone
that lay nearby the waterfall where she sat. She covered it with
some watergrass and returned to her duties.

Several days later when she made her morning visit to Long
Man to bathe and pray in the sunrise, she heard some noise
in the bushes that grew near the waterfall. Peering intently at
the bush, she saw a child hiding mischievously among the
branches. She called to him, but he vanished at the sound of her
voice.

She returned home and went about her tasks, saying nothing
to Kanati about the boy. Months went by. Selu gave birth to a
son, and he grew rapidly. She often thought she saw the wild
boy half hidden among branches or moving among the play of
light and shadow when the wind blew, but she was never certain he was there. She grew certain that she heard two boys
laughing when her son went out to play, but still she said
nothing.

One day she and Kanati were sitting beneath the arbor, and
she again thought she heard two boys' laughter drifting up to
them from the river. When the child returned that evening,
Kanati asked him who he had been playing with all day. "I
don't know," the child replied. "He comes out of the water
when I go down there, and he says he's my elder brother. He
told me that his cruel mother threw him in the river when he
was tiny, and he has no home or any place to stay except
there."

That night after the boy was asleep, Selu told her husband
about the strange blood on the path and what she had done.
They agreed that their son should be instructed to bring the

other boy home with him, but they thought he might not readily come, so they made a plan. Their son would be told to go and play as usual with the wild child, and when he had an opportunity he was to grab the boy and hold him firmly while calling for his parents.

The next day the lad went to the water, and when his play-mate appeared he did as he was instructed. The wild boy fought wildly to escape, but his brother held valiantly to him until Selu and Kanati came and together hauled him home. He was frantic, wriggling and trying to fling himself free of their grip, shouting to them to let him go. "You threw me away," he cried. "Why should I go with you now!"

But he seemed to accept the situation once they brought him into their house, and eventually he gave in to their care and in-struction. But in the meantime the old people discovered the child was gifted with magical powers, so they named him Inage-Utashunhi, Wild Boy.

In spite of the fact that he gave the old folks the impression that he was reconciled to their rules, Wild Boy delighted in es-capades in which he enlisted his younger brother. One of these adventures resulted in the freeing of the game, which meant that the easy days of hunting were ended forever. Another led to Selu's death.

Having noticed that their mother would go out to the small storehouse just beyond their dwelling and would return with ears or kernels of corn and perhaps some beans, Wild Boy in-vited his brother to join him in another spying adventure. They waited until Selu had made her way up the ladder that rested against the wall of the building, watching her unlatch the tiny door and duck inside. Quietly the boys climbed up the farther pole that the storehouse stood on and removed a small piece of dried clay they had previously readied for that purpose from the lower part of the storehouse wall. Peering inside, they could just make out Selu in the dim rays of light that filtered through small cracks along the walls.

They saw her place a sieve on the floor then step over it, planting her spread legs on either side. She began to chant and sing softly, and as she did she raised her skirt and touched her-self between her legs and rubbed her belly briskly. In a short time, ears of corn began to emerge from the place between her legs and fall to the waiting container.

When seven perfect ears of corn had been thus produced, she lowered her skirt and opened her bodice. Baring her breasts, she leaned over a second bowl and began to pull at her nipples like a woman does to express extra milk when she is nursing a baby. As she did so she again chanted and prayed softly, and shortly the green slender tubes, beans, began to emerge from her nipples and fall into the waiting bowl. When she had expressed a sufficient quantity, she straightened and closed her bodice. Taking the containers, she left the storeroom.

The brothers were aghast. "This is dreadful," Wild Boy exclaimed. "She's a sorceress, just as I thought. That's why she threw me away at the beginning. We must kill her before she destroys us." His younger brother, accustomed to following his lead, concurred.

They went back to the house and entered the cooking room where Selu was roasting the ears of corn. As they entered, she knew their thoughts, even though they were silent. Calmly, she said, "You have seen me, and now I must die." They stood silently regarding her. "Well," she said, "that's all right." She continued evenly, "It's time for my transformation, and you were made to assist me in it.

"Now listen carefully. When I am dead, make a clearing in front of the house. Take my body and drag it around the clearing seven times in a circle. Then drag me seven times over the inner part of the circle and stay up all night and keep vigil. In the morning you will have plenty of corn."

The boys killed Selu and cut off her head, which they mounted on the roof of her house facing the west, telling her to watch for her husband. Then they set to work to clear the ground, but being lazy and self-indulgent, they cleared only seven small areas. Because they failed in their obligation, corn grows only here and there instead of over the entire earth as Selu had intended. Then they dragged her body over the spots, but stopped after doing so two times. Wherever her blood fell on the ground, corn sprang up. Then they kept watch all night, and by morning it was mature.

That morning Kanati returned. He did not see Selu anywhere and asked his sons her whereabouts. "Old man," Wild Boy said insolently, "look above you. There is her head." And he gestured with his chin and pursed lips toward the rooftop. "We killed her," the younger boy added, "because she was a witch.

We were afraid she would kill us since she tried to kill my brother before."

Kanati was sickened and angry at the sight of his wife's head perched lifeless on the housetop. But he said only that he could not stay there any longer, and turning his back on his home he walked away. Reaching the wolves' settlement, he told them what had transpired and asked them for help in ridding the planet of the two boys. But Wild Boy, using his magic, was aware of Kanati's plot, and together he and his brother prepared a defense. When the wolves came, they were ready. With magical defenses and a ready supply of arrows, they trapped the wolves within a magic circle from which they could not readily escape and shot most of them. Those who managed to flee through the small opening through which they had entered the magic circle were chased by the boys into the swamp, where they perished in sudden bursts of fire created by Wild Boy. Having dispatched the wolves, the boys resolved to follow Kanati. Through the use of a gambling hoop, they located the direction in which he had traveled and swiftly made after him.

The hoop had indicated that Kanati had gone toward Sunland, and the boys went swiftly in that direction. And though Kanati tried numerous times on the journey to shake them off, always Wild Boy's magical skills were superior to Kanati's ploys.

Finally they tracked him to the end of the world, where the sky vault meets the ground. They waited until the vault raised and went through the perfectly square opening. Across the waters they saw an island, its steep cliffs rising a hundred meters into the sky. Using Wild Boy's magic, they soon found themselves outside a townhouse, where they saw Selu and Kanati sitting together under a grass arbor. The old couple received them happily, seeming pleased to see them. The boys remained in that place for seven days; then following the old ones' instructions, they removed to the Nightlands, where they still reside. They are Thunder and Lightning, and their magic made the earth ready for the coming of the human beings, because everything we see around us was put in place during those times.

MAKING SACRED,
MAKING TRUE

In the native world, major gods come in trios, duos, and groups. It is the habit of non-natives to discover the supreme being, the one and only head god, a habit lent to them by monotheism. Because of this, Changing Woman is often spoken of alone in the literature of the bilagáana, the white people. But in the texts, as in the lives of Diné, singularity is sad and undesirable. Belonging to a people—a community, a clan—is a necessity for all beings, human, holy people, animals, everyone.

Changing Woman is a model for Navajo women. While changeable, she is not fickle. She is independent, resourceful, and capable. Her powerful sense of self does not depend on caprice, coyness, self-deprecation, or self-centeredness, but is derived from a perspective of dignity, equality, balance, and reason. She looks to the harmony of the whole over vast lengths of time for a definition of the good.

I have composed this version of Changing Woman and White Shell Woman from a variety of sources (Reichard 1950, Haile 1981, Moon 1984, Zolbrod 1984) and versions told by Navajo friends. I have stayed as true to the sense I have of the rhythm and presence of the land of the Diné as I could.

I must say, I see Giant Spruce Mountain as Mount Taylor, near whose base I was raised, though I don't think they're the same. Mount Taylor, known as the Woman Veiled in Clouds to the nearby Keres, might well be Changing Woman. She changes noticeably in the seasons, and she is a self-defined lady indeed. Yet her being is inextricably part of the surroundings she graces with her soaring, big-breasted presence. She is situated along the eastern reaches of the homelands of Diné, in central New Mexico, part of the sacred Four Corners area. The Navajo entered the area sometime after the twelfth century (Christian time), a time when much upheaval and transformation was occurring throughout much of pre-European America. Intermixing with the Anazazi, an Old Pueblo culture, the Athabascan-speaking Diné incorporate many spiritual features of the supernatural world of the region into their religion and way of life. Because of their intermixing and their tenancy in the same area, their stories of White Shell Woman and Changing Woman are very like our Keres Pueblo stories of Nau'ts'ity, Ic'sts'ity, Iyatiku, and Spider Woman. But their way of life, social organization, language, and religion are distinct from those of Pueblo people in many particulars. Their nearest Pueblo neighbors are the Hopi, the Zuñi, and the Keres, and they have the greatest similarities with these three and, I might add, the greatest differences.

In Diné Bahané: The Navajo Creation Story, *Paul G. Zolbrod says that Talking God (Haashch'e'eelti'i) and Growling God (Hashch'eoghan) and the other supernaturals featured in the Navajo story of creation and in their Chantways are holy people, as the Navajo term "Yei" is rendered in English.*

> *The Holy People are unlike the earth-surface people who come into the world today, live on the ground for a while, die at a ripe old age, and then move on. These are intelligent people who can perform magic. They do not know the pain of being mortal. They are people who can travel far by following the path of the rainbow. And they can travel swiftly by following the path of the sunray. They can make the winds and the thunderbolts work for them so that the earth is theirs to control when they so wish.   (1984, 48)*

> *It should be noted that while Zolbrod's depiction of the Yei is a beginning description of them, the powers he names are largely those the more advanced shamans share. The Yei, I think, go beyond shamanic prowess, as they go beyond human identity or human consciousness. They are not earth-surface people. They are not "five-fingered beings."*

When Changing Woman was born, she was found among flashing lightning so bright it was blinding, a rainbow was showering the peak of the spruce-covered mountain with brilliant colors. First Man of the Emergence People heard her crying, though he was blinded by the light of rainbows. Just as he first heard her

crying, the light vanished and dark rain began to fall. He couldn't
see, but he went toward the sound of an infant's cry.

First Man, maker of much of the earth, had gone up to the top
of Giant Spruce Mountain to find out what caused the strange
phenomena he and his family could see from below. For four
days a cloud had covered the peaks, first only the top, then a
greater portion each day until on the fourth the entire mountain
was cloaked in a dark, heavy shroud. He, First Woman, and
their only surviving son and daughter were in the vicinity because they had been forced to flee the alien monsters who
sought to destroy the people. These four were the only survivors, and they were desolate. They believed they could not continue to live. They had no heart left to go on. He determined to
climb the mountain in pursuit of good fortune, following the
rainbow, the trail of the cloud, the scent of the falling rain, the
lightning tracking down from the sky, all pointing to the source
of the mystery he sought to explore.

Perhaps he hoped to discover some reason to continue with
their struggle. I suppose he didn't know what else to do. So he
went in pursuit of long life and happiness for his people. Even
on the edge of darkest despair, he sought for a reason to hope,
to go on.

The day Changing Woman came to earth, she was found in
the midst of the dark cloud that had shrouded the peak—amid
the rainbow, amid the lightning, amid the rain. Her coming was
mysterious. She signaled her presence with a thin wailing cry
so that First Man could find her despite shattering brightness,
suffocating darkness. But what he saw as he reached the place
of the crying—when the lightning stopped flashing, the rainbow muted to a familiar, soft hue, the rain lightened into a fine
mist, and the dark cloud thinned and evaporated into a serene
sky—was not the tiny infant he expected, but a small turquoise
figure. It was the size of a newborn but proportioned as a full-
grown woman.

Who could it be? What sort of mystery did he behold, lying
quiet and still at his feet?

Mystified, resourceful, First Man picked up the figure and
carefully carried it back to First Woman and the rest. "Take it
and care for it like one of our own," he said.

When Changing Woman was born, alien monsters bent on annihilating the people controlled the land. Talking God and Growling God and the other holy people who had helped create the Emergence People also helped them now. Two days after First Man took Changing Woman home to his wife and daughter to care for, Talking God came and signaled them to meet with him at the top of the mountain in twelve days.

When they arrived there, they met Talking God and Growling God, Blue Body and the Wind, along with Wind's brother Darkness and the brothers of the Woman Who Becomes a Bear. Also at the gathering the Emergence People saw the Image-Bringing People, the Daylight People, the Blue Sky People, the Yellow Light People, and the Darkness People.

Standing among the Daylight People, Talking God stood holding another small female image made of white shell. The Emergence People saw that this figure was identical to the turquoise figure they had. In a ritual manner, Talking God and Growling God laid out the two figures and two ears of corn, placing them between two soft skin blankets. They made a circle with an opening to the east so that Talking God and Growling God could enter and leave freely.

When all was in readiness all the people chanted and sang until the two gods who had been hiding in their house in the east came around the circle and entered, parting the two buckskin blankets. They asked Wind to breathe life between the soft skins. Three times the chanting and singing, the entry and parting, the request and leaving occurred, and yet a fourth time the sequence was repeated. On the fourth round, the gods did not ask Wind to breathe between the blankets, but instead they thanked him for already having done so. And the turquoise figure was the Air Spirit Person Changing Woman; the shell figure was now White Shell Woman; the white ear of corn became White Corn Boy and the yellow ear of corn had become Yellow Corn Girl.

After this, the two gods sent White Corn Boy and Yellow Corn Girl to live among the holy people, and everyone returned to their homes, leaving Changing Woman and White Shell Woman alone on the mountaintop. They were newly made Air Spirit People, left with no instruction about where to go or how to proceed.

After eight days of waiting to see what their life would be, four days where they had been given life and four days farther up the peak where they could see all the earth spread out below them, the Air Spirit Women were feeling lonely. Changing Woman spoke to her sister, saying she had been wondering if the sun was also an Air Spirit Person. Eagerly, White Shell Woman admitted she'd also been lonely. She said she had wondered if the water in a lively brook that flowed clean and sweet from the mountainside was an Air Spirit Person.

Boldly, Changing Woman suggested that they should each pursue their thought. She, she said, intended to watch Sun carefully every day to see if she could discover the exact nature of the being who sailed so serenely overhead.

True to her word, the next morning Changing Woman went to a sunny spot at sunrise and lay upon a flat rock where she could watch Sun make his way over her throughout the day. She wore no clothing, for they had not been given any other than the buckskin blankets that they used against the chilly nights, and as she reclined she spread her legs comfortably, making it possible that Sun's rays could fully warm her.

Following a like inclination, White Shell Woman that same morning went to a waterfall along the brook's path. She found a shallow place where she could lie comfortably and, like her sister, let her legs fall open so that the spray washed gently over her.

For four days the sisters spent many hours contemplating the beings they hoped to contact, hoping thereby to gain a mate and to assuage their loneliness. Then for four days they stayed near their camp at the top of the high peaks of Giant Spruce Mountain. All but consumed with longing and loneliness and that odd feeling that Diné say girls on the threshold of womanhood feel, on the fourth day White Shell Woman felt a movement low in her belly. She let out a small cry and told Changing Woman what had happened. Changing Woman assured her that it was good. The feeling was that of life moving within her, she said, and added that she herself had felt a movement within herself earlier. She was triumphant. Hadn't they spoken in the long days just past about the possibility of making beings like themselves, just as they had been made? It seems they had succeeded in doing so.

In another four days they felt their labor begin, and soon each gave birth to a son. The son of Changing Woman was Monster Slayer and his brother was Child of Water. Together they would slay all the alien monsters but four and make the earth a place where the human beings, the five-fingered beings as the Diné call them, could live and flourish.

The four monsters they didn't slay were Old Age Woman, Cold Woman, the Poverty Creatures, and Hunger Man. Monster Slayer wanted to destroy them, because he had promised Sun, his father, that he would eradicate all the monsters. But his mother, Changing Woman, had told him that he had been successful against all the monsters she wanted destroyed. "Some things are better left as they are," she told him, as Indian mothers have been telling their children since that time.

Of course, he didn't listen. But when Wind whispered to him where he could find each of these monsters, he sought them and discovered the wisdom of his mother's words. As Old Age Woman pointed out, killing her would mean that the five-fingered beings would have no reason to have children. And when a boy reached his sexual peak, or a girl reached her womanhood, they would not engage in sex and much of the joy and depth of their lives would be lost. Nor, she added, would they grow and thrive if she wasn't there to quietly and slowly sap their energies so they would age. Youth would lose its meaning, and wisdom would be unattainable. That's what she said.

Cold Woman didn't mind dying, as she made clear to Monster Slayer. She was wretched as she was, she said, and dying would be very welcome. But the problem with her disappearance was that the heat of the sun would wither all of life without cold to lessen its blast.

The same thing happened with the Poverty Creatures, who informed Monster Slayer that their job was to help people care about themselves, their families, and the earth. Without the threat and fact of poverty, they said, no one would have any reason to be inventive, no one would ever make anything new. Thus, the five-fingered beings would not use their creative natures and they would languish being less than their fullest selves.

Monster Slayer then sought and found Hunger Man, but Hunger Man explained that without him there would be no reason for people to cultivate plants. They would lose their taste for cooking and eating. Many of the pleasures of being together

would be denied them. They would not learn to tend to live-
stock and would miss most of all their close relationship with
the sheep.

In the end, Monster Slayer returned to his mother and agreed
that her assessment of the situation was the right one. "Some
things are indeed better left as they are," he said.

In order to get the weapons and skill to destroy the alien monsters, Monster Slayer and Child of Water had had to make a
long, dangerous journey to Sun's house. It was with the help of
Spider Woman that they were able to find their way to Sun's
eastern home. They had inadvertently gained the interest of the
alien monsters and fled their home in an attempt to protect
their mothers from harm. In their confusion, they fled along the
Path of the Rainbow blindly, not realizing that they had taken a
forbidden way. In time they came to Spider Woman's house,
which was beneath the ground. They climbed down into her
house at her invitation, and at her urging told her their story.
They said they did not know who their fathers were, but that
their mothers were Changing Woman and White Shell Woman.

Spider Woman told them she recognized Monster Slayer as
Sun's son, and that she would help them get to his home far
above them in the sky. The way was perilous, she warned
them, and they would face many alien monsters who lived between earth and sky.

"But I will give you this hoop," she said, showing them a
hoop made of the feathers of Monster Eagle. "You must hold
this before you and face your attacker boldly, without fear.
Then sing the chant I will teach you, and you will be safe."

Not only did they face the peril of the alien monsters, she told
them, but four great dangers stood along the way they must
take: the great rocks that crush, the knife-edged reeds that rend,
the needle-spiked cactuses that pierce and shred, and the boiling sands that sear all who pass.

"You must use the hoop to pass through these perils and per-
severe. If you fail, all will perish. Do not be alarmed that your
father is not glad to see you. He will probably be almost as difficult as the alien monsters or the dangerous places. Be quiet and
do as he says. I have helped you because this is your task to do,

and now you have the power to get help for yourselves and your people."

As they left her place, she bid them good-bye. "Go on your journey, and walk in beauty," she said.

After many fearsome events, they finally came to the house of Sun. There they faced his suspicion and met the trials he had set for them, but when he finally accepted Monster Slayer as his son, he tried to set a condition on the youths' use of what he had taught and given them. His condition was that they make an agreement that Changing Woman would become Sun's wife.

Of course Monster Slayer knew his mother better than that. A woman of decision and ability, she would brook no agreements on her behalf. "She makes her own decisions," he told his father. "You'll have to ask her yourself."

When all but the last four alien monsters were finally destroyed, Sun came to check on the youths' progress. On receiving their report, he agreed that they had indeed done well. Then he asked the young men to pass a message from him to Changing Woman. He wanted her to meet him at the summit of Giant Spruce Mountain in the space of four days.

At that time, Changing Woman, seeing that her son was grown and the alien monsters defeated, felt the urgings of her inner self to leave there and find a place of peace for herself. She told her son and White Shell Woman what she intended.

White Shell Woman agreed with her decision to go, saying that she too was weary of mothering and warring and wished to live alone for a time.

On the day she and Sun were to meet, Changing Woman climbed to the summit and went to the place where she had sought him as a mate. As she sat remembering the one time Sun joined her, she recognized how much she had changed, how the tumultuous years of their wars with the alien monsters had firmed her nature. "I am not the maiden I once was," she thought. "I have become a woman, secure in my judgment and decision. What I once longed for seems not so attractive now. I was born amid the rainbow. Dark cloud and male rain attended my first cry. The turquoise mountain was my beginning, and the Air Spirit People are my home."

She remembered, not without bitterness, how warm and sweet Sun had felt inside of her the only time he'd come to her,

and how she had longed over the years to feel him inside her
again. She had told her son of her anger at him. "Once I longed
for him and opened myself to him. It was a partnership I wanted.
But he has not returned to see me even once, not once has he
even spoken to me. Now he wants to see me, I wonder why.
Maybe he wants to brag about his son," she had said.

Engrossed in her memories, Changing Woman did not at first
see Sun as he approached her. He came toward her, deep bronze
and radiant, smiling. And he attempted to embrace her, but she
demurred. She longed for peace as she had once longed for
companionship, having tasted motherhood, and having raised
her son and endured dangers and heartache. She wasn't sure
she believed in her maidenly dreams of crystal fastnesses and
shining joining. She knew the beauty of winter and summer, of
sky and earth, and within herself she was content.

Sun knew her thought, but he hoped to change her to his
way of mind. "Our son agreed that you would become my
wife," he said.

"What difference does it make to me what someone else
agrees to?" she asked. "Unless I enter into an agreement myself, there is no agreement. No one else decides for me."

But Sun persisted. "I gave you a son and helped him defeat
the alien monsters. For that, you owe me," he said.

"I did not seek your help, as you know," the lovely woman
said. Her face was serene and clear in her certainty. "You gave
what aid you chose, and then only because your trials committed you. You had no choice in that. Monster Slayer is as
much your son as mine."

And Sun withdrew, moving away for several paces from
the woman he wooed. He searched his thought carefully and
found there the loneliness and dreariness of his splendid and
inexorable life. He found there an exhaustion with same-
ness, with what he could not change. Determined to end his
pain, he at last turned to Changing Woman. "I need you," he
said simply, revealing his true mind. "Please come and live with
me. You are alone and I am alone. What good is it, to be so
lonely?"

Changing Woman heard the loneliness in his voice. She knew
that it matched the loneliness of her own heart. But while she
understood the rightness of his thought, she also knew there

were certain matters he should understand. Quiet a while, she at last responded. "If I come to live with you, you must give me a fine hogan in the west, as fine as the one I have heard you have in the east.

"Build it on the water so I can be free of earth peoples' quarrels. I have been too much involved in war. Around my hogan you must plant white shell, blue shell, turquoise, haliotis, soapstone, agate, redstone, and jet because I wish them always near me in their beauty. And as I shall be lonely during your long days away, you must give me many elk, buffalo, deer, long-tails, mountain sheep, jackrabbits, prairie dogs, and muskrats for companionship.

"Should you make a house for me where I can live in peace and where I can walk in beauty, then I will consider becoming your wife," she said gravely.

Sun was offended at her demands. "Who are you that you should make these demands," he blazed.

"I am the wife you long for," she replied softly. "Think about it. It is you who long for our match. I would be as content to remain alone. And you are bored and life to you is dreary, for you are of the sky, and always must be the same. I am of the earth, and I change with the seasons. You are always moving while I remain in place. In these ways, we complete each other, make the world of being whole.

"You and I are of the same spirit stuff, and so we are of equal worth. As unlike as we are, we are similar; and if there can be no harmony between us, then there can never be harmony any place in the universe.

"If such harmony is to occur, then you must take my needs seriously and treat them with respect. My requests must be important to you. Every exchange between us must be equal. What I take from you, I give in equal measure. That is how it must be."

Sun was silent for a time. Then slowly he went to her and his heart was clear. This time they embraced as equals, for Changing Woman could see that he understood.

Finally the day of Changing Woman's departure came. Two groups of holy people, the Mirage People and the Ground Mist People, came with her to herd the animals accompanying her. Before she left, she said good-bye to White Shell Woman, Monster Slayer, and Child of Water. She told the boys they were now men who could stand on their own.

During her journey, her body changed dramatically. Her breasts became full and heavy, her hips spread and rounded, her belly filled out, and the fullness of her womanly beauty shone. During the journey also, the herds swiftly became numerous, many breaking away and going to range all over the continent.

Four days after they left her home, they arrived at the mountain known as San Francisco Peak in the language of the whites, where Changing Woman and the holy people with her stopped to perform a certain ceremony. Laying her across the top of the mountain with her head to the west, the direction she was heading and where she would live with her husband, the holy people stretched out her arms and legs and massaged her body. Changing Woman told the people to do the same with all maidens who reached puberty, which the Diné do even now, attempting to mold the bodies of maidens into the lovely lineaments of Changing Woman.

So Changing Woman moved to her western home, to become the wife of Sun. It is said that when they are having difficulties in their relationship, the harmony of the whole world decreases and many suffer.

After Changing Woman went to the west, White Shell Woman, Child of Water, and Monster Slayer also moved away. They went toward the San Juan Mountains. In the San Juan valley, where two rivers join, the men stopped. There, they declared, they would make their home. They can still be seen in the shimmer of light when the water rises from pools formed by a summer rain. In the moist, bright air you can see their forms shimmering.

White Shell Woman continued alone to the mountain near the emergence place of her people long ago, before they fled the alien monsters. In her heart she longed for them, and for the earth-surface people who would come. For four days she wandered from peak to peak, sleeping in a different high fastness each night. As the days passed, she recognized her loneliness. "I should have listened more carefully to my sister," she thought. "She cautioned me against coming here alone, fearing I would be lonely."

On the fifth day, she heard the familiar sound of Talking God approaching her. Soon he was with her, and she told him all that had transpired and where she and Changing Woman had gone. "Now she has gone to the west, and I have returned here. I long for companionship," she confided.

Talking God told her he would return in four days' time, and he went away. While she awaited his return, White Shell Woman made a strong house, one with a door opening to the east and a window facing west.

When four days had passed, Talking God returned, and with him were a number of holy people, including Changing Woman, who carried two soft buckskins over her arm. The other holy people had brought two ears of corn, which they carried into the house on a turquoise dish.

Talking God arranged the corn within the buckskin, and through his powerful ceremonial force, they transformed the ears of corn into two people, one male, one female. They were brother and sister. When they were finished, White Shell Woman led them into her hogan. She was very happy.

Some time after the ceremony, Talking God returned and introduced these five-fingered beings to two other kinds of beings, one male and one female. They were Sky Mirage Boy and Ground Mist Girl. He gave White Shell Woman two ears of corn and told her, "Grind them, but only one grain at a time."

White Shell Woman told Sky Mirage Boy and Ground Mist Girl that the man and woman who lived with her were made out of corn, and that as they were brother and sister they could not marry. "But children must be born for the people to become stronger and prosper," she said. "Maybe you can each marry one of them, then all will be well."

Following her advice, they did, and so the earth-surface people came into being. Soon each couple had children, and their households were thriving.

White Shell Woman chose one of their daughters for her companion, and she loved the child dearly. The child lived with her and slept with her at night, keeping her from being lonely, filling her heart.

But twice Talking God came to talk to her out of the hearing of the people. The second time, she spoke to the child, saying, "Grandchild, I must leave you. The holy people have sent for me, and I must go. I won't forget you or your people, be sure of that," she said. Then she vanished into the shimmering mountain air.

Four nights after she vanished, the child had a dream of her, in which White Shell Woman said she was well and happy. "The holy people have built me a house of white shell that is beautiful," she said. "I will live in that house forever. I don't think I will be seeing you again, nor will you see me in this form. But I won't be far. Look for me when it rains. The soft falling female rain, the corn that grows because of that rain will encompass me. Look carefully with a good heart and you will see me in them sometimes."

And when she awoke, the child told her people what White Shell Woman had said. "'Look for me in the soft, gentle rain, and seek me in the growing corn.' That's what Grandmother told me," the child informed them. "That's what she said."

STRANGE BURNING

There are a number of stories about Six Killer in the various collections of Cherokee myths and legends. She is (or was) the major deity of the Cherokee, the Apportioner, or as I have put it, the Measurer. For horticultural people, particularly in the kind of climate the Cherokee homelands enjoyed, a major function of the sun is to measure time. Calendars among the horticultural peoples are based on the sun's daily and seasonal positions as it moves between a northern and a southern point over the year. Knowing the measure of time is important for ceremonial reasons more than for economic ones, and the distinction is significant. Tribal people, pagans, do not center their lives on belongings, so economic considerations are not of primary concern for them. They believe that our physical needs are taken care of as a consequence of our meeting our spiritual obligations, and fulfilling those obligations depends on our harmony with the universe. We can tell a great deal about what obligations are upon us by knowing "what time it is," that is, what day and therefore what spiritual currents or forces are operative. Thus the function of Measurer is central to the prosperity and spiritual survival of the Cherokee Nation.

In pre-Christian civilizations, the function of measurer fell upon women and involved concerns other than solar movements. Women measured out the goods—foodstuffs, clothing, decorations, housing, and implements. They kept the stores and provided the sustenance. This was one of their spiritual obligations, and I think a major reason that obligation was seen as women's work was because it was the obligation of female supernaturals. Similarly, among many indigenous peoples major administration of justice was in the hands of clan matrons because the measurement of harmonious and balanced behavior by and among individuals is goddess work and thus, logically, the province of the feminine.

It is popular in modern America to believe that politics determines

84

destiny, but the traditionals say that the spirits are a more significant factor in human lives than politicians. The power of Six Killer—political, ceremonial, and spiritual—was great, judging from the stories still told about her.

In this retelling, I have strung several shorter narratives together, striving to create a sense of the fullness and complexity of her being. It is clear to me Six Killer was not seen as a one-dimensional divinity.

Sutalidihi, Six Killer, Sun Woman, lives in a house beyond the eastern sky, and each day she climbs the great arching path and travels to the west, returning each night along another path that runs on the upper side of the vault of the sky. Very long ago, long before there were any Cherokee, Sun Woman became too radiant for even the Nunnehi, the immortals of the upper and lower world. Needing to make some adjustment to her great power, their magicians chanted and prayed until they prevailed on Sun Woman to move upward a handsbreadth, but the radiance from her body was so great the heat it emitted still scorched all below. Again the ancestors of the Ani Kutani prayed and chanted, and at length Six Killer, Sutalidihi, was able to raise herself another handsbreadth. Still her profound radiance was searing; still they entreated her to make the enormous effort to move another handsbreadth higher. At last, together the Nunnehi conjurors and Six Killer succeeded in moving the great stone vault that constituted her pathway a full seven handsbreadths higher so her heat would not be unendurable to earth life.

The wise ones call the place Six Killer walks Gulkwagine Digalunlatiyun, the seventh height, because her place is the highest. The priests and holy people know Six Killer as their highest deity, for do they not call her the Measurer who determines the division of time into day and night and the duration of the four seasons? Is Six Killer not Grandmother of the Sacred Fire, Atsila Galunkwtiyu, the Divine Flame? Certainly no ceremony can be attempted without the presence of Sutalidihi in her guise of Ageyaguga, the Ancient One. Even the Nunnehi, the immortals, and the Yunwitsansdi, the little people, give her honor in their rites.

Does not this everlasting fire, from which every fire in the seven districts is rekindled every Green Corn time, exist permanently only in the central sacred mounds at Nikwasi and Kituhwa, whose warriors and strong women are still straight in the old ways? Does not her earth-fire burn still, deep within the heart of those ancient structures, just as her radiance nurtures and sears life on earth? Is it not true that because so many of the human beings no longer honor her or her daughter, fire, that her great anger threatens to unleash itself and consume us in its flame?

They say that long ago, when Sutalidihi was very young, a suitor used to come to her asi, her sleeping lodge. It was the custom for suitors to court women in the dark, because they did their wooing after the woman had retired for the night. But Six Killer was young, and she became curious about the identity of the man who came to her each night and filled her with delight. So she decided she would investigate the matter, and to this end she coated her hand with ashes from her banked fire. When her lover entered the asi, she welcomed him warmly. Caressing his face softly, with concern in her tone, she said she found his face cooler than usual. She asked if he felt ill. He said he was well, and the night proceeded as usual. But the next day, Six Killer realized that the one who had so delighted her with his caresses was her brother Geyaguga, for his face was smeared with ash. Realizing he had been discovered, he fled in shame, ever keeping himself separate from her. He is known to the old people as Red Man. He is called Nunda, Sun, or more fully, Nunda Sunayehi, Sun Living in the Night, just as she is commonly known also as Nunda or Nunda Idghi, Sun Living in the Day. To the white people they are called the sun and the moon.

Once, long after the marking of her brother, seven young men of the priestly caste, the Ani Kutani, determined to travel to the region where Six Killer made her dwelling. They longed to see her, and like their entire clan they were arrogant and did not recognize their proper place in the balance of the universe. They believed, like the privileged people of today, that nothing was too sacred for their interference. They thought they could do whatever they wished, go where they liked, trample on the lives of others who were not Ani Kutani. In times to come, the rest of the people would rise up against them. Though the Ani

Kutani held all the spiritual and mystical knowledge that the people needed to maintain the fullness of their religious and secular lives, the arrogance and uncaringness would grow so monstrous that all of them—men, women, and children, the aged, the infirm, everyone—would be slaughtered in a long battle with the other clans.

It was the sort of arrogance that would result in their ultimate destruction that led these seven lordly young men to venture eastward. Their journey was a long one. They first met people who were familiar to them; but as they traveled on, they found themselves among people whose demeanor, languages, and customs were alien to all they knew.

At last they came to the place of the sunrise, where the sky and the ground meet. The sky was a vault made of a solid substance they thought was stone, and it raised and lowered, revealing a doorway between sky and the ground. As they watched, Six Killer emerged through the open door of the raised vault and made her way westward, climbing quickly far above their heads, along the inside of the arch. They could make out her humanlike lineaments, but the brilliance of her aura was so great that they could not discern anything more about her. Thinking to fool Nunda Idghi, they waited until she had moved far above them then made for the still open door. The first one to enter the opening did so just as the solid vault lowered. He was crushed beneath its great weight. The six remaining men fled, returning home at last. But strangely—perhaps because their journey took such a long time, or perhaps because the events they had witnessed and the magic they had engaged in to make the journey in the first place claimed all their energies—they returned old men. Some say that the name Six Killer comes from that event, proving once more that her power is supreme. Humans, however great they believe their knowledge and power to be, dishonor her at their peril.

Once a clan of magicians determined to kill her because she wouldn't respond to their will. Their disrespect infuriated her, and she raged at them continually, causing them to burn and sicken with illnesses they could not cure. Their skins erupted in painful and deadly swellings, their limbs and organs developed horrible pains, their very life-fire turned on them and degenerated into growths that ran like wildfire through their beings, leaving nothing healthy in place. So many died that everyone knew someone who had been afflicted. The people of the seven districts were filled with fear, sorrow, and anger. They demanded that the conjurors (as medicine people are called among the Cherokee) and the priests stop the killing.

To this end, they consulted with the little people, the Yunwitsansdi, whose magic was even more powerful than their own. It was known that Six Killer stopped at her daughter's temple (townhouse) every day about midpoint in her daily journey across the sky. It was determined by the shamans of the Yunwitsansdi that the best way to destroy Six Killer was to lay an ambush there.

They transformed two human men into snakes, Spreading-adder and Copperhead. The two made their way, by means of the incantations of the Yunwitsansdi, to the door of Six Killer's daughter's temple to await Six Killer's arrival. At the appointed time, Six Killer, the Measurer, appeared. Spreading-adder made ready to spring at her, but her brightness so blinded him he was able only to spit out a stream of yellow slime. As she swept past Spreading-adder into the townhouse, she conjured him, fixing him in the snake form he had taken. Henceforward he and his descendants would only be able to spit slime at their would-be victims. This so frightened the man who was transformed as Copperhead that he fled without attempting to molest the goddess.

Defeated, the conjurors and priests returned to the people empty-handed. They told the people that Six Killer the Woman God was so jealous of them that she would not stop her assaults on the innocents. She was bent on destroying them all. They told the people that she was angry because when they looked at her they squinted and grimaced, but when they looked at her brother who followed her ever in shame, they smiled. They did not tell the people that her rage was directed at the presumption of the priestly and shamanistic clan who abducted women from other clans whenever they desired, driving their hapless victims to suicide, leaving families—even husbands and children—to grieve. They did not mention that her power as Measurer meant that she measured the actions of even the Ani Kutani, and when she found their actions abhorrent she let her displeasure be known and felt by all. For after all is said and

done, all are responsible for the well-being of the planet and of
each other.

The sickness continued, striking every household. The people
feared that not one human would be left if it didn't stop, so
again they called on the Ani Kutani to use their arts and skills to
bring the suffering to an end. Helpless in their own power and
inexplicably unable to consult with the immortals, the priests
again consulted with the Yunwitsansdi. Their advice was the
same as before: they would ambush Sun Woman as she entered
her daughter's dwelling, but this time they would send two
snakes whose deadliness could not be bested.

Again they transformed two priests into serpents. This time
one became a diamondback rattler and the other was transformed into the fearsome Uktena, a monstrous beast whose
name derived from the lethal potency of his glance, and whose
head was crested with two horns and with a triangular sheet of
pure crystal that was perfectly transparent except for a thin red
streak that ran down its center. So fearsome and powerful was
this being that no one doubted his ability to destroy Sutalidihi.

But Rattlesnake, being anxious to see the end of Sun Woman,
rushed forward to the door of her daughter's house and when it
opened he struck, killing Sun Woman's daughter instantly. Hor-
rified, he fled, returning to the camp where the priests and the
little people's shamans waited. Seeing the error, the Uktena was
filled with rage, and also quit the scene. Indeed, his anger grew
dangerous, becoming second only to the fury of Sun Woman.
He had become her adjunct in some mysterious way, a result
that was not at all part of the little people's plan—or was it? He
became so dangerous to the humans that the little people conjured him upward to another plane, where he still resides, coming forth only at the behest of holy people, wizards, wise ones.

When Sutalidihi discovered her daughter's body, she returned
to her dwelling beyond the sky vault, and the land lay in darkness. The people did not die any longer, but in that long darkness they sorrowed and feared. Surely they would starve. Surely
they would perish of spiritual malaise. Surely they could not
dance, they could not go to the water and clean their inner and
bodily selves. Surely their worship services could no longer
bring them into harmony with all that is. With Sun Woman vanished, the whole earth mourned and would not bring forth life.

Once again the wise ones among the people went to the little people, the Yunwitsansdi. They were told that in order to bring Sun Woman forth they would have to travel to the Shadowlands to the west and return with her daughter. Seven men agreed to make the journey, and the Yunwitsansdi equipped them with a box and seven sourwood rods, each a handsbreadth long. They told them that when they arrived all the dead would be dancing, and that they would find the young woman alone. Each was to strike her with his rod in turn, and on the seventh blow she would fall unconscious. When that occurred, the men were to place the ghost woman in the box and seal it. On their return journey they were not to open the box, no matter what the ghost girl said.

So the men set out. After a journey of seven days, they found the camp of the ghosts in the Shadowlands to the west, just as they had been told, and as promised, a dance was in progress. Sun Woman's daughter stood alone just outside the circle, and the men drew her a little distance from the dancers, surrounding her and each in turn striking her with his rod. When she fell unconscious at their feet, they placed her in the box and sealed it before starting home.

But before they had returned to the settlement, she began to plead with them to open the box, complaining of hunger, thirst, and finally, suffocation. Frightened, one of them opened the box a crack. As he did so, they felt a rush of air, and immediately heard the sound of a bird's wings beating through the air of the surrounding darkness. As it passed over their heads, they heard the Kwish! Kwish! Kwish! cry of the redbird, the ghost of Sun Woman's daughter had become Redbird, and the sacred fire of the Ani Kutani had fled, never to be recaptured.

Returning empty-handed to the lodge where the conjurors of the people and of the little people together awaited them, the priests opened the box and found it filled with cold ash, the spirit within having fled. Their despair was great, for by their foolish lack of determination they had not only ensured that Sun Woman, Six Killer, would continue her mourning, but they would forever after be unable to bring any of their own loved ones back from the land of the dead.

Aware that the people had begun to mature, that they had

learned that their powers were limited and their wills were not as strong as their desires, and seeing that the necessary quality of humility—which is nothing more than realizing that every- one has a proper place and a proper power—Sutalidihi relented. When the people began to show they respected her and trea- sured the spiritual and mortal gifts she bestowed upon them, she left her house of mourning and smiled once more.

THE DAY THE END BEGAN

In 1519 tiny Hernán Cortés and his band of equally small but hardy adventurers disembarked on the coast of Yucatán. They were intent upon conquering and claiming the new world and its inhabitants for Crown and Church. Their party consisted of five hundred men and sixteen horses. In March of that year, the people of Tobasco gave the slave woman Malinalli to Cortés; and by the end of the year, with her considerable assistance, he had entered Tenochtitlán, the center of Mexica civilization, and swept the emperor and great speaker Moctezuma from power.

How a twenty-seven-year-old soldier with five hundred men, sixteen horses, and a young woman as his diplomat succeeded in overthrowing a confederacy that controlled a land area larger than Spain is an intriguing tale. The Aztec confederacy, which claimed a population of ten million, was filled with great cities and numerous towns and villages and boasted of well-trained armies of thousands of courageous soldiers. William Brandon in his history of Native America, The Last Americans, writes that "the Spanish had superior weapons— but not that much superior" and notes that the quilted armor the Aztec soldiers wore was superior to Spanish armor. He goes on, "Throughout the first march on Mexico, after they were joined by Malinal, the Spanish were forced to fight in only one instance. . . . Otherwise, the road of their first penetration into the country . . . was paved by a string of diplomatic victories as remarkable as so many straight passes at dice" (1974, 101).

What happened was due in far larger part to what time it was than to military or diplomatic strategies. That year was Ce Acatl, One Reed, the year when the god Quetzalcoatl, Precious Twin (quetzal is the name of a green-feathered bird and can also be translated "precious" or "beautiful") or Morning Star—whose twin was Evening Star—was to return. He had made that promise long before, when he

*had left the people and gone, like Naotsete, to the east. He had taught
a reasoned and gentle spiritual way, one that differed markedly from
the course they had taken. Instead of the sacrifice of other humans, he
taught them to sacrifice themselves, as the Goddess Tonantzin was
said to do continually in the interests of the life and prosperity of all.
One mode of self-sacrifice was to pierce their tongues and draw lengths
of a certain grass through them. The name of that grass in Nahuatl,
the language the Aztecs spoke, is malinalli, "penance grass."*

*Cihuacoatl, Serpent Woman, was one of the two major goddesses of
the Mexica group of Aztecs. Her primary priest was Tlacaelel, whose
office was often referred to as cihuacoatl. The other goddess central to
the Aztec cosmogyny was Coatlicue, Serpent Skirt. Her priest was
Moctezuma II, whose office was sometimes called quetzacoatl, more
often tlatoani, "great speaker," or uelatoani, "emperor." The emperor
ruled with the help of a four-man council of elders and was elected to
office by noblemen from their ranks.*

*Serpent Skirt was often seen in conjunction with her son Huitzilo-
pochtli, "Blue Hummingbird on the Left." This god was associated
with the sun and was one of the aspects of the god Tezcatlipoca, Smoking Mirror. The fire in which he lived burned at the portal of Coatlicue's temple, and it was here that captives were burned, to feed the
Earth and her heart, Huitzilopochtli. They did this so that the goddess
could continue to give life and prosperity to humankind.*

Long ago, just before the coming of the white man, the cihuacoatl, the sacred priest of Cihuacoatl, Serpent Woman, sat
among his advisors. He'd had a disturbing dream the night before, and he had called his prophesiers and shamans to him,
hoping they could interpret the dream in a more hopeful way.
Tlacaelel was still shaken from the experience. It had surely
been no ordinary dream, its vividness and clarity marked it un-
mistakably as prophecy. And, well he knew, the Great Serpent,
his goddess, did not send lightly messages of such import. The
book of destinies and his own training told him that One Reed,
the time of the end, was upon them.

For years the signs of calamity had grown, though the New
Fire ceremony had gone as it should eleven years before. The
priests had extinguished and rekindled the fire of the Lord of the

Dawn, the Lord of Time, Xiuhteuctli, whose abode was within the dark earth that lay before the figure of the Great Goddess Snake Woman, Cihuacoatl. It caught quickly in the empty breast of the great man they had sacrificed, and it flamed hungrily. From this sacred flame they had built the great bonfire that signaled to all for many miles around that the world would continue, the sun would emerge again from within the earth. From that bonfire, flame was borne by runner without mishap to the central fire house at the great temple of Blue Hummingbird, god of war and sacrifice, and taken from there through the districts to every temple and thence into every household.

But other omens were not so hopeful. One who knew what time it was knew the inevitable flowering and withering. Now was the time of the end, and the withering was upon them. Ah, fate, he sighed, remembering the words of the song:

> *We only came to sleep*
> *We only came to dream*
> *It is not true, no it is not true*
> *That we came to live on the earth*
> *We are changed into the grass of springtime*
> *Our hearts will grow again green*
> *And they will open their petals*
> *But our body is a rose tree*
> *It puts forth flowers then withers.*

The cihuacoatl felt downcast. He knew that the signs were upon them, and that all they could do was meet their fate as befitted a great nation, submissive to the turns of destiny, ever in the hands of the gods. He cast about in his mind, searching for a sign that would say otherwise. But he could not deny what had occurred in the past few years.

The great pillar of fire, the goddess that had sent the last rulers, the Toltecs, to their graves, had been seen every night for four years. A temple had suddenly burst into flame and burned with unearthly swiftness to the ground; the ceiling beam in the school of music sung a prophecy of the death of Anahuac, the Land between the Waters. Worse, a second temple had been struck by lightning, and that out of a clear sky. Surely Blue Hummingbird, Huitzilopochtli, was warring, perhaps in his death throes. For no reason, except the obvious one, the lake had risen suddenly, drowning some, destroying homes, showing the power of the Precious Twin was rising. And a star serpent had fallen screaming to earth in full light of day. Most terrifying of all, Serpent Woman, the Great Goddess, had been heard weeping in the night, wailing through the streets of the calpulli, the districts, "Oh, my beloved children, where will I hide you?"

He sent a message to Moctezuma, his priestly counterpart and lord. Together these two great leaders, himself the high priest of Cihuacoatl, Serpent Woman, and Moctezuma, ueitlatoani, emperor and great speaker of the Great Goddess Coatlicue, Serpent Skirt, had labored in every arena to stave off the dictates of time. But Time was the first child of the universe, and each of his steps gave life to each day in every year, every age, every eon. There was no changing what each day contained, since time began.

This year was Ce Acatl, One Reed, the year of Precious Twin's return. Nothing could stay the hand of fate, not all the sacrifices of every man, woman, and child in the whole polity. But they tried. The temple walls were thick and black with blood. Blood ran over the lip of the great bowl Moctezuma's father had commissioned. The penitents, the long hairs, roamed the streets in ever increasing numbers, their torn skin and wildly uncombed hair bearing witness to the harshness of their discipline. War was everywhere, and more blood spilled. It ran in rivers throughout the land, from sea to sea it poured, and still there was no stopping it. The emperor himself had built a great new temple to his goddess and one to her son Huitzilopochtli, Blue Hummingbird. What more could they do to assuage her hunger and to moderate the fate that awaited them?

One Reed, the year Quetzalcoatl would return. Surely it meant that the cycle would end in thirty-nine years. Whatever would happen after the predicted return of Quetzalcoatl, Precious Twin, the Wind, the Whirlwind, the Morning Star, the god who forbade human sacrifice, who insisted that all should sacrifice themselves instead of others, sacrifice their own extreme appetites and their comfort, so that Sun, Tonatiuh, He Who Goes Forth Shining, the Eagle, the Ruler of Fate, would continue to emerge from the innards of the Great Mother Tonantzin, and she would continue to bear corn, children, and light? Whatever would happen to them, the priesthood, the people of Anahuac, the tribe of Mexica, when Quetzalcoatl returned? At the end of this cycle would Sun remain unborn and all humankind be devoured by demons?

His brother Moctezuma and his large retinue entered the great hall where Tlacaelel, Serpent Woman's high priest, sat surrounded by his company. Equal in status, distinct in function, these men were responsible for the considerable prosperity and spiritual welfare of the Aztec Nation. Having greeted Moctezuma and seen to his comfort, Tlacaelel recounted his dream. Silent for a time, Moctezuma considered his *quate's* words. Then he signaled to one of those with him. "Bring the mirror," he ordered.

A heavy quiet had descended upon the gathering. All knew of the events of the past years: the putrid death that swept devastatingly through the population—surely a sign of the return of the time of the beginning, of Nanahuatl, the Ulcerated One, He Whose Body Was Running Sores. There was also a rumor that strange beings had been seen upon the waters and lands far to the east, where the death had already devastated millions.

Soon the sacred mirror was carried in. With great ceremony they bared its dark surface to Moctezuma the emperor, he who alone was empowered to gaze within its depths. Smoking Mirror, the other face of Blue Hummingbird, had come with them from their homelands, far in the past. It had shown them the being they called Tezcatlipoca, Smoking Mirror, standing within the ruined temple they had left behind centuries before in their flight from defeat. He had shown them their path, had told them they would rest when they saw an eagle perched upon a cactus in the center of a lake. They had traveled long until they had found the place, naming it Mexico-Tenochtitlán, place near the cactus. Mecitli, Grandmother Maguay, had brought them into existence, the tribe of the Mexica, and she was their dear Creator and Grandmother.

Fearing what would be revealed, Moctezuma turned his gaze upon the obsidian surface and held it there. His breathing slowed and his form relaxed. He saw a large ship, different from those of the Maya, their neighbors to the far east, and saw it disgorge bearded warriors astride antlerless deer. He saw the figure of Quetzalcoatl, crowned with cactus and spread upon the tree of life. "Ah," he thought. "It must be so. They will conquer us, we who have been victorious over all." Then the scene shifted and he saw a bird, its ash grey almost lost in the smoky darkness of the mirror. It flew toward him and he jerked his head aside automatically, and it flew past him into the room, vanishing.

The room was filled with silence. They all knew it was not more reasonable to wish to change the times than to wish to change the annual movement of Morning Star and his dark twin Evening Star. Their emperor told them that he had seen Precious Twin, Morning Star, crossing the face of the Shining One, Sun, and because of this their path was determined. He said that they would face the coming armies with fortitude. He would go east to the place where the Dragon God, Precious Twin, would touch land and there offer him his choice of garb from the four gods they served. The choice of garments would seal their fate, and make known the god's intention.

There would be no gainsaying One Reed's victorious emergence into the life of his people as he had promised long ago when he had gone eastward, away from them. "When One Reed climbs the tree of life, leaps into the sky, it is time again for returning the balance from death to life, from war to peace, from conquest and destruction to reconciliation and healing," Moctezuma counseled. "That time is upon us now. Did I not myself see Precious Twin sail across the face of the Great Shining One only eleven years ago? However bitter our fate might seem, it is as it should be, and we could ask no more," he said.

Then he reminded them, as was his duty, of the events that faced them. Quetzalcoatl would return, carried upon the tree of life, crowned with cactus thorns. At the time of his coming, when One Reed would have returned and the cycle been fulfilled, a new order of living would begin. But it would begin in the slow degradation of the people who were faithful to him. It would be a dreadful time.

For nine xiuhmolpilli, nine bundles of fifty-two years, they would sink into a morass of poverty, ignominy, disgrace. They would become a people spurned and spit upon. Not only the Aztecs, the people of the sun, but all the peoples of the great lands surrounding them.

"But we know how to suffer, and how to endure. Making sacrifices to our gods is not new to us," the emperor said. "And as we pulled ourselves up from the last disaster, long ago, so we will rise up again. At the end of the cycle of descent, we will ascend. We will once again lead the world into its proper place of balance. We will lead the people into the second era of Tula, the peaceful land. We know there is nothing on earth we own, not even our lives. All is the gods', all is the Great Mother's, she who gives us life and takes us back into her womb."

Then the tlatoani, the great speaker, directed the cihuacoatl to speak to the people and tell them to prepare. The signs were clear, and their part was clear. They would make ready for the coming of the god. It only remained to discover which face that god would wear. It was their duty to submit to whatever the gods decreed.

Moctezuma withdrew. He went from Tlacaelel's great hall to the temple of his own goddess, Coatlicue, Serpent Skirt. Before her statue he studied her fearsome lineaments. The monolith was huge, standing firmly in the courtyard of the great temple he himself had had built. It was in an attempt to honor her, to let her feel his devotion and spare her children that he had done so. Gazing up at her, he eyed the stonecarved rattlesnakes that formed her skirt, whence her name. He studied the skull that hung about her middle, the hearts that formed her grisly necklace, reminders that she hungered and would be fed on human hearts offered in exchange for all her gifts. The hands in that same necklace fed the nobles like himself when the limbs of the offering had been severed and bits of sacrificial flesh were passed among the celebrants. The Great Dragon Lady whose effigy stood before him was fearful indeed in her power. Movements of her body caused the earth to writhe and tremble, raising mountains suddenly, and as suddenly creating deep canyons.

He feared her as much as he loved her, and he recognized that her power lay as much in her continual sacrifice as in her primacy. Was she not the first and greatest of the gods, the source of food and life? Her head was not part of the carving; she was more fearsome than one could safely look upon, so in place of her visage reared two great heads of rattlesnakes, fangs bared and touching. To his eye, those great heads closely resembled eagles standing beak to beak, and the comparison suited his sensibility. Were not reptiles and birds all but the same, one of sky, one of earth, but somehow united as they were united in the person of the strange god who chose to return with his teaching of peace and penitence, sacrifice of self rather than of others?

Weary, Moctezuma bowed to his goddess's taloned feet, and began the long descent.

Tlacaelel stood a time after Moctezuma left. He was still caught in the intensity of his dream, and while the great speaker's words had confirmed his own knowledge, it did not restore his sense of purpose. The signs were too many and too complete for there to be any question that this was the age Precious Twin had referred to in his promise to return. But that was not what troubled the high priest.

No, his uneasiness lay in a certain anomaly, a pattern that seemed to emerge from the murk of events that pointed to something other than, or more than, what he knew or believed. He could imagine the end of all that is. Simply, when the fire was extinguished at the end of this period, it would not be rekindled.

Long ago, the god Mixcoatl, father of One Reed, had used a fire drill to ignite the first fire, and for ages after they had followed his example at the time of the New Fire. Every fifty-two years, they had repeated the ceremony, and for all the years of their count the sun had agreed again to be born, the great dark womb of the Mother of Night had birthed him again to give the people light. Nor did the omens signify that time was almost at an end. As the great speaker had said, they would live.

But of what would that living consist? For many ages the gods had contended, war and peace, famine and plenty, death and life. There was no lack of unity in that, it was simply the order of the universe, a universe that was born and reborn from the womb of the Mother, as the gods had emerged from the womb of Star Skirt, as the spirit of the sun was born from the womb of Spirit Woman, as men emerged from the wombs of their mothers. As he thought, he could picture Star Skirt, her belted skirt of studded leather strips swirling about her legs.

He could not imagine that the goddess would die, nor her children the gods. Yet something of that fear seemed to haunt his thought, a knowing which he could form in neither words nor image. He felt as though the heart that beat strong and steady within his chest would burst. The pain within it came from the flint knife of the goddess, Flint Knife who was her firstborn, the Knife that was her Sacred Tongue. She, Coatlicue, the goddess of all the heavenly beings and mother of all the gods, seat and source of divinity, the profound authority over all. He felt again the stabbing pain of his heart.

How many hundreds of times had he sent the avatar of Knife, bundled as though a newborn child to the marketplace to be set by some peasant woman to watch? When the day was done and the bundle unwrapped, the knife revealed its face and soon captives were brought to the temple of his goddess to give their lives so the people could prosper. The pain he felt now told him she hungered, but it told him something more, something he could feel in his dream, but could not say.

Signaling to a few of his assistants, he went out. Soon they came to the tellen, the low enclosure that was the sacred precinct of Cihuacoatl, Serpent Woman. Struggling not to hold his hand pressed against the painful stabbing in his chest, he recognized that this was a further sign, one for him alone, given by his goddess the Great Serpent.

In the beginning, after Star Skirt had given birth to Flint Knife, it had fallen to the earth and been used by one of her later children, Mixcoatl, in a war to compel the other gods to provide their parents with food. After the battle, he had continued on in the ways of the hunter and warrior, prepared always to see that his mother was fed. Along his way he met the great goddess of the earth and she gave birth to his son, One Reed, Quetzalcoatl.

Quetzalcoatl had a mission to wrest form from chaos. This he performed in concert with his brother Tezcatlipoca, Smoking Mirror. Over and over they compelled the Great Dragon to bring forth life, form, from her formlessness. In the doing, Tezcatlipoca had wrested her from chthonian turbulence and held her by the jaw above it. That jaw was still the marker for the beginning of days on their sacred counts. Their lives depended on her captivity, and their lives went to feed her so she could produce food for them.

But it was not so clear as that. In the beginning, the god Tonatiuh—the son of Cihuacoatl's sister goddess, Coatlicue—had agreed to sacrifice himself to become the sun and had leapt into the fire the gods had set. But once in it, he refused to rise unless he was fed with the hearts and blood of the gods ringed around him. Morning Star had leapt into the fire to slay the treacherous Tonatiuh, but was himself slain. Because of his loss the gods submitted to Tonatiuh's demand and immolated themselves. Thus it had continued since, humans following in the path set them by the gods, sacrificing themselves to the hunger of To- natiuh so all could live, sacrificing themselves to the hunger of Cihuacoatl so she would continue to bring forth food.

But Morning Star was not defeated. He had disappeared for a time, reappearing as his counterpart Evening Star, then return- ing again as himself. And he had taught them another way, the way he had defended by giving himself to the flames and tri- umphing over them. But his way was strange, and it was only pe- riodic. How could they not fall into the flames? How could they leap into them and emerge again, reborn? Was that not what his tlatoani, his emperor, had promised them? That somehow, however strange their transformation might be, they would again rise in the spring sky, whole and precious once more.

Tlacaelel entered the Tlillan, the great cave the Mexica had built for Cihuacoatl's worship. The soot-covered walls crouched over the figure of the goddess and the images of all the gods of Anahuac, the Tecuacuiltin. He glanced to see if the last image that had been removed for a ceremony in its faraway village had been returned. Not seeing it, he determined to have an assistant see to its whereabouts. Standing before the effigy of the god- dess, more aware than usual that he must be careful not to touch her figure in any way, he swayed as his dream arose to engulf him.

He was confronted by her chalky, white-robed figure, her jawbone clean of any flesh, her mouth stretched wide in hun- ger. Her long, writhing hair seemed whipped by strong winds, and her headband of two knives gleamed in the soft light that surrounded her in an eerie glow. He felt himself recoil from her hideous appearance, even as he yearned toward her violent strength.

He was again awed by her giant dimensions. He saw on her back the knife of sacrifice, bundled like a child in her tilpa, her robe. For a moment all he could register was her great size and the purity of her white skin, how she stood white on white, the vision underscored by the startling black gleam of her obsidian earrings. As he stood, dazzled with horror and love, she changed into a beautiful young maiden, eyes enticing, hair flowing in long black coils about her shoulders and down her back and breasts. She extended a lithe young arm and beckoned. The snake bracelet on her wrist flicked its tongue as her fingers curved inward in her gesture, its eyes shining like rubies in the sun. And as swiftly as she had become the lovely young woman, she again shifted her shape, transformed into a long, bronze serpent. She coiled and made as if to strike, then slithered toward the portal, then through it to the fire of Xiuhteuctli, who was the heart of Earth. "Feed me," she said in tones that rang along the stone walls and tumbled along the stairs as the captives' dead bodies tumbled after her feeding time. "Feed me well. There is unrest among the people who know you do not attend to your duties. They have seen the signs I send, and they know full well why disaster is upon them. I will send many more sacrificial knives, my infants, so they may know I remain underfed. They will be your destruction if you do not heed me well."

"No, my Lady," the distraught priest protested. He fell to the stones, prostrating himself before her. "I will see to your needs, my Lady, of that you may be sure."

"I may be sure that my hunger will be assuaged. Many will be the captives that die in this new era. Many will be the hearts and great will be the supply of fresh blood. I will eat, my priest, I will eat. My son Huitzilopochtli will ensure that I am fed, that all my sisters and brothers are fed. He ever brings war to that end, I ever urge him to greater wars.

"Remember, in the new time," she said more softly, "when the god Precious Twin has returned among you to feed me on your own blood, wrung from your own flesh. There will come one, a human woman, whose tongue is sweet. It will rain blood upon you for generations. They will call her Malinalli, Grass of Repentance, and so she will be. She will lead you to give your blood and suffering to the great goddess Tlazolteotl, Eater of Filth, so you nobles, descendants of Tula, might cleanse yourselves of impurity and find a warrior-priest's paradise in the end.

"This I have told you," she sighed as the vision began to grow

dim and the voice retreated into soft echoes from the sooty
stones. "This you must heed."

Slowly the cihuacoatl, the snake priest, recovered himself. He
stood painfully, his knee throbbing from a blow it had received
as he fell to the stone. He looked slowly around him. There was
no sign of her. No sign that she had ever been there.

After a moment, he spoke to one of his assistants, telling him
to see to ordering captives from the great speaker and the warrior clans, the Eagles and Ocelots. Surely their store of prisoners
would yield a particularly pleasing sacrifice, he said, his voice
gruff and thick with emotion. Then he turned on his heel and
strode out of the Tlillan, into the slanting rays of the late afternoon sun.

Would his goddess fade in this fifth world as he had seen her
fade in his dream? Was that what haunted him? Shaken at the
enormity of his intuition, one that he knew with absolute certainty was correct, the high priest retired to his sumptuous
chambers, threw himself into a chair and wept.

RITUAL MAGIC
AND ASPECTS OF THE
GODDESSES

Cosmology is the study of the ordered arrangement of the universe, and in an arcane sense this section is a cosmology. The cosmogyny that unfolds is essentially laid out in the eight stories that compose this section, and they combine to provide a multifaceted picture of concepts the preceding stories introduced, knitting them to ritual as the mediating principle between human and supernatural. As we have seen in the void there is energy, and it is an energy that is self-aware. It is thinking. Nor is it a singular phenomenon, but multiplicitous, for intelligence cannot arise from the absence of intelligence, nor can variety arise from uniformity. The singular can no more give rise to the many than the many can become the singular. However we look at it—the multiverse that surrounds us, there is no such thing as *only,* no such thing as *one.* That we think otherwise is testimony to the depth of our patriarchalization. Snowflakes, leaves, humans, plants, raindrops, stars, molecules, microscopic entities all come in communities. The singular cannot in reality exist.

The void, or the Great Mystery (Great Mysteries would be more accurate), is not an object but a period; it consists of events. The events that transpire have neither beginning nor end. They simply are always and everywhere. (Location or place is also event, verb not noun, process not product.) The events of the void have names or intelligence-locations (processes) and action. All is mind—or perhaps it is more exact to say everythings are intelligence-bearing. But that can't be said in English, a monotheistic language structured in terms of hierarchy, individualism, objectification, and stopped motion. "Everythings are intelligences" is ungrammatical, nonsense. Yet however ungrammatical the construct may be, it is accurate.

The essential nature of the cosmos is female intelligences, that is, goddesses. There are several rather than one, indicating that multiplicity is a fundamental characteristic of all that is. The primacy of relationship is also expressed in the kinship of the creatrix intelligences, pointing to the basic organization of the multiverse or cosmos. As the multi-intelligences think in relationship contexts, ritual magic operates. Out of this particular mode of thinking—the primal, the cosmogynological, the ritual magic—all that are continue to exist enduringly, continuously. What changes or transformations occur are simply vast energy/intelligence fields doing what they do, doing it in concert, in harmony, and in significance.

The fundamental order of the multiverse thus is ritual, magical, transformative, and it is enduring because change is a basic characteristic of thinking. Further, relationship and thinking are basic characteristics of change. You might say that ritual magic is a three-way street, a three-legged process, a journey along a three-pronged road, and that three-part structure is eternal and infinite.

With the goddesses, the sacred twins or brothers are entities and expressions of this tripartite process, and they remind us that the masculine expression of multiversal energy/intelligence is movement of a dual, but not oppositional, nature. The duality that the masculine (which is a special case or subset of the feminine) embodies is complementary in essence, though that complementarity sometimes takes a form that appears adversarial or polar. The most notable characteristic of masculine intelligence is its periodicity, especially when considered against a background of endurance which is feminine. The warrior sings: I die, but the earth continues forever. Beautiful Earth, you alone remain. Or the anishinabeg claim: Woman is forever, eternal. Man comes from woman and to woman he returns.

Thus male energy is a certain kind of movement, as divine or mysterious in nature as female energy, but arising from it and returning to it. It is that kind of motion. Movement, motion, is all that is (all that are); matter is a special case of motion, and all motion is material because verbs are *names* at base. The Lakota say "God is moves." They characterize the Great Mystery as Skan, Sky That Moves, Wind. White Buffalo Woman is She Who Sends and Calls Back the Winds. The Navajo put Wind into the tale of creation and Wind, (Nílch'i) who moves, is the intelligence-being of Changing Woman, who is herself of the Air Spirit People.

Yellow Woman is taken by Whirlwind Man to his mother's home where she grinds corn as is the duty of a bride, to make a gift of her skill to her groom's mother. Whirlwind takes her and so she is possessed of power; not that he gives her power, but that he recognizes her power and therefore takes her home. Yellow Woman is ritual magic, and the story, like its companion tale, explores some of the meanings of her identity, as well as that of her sisters and their four-way relationship as it pertains to the working of magic and the place of ritual in magical operations.

The Yellow Woman stories and the other stories in this section explore the significance of ritual magic as a female identity, and they do so in a sacred manner. They explore sacred thinking, demonstrating that to think in a sacred manner is to participate in the ritual that is the time or location of a magical event. The story of Yellow Woman and Whirlwind Man, like the stories of how Grandmother Spider brought the light, Older Sister and Younger Sister, and the rest included here, is a magical event—not only as told but simultaneously as enacted. Both, not either, are necessary if the exploration is to bear the fruit of intelligence, if its significance is to be adequately conveyed. The stories in this section are all ritual-magic-stories (ritual AND magic AND stories). They are not stories about pretend beings such as populate children's literature, cartoons, and popular films. They are stories for pilgrims along the path, for those who are students of the woman's medicine way. When these stories are entered as a room is entered, as wilderness is entered, as the surf (and self) is entered, one moves into mythic space and becomes a voyager in the universe of power.

This section is concerned with the roles supernatural female intelligences play as mediators between the mortal and supernatural worlds. These goddesses and demigoddesses are agents of negotiation and as such inhabit the borderland between the purely supernatural and the purely mortal, two energy-modes that are connected at certain points along their respective spectra. When Yellow Woman mates with Sun Man, the twins result. It is fairly evident that this story is about planting. It is less evident that a connection between planting seeds in soil and planting seeds in Woman have analogous results: the bestowal of supernatural life that provides nourishment to the people.

The arcane implications of the story (of which my rendition is a fragment of a long cycle) are clarified in the story that follows. Yellow Woman who in the first story is an outcast who lives with her mother outside the community is in this narrative one of four sisters. The energy of female intelligence takes on many guises, reminding us that identity is formed by context and is a function of ritual purpose rather than of self-will or individuation. As an abductee, captive of holy forces, Yellow Woman effects the ritual her sisters devise to find her. Her return is contingent on her familial connection, which is the intelligence that renders the ritual the story embodies potent.

Community imparts power to Grandmother Spider's magic in the next story—one in which she operates as a supernatural or immortal rather than as a goddess or creative principle; while in the story of Qiyo Kepi we see the creative power of a full-fledged medicine woman at work. In her hands, water is a sufficient curative because her powers are enormous. She can shake her moccasins and populate the terrain with a variety of creatures.

White Buffalo Woman is a priestess; she is wakan̲, that is, sacred, powerful. The magic she manifests is not as important as the power of the teaching she brings. Rather, magic underscores the teaching, contextualizing the nature of right relations between the people and the mysteries, enabling them to navigate the borderland path that runs along the boundaries of the mortal and immortal domains.

Another kind of ritual magic is addressed in the story of Older Sister and Younger Sister, despite its echoes of the stories of Yellow Woman and Whirlwind Man and Qiyo Kepi. Like the former, the abductions result in a gift from the immortals to the people, though the gaining and giving of the gift necessitates the transformation of the women into immortals and entails their final separation from their community.

Each of the stories speaks to the isolation of the sacred women from their human communities in one way or another, indicating that the pursuit of sacred power requires the sacrifice of belonging, the loss of the familiar, and the attendant loss of identity and place. In a number of regards, the stories and the rituals they embody tell us that sacrifice of deeply personal needs is required of all who walk the path of power. The stories of Oshkikwe and Matchikwewis, which I wove together for the story that appears here, contain the poignancy of sacrifice but also much of the humor and balance that accompany experiences of the sacred.

With Clear Sky and Fair Maiden, the poignancy of transformational operations, manipulations whereby beauty and sorrow combine, becomes the empowering agency of creative ritual magic. In this story the creative prowess of female intelligence becomes once more the theme, drawing this section to a close that mates it with the section preceding it.

THERE IN THE NORTHWEST

Yellow Woman, or Yellow Corn Woman, is a model for how to be a woman. She is a sacred being as well. Infused with the breath of Naya Iyatiku, she empowers ceremonies and households, rabbit hunts, and the change of season. Many stories about her have been collected, and choosing among them was not an easy task. She is a many-faceted being whose adventures say as much about a people's philosophy as about their spiritual history—a variety of history that is central to Indian people's lives and virtually unknown in the Western world.

With difficulty I have chosen only two of her stories to recount in a two-part narrative. In the first, she gets with child, as they used to say in my grandmother's time, and her children are the Little War Twins, Masewe and Oyoyowe, the twins who become Grandmother Spider's companions and whose duty it is to protect the people and keep the lines of communication between them and the immortals, the katsina, clear.

In the second, she is abducted by Whirlwind Man, a being who can be seen often in the land of my birth. He dances along the plain madly, a dervish of giant proportions. I was taught to call his manifestations dustdevils, "chindi" my best friend said the Navajo call them.

Once one chased my husband and me down from the west mesa above Albuquerque. It followed us along the road where we were parked back to the nearby road we had driven up to get there, and then followed us, standing and simultaneously whirling and, I swear, shaking his dust fist at us from the cliff as we fled down the road it paralleled. Funny. I haven't gone back to that spot in the twenty years since.

1.

Long ago, Yellow Woman wanted to go gather piñons, pine-cones. It was that time, and all the people were going. The forest would feel so good in that later month, after so much heat. She begged her mother to take her. Now Yellow Woman and her mother were outcasts in the village. No one would play with the girl, and she was often lonely. Her mother felt sorry about this. She knew that they would not be able to join the rest in the gathering. But she agreed to go anyway. She gathered the provisions they would need, and some blankets on which to carry the piñons, and soon after the other villagers left, she and Yellow Woman followed. They gathered piñons, though they had to keep to themselves.

One afternoon, Yellow Woman was alone gathering the piñons. She heard soft footsteps near her. Looking up, she saw a handsome young man staring at her. She did not recognize him, but she smiled at him. She thought he might talk to her, and she was lonely.

The youth smiled back, and they began to talk. She told him a little about herself, and he told her that he came from the east, far away, from where the sun lived. He told her some fine tales about his journey to her land, and she was very entertained. After some time had passed, he took two piñons out of the pack he had been carrying. "I want you to taste these," he said. They were fine, fat piñons, so she took them, and cracking their brittle shells by biting them carefully, she pulled them apart and removed the fat sweet nuts and ate them. They tasted very good. When she had finished them, the youth stood up. He said he had enjoyed talking to her, but that he had to be on his way. The long sun of late afternoon was slanting through the pine-trees, making a golden haze on the dark air in the forest.

Yellow Woman bid him good-bye and watched as he disappeared into the golden haze. "My, what a fine young man he is," she said aloud, and she stood dreaming for a time. Then she noticed that the air was beginning to chill, so she gathered up the piñons she had picked, and putting them into her blanket, she turned and went back to her camp.

Some time after she and her mother returned to the village, Yellow Woman gave birth to twin boys. They grew very rapidly, and in no time were frolicking about the yard and asking their mother and grandmother all sorts of questions. As they grew they learned how to hunt, how to plant and care for corn, and how to weave—all the things a boy should know.

One day they asked Yellow Woman who their father was,

and she told them he was the sun. They begged to go and find
him, and she agreed.

So they began their long journey, provisioned with food their
grandmother had made them. Along the way they had many
adventures. They met up with Old Spider Woman, who vowed
to help them. She told them some secrets they would need to
know when they got to the sun's house, and she explained the
tests he would put them to so he would know they were truly
his sons.

After they got there, they were greeted by the sun's wife,
who was quite annoyed when they announced to her that they
were the sun's children. "Humph," she said, "he says all he does
while he's gone all day is check on his people." But she treated
the boys courteously enough, giving them some food and a
place to rest from their long journey.

That evening the sun went in to see the boys who claimed to
be his children, and he told them that there were a number
of tests they would have to meet to prove themselves his sons.

They agreed, and because of the knowledge and power they
had gotten from Grandmother Spider, they passed all of the
tests and were welcomed by the sun as his children.

He gave them many gifts, for themselves and for their mother
and grandmother, and he sent them home. And with the powers they had learned from him and Old Spider Woman, they became the helpers of the people for a long, long time.

They even created some of the earth's features. They made
canyons with their lightning bolt arrows, and they saved the
people from the great serpent when he raged over the flooded
lands of the first village.

In later times, they were turned to stone and stood on the
side of one of the tall mountains where they guard the people
even now. They live with Spider Grandmother, the keeper of
the fire, the bringer of light, the mind and maker of the world.

2.

There in the northwest, long ago, Yellow Woman was with her
three sisters, Blue Woman, Red Woman, and White Woman.
They had been working together making clothes. They made

leggings and women's belts and painted them like flowers. Thirsty, they looked into the water jars and saw that they were empty. They said, "We need some water."

Yellow Woman said she would go, and taking the jars she made her way across the mesa and went down to the spring. She climbed the rockhewn stairs to the spring that lay in a deep pool of shade. As she knelt to dip the gourd dipper into the cool shadowed water, she heard someone coming down the steps. She looked up and saw Whirlwind Man. He said, "Guwatzi, Yellow Woman. Are you here?"

"Yes, I am here," she said, dipping water calmly into the four jars beside her. She didn't look at him.

"Put down the dipper," he said. "I want you to come with me."

"I am filling these jars with water as you can see," she said. "My sisters and I are grinding corn, and they are waiting for me."

"No," Whirlwind Man said, "You must come with me. If you won't come, well, I'll have to kill you." He showed her his knife.

Yellow Woman put the dipper down carefully. "All right," she said. "I guess I'll go with you." She got up. She went with Whirlwind Man to the other side of the world where he lived with his mother, who greeted her like his wife. "Come down here into the south room," Whirlwind's mother said. And so Yellow Woman did.

"Don't run away," Whirlwind Man told her. "I belong to the wind. That is why we are accompanied by dust and wind-gusts when we travel. We run very fast, so you stay here with mother." That's what he said.

The jars stayed, tall and fat and cool in the deep shade by the shadowed spring.

After depositing her with his mother and sisters, Whirlwind Man went out hunting deer while Yellow Woman was set to grinding corn, as was the proper duty for a new wife.

But her sisters missed her. They went to the spring to find what had happened to Yellow Woman. They found her jar, carefully placed upside down on the smooth rock that surrounded the spring. They found her tracks, going westward from the spring a short way, then abruptly ending. They looked southward, fearing someone had abducted her, but found no trace. "Oh, we must find our sister," they said, alarmed. "I wonder how we will find her!"

"Let us mix dirt and valuables," they said. They returned to
their house and selected a beautiful long-neck jar. Into the jar
they put water, a mixture of dirt, ground turquoise, shell, and
coral and added sweet corn flour. After a time they added medicine, and later some beads. Then they stirred it, until Blue
Woman judged it was right. She called on Grandmother Spider,
Ts'its'nako, saying, "Grandmother, you must help us to make
this large fly alive. We need to find our sister who is lost. Therefore we need this fly." Then Blue Woman covered the jar with
her shawl saying, "Enough. After four days you will be alive."

Four days later, the fly emerged from the jar when they removed Blue Woman's shawl. They solicited Fly's help in finding
Yellow Woman. "We don't know where she went, poor one,"
they said. "Please help us find her."

Fly agreed, and soon he was aloft. He went northward and
into the northeast. By the evening he had circled around and
was back in the southeast, where he reported to the anxious
sisters that he had failed to find Yellow Woman.

The next day he searched the east, circling all over the southeast. But still he didn't find her. "Maybe she is still alive," he
said to the sisters on his return. "I will go out early and search
some more."

So the next day he searched the southwest, and he searched
again in the northern part of the day's search pattern. Finally,
toward evening, he found her.

He climbed to the top of the ladder of Whirlwind Man's house
and waited. Soon he heard Yellow Woman's voice. After a time,
he began to sing: "Yellow Woman, Yellow Woman, I have come
for you," he sang, and repeated, "Yellow Woman, Yellow Woman,
I have come for you."

Yellow Woman heard him and went up the ladder northward
and looked all around, but she saw no one. "I wonder if somebody is singing somewhere, and he says my name," she said.

Then she heard it again. "Yellow Woman, Yellow Woman,
I come for you," Fly sang, and repeated the refrain, "Yellow
Woman, Yellow Woman, I come for you."

That time Yellow Woman spotted him. When he had greeted
her, Fly told her her sisters were looking for her. "I was stolen
by Whirlwind Man," she said. "That's why they couldn't find
me. He is not here now," she said. "He is out hunting. He will

return this evening," she said. "Let me tell him that tomorrow you will take me east."

Fly agreed, and asked if he could go. He wished to report to the sisters that he had found her. Yellow Woman agreed but said, "First let me feed you." And she set some roasted meat and wafer bread before him. Fly dug right in, but the meat was hot, and he burned his mouth. He could not speak, only hum. "Rrr," he said.

"Oh, poor one, he has burned himself," Yellow Woman exclaimed.

Fly only nodded, and soon he made his way up north and flew eastward to Yellow Woman's house. The sisters greeted him, but he could only hum and nod. "Oh, poor one," they said. "Somebody has hurt you." Then they asked if he had found Yellow Woman, and he indicated that he had. Joyfully, they gave him some food, and many thanks. "From now on, because you have helped us," the goddesses said, "you will never be hungry. When your kind increases you will eat every kind of food, even rotten meat and food that is very sweet." After he had eaten he left, flying southward.

When Whirlwind Man returned home, Yellow Woman told him that Fly had come for her. "Surely you will take me back tomorrow," she said. Whirlwind Man agreed, but said first he would make shoes for all her sisters, and leggings. He also wanted to send dresses for all of them.

The next day he and his mother readied dresses, shoes, leggings, and packs of venison, placing them on a mesa top that lay southward of their house. When all was in readiness, he signaled Yellow Woman, telling her to sit among the bundles.

Whirlwind Man readied himself for the journey, adorning himself with Jamestown Weed flowers and rubbing his body with their petals. Then he drew the woman and the bundles into his vortex and carried them quickly to the spring where he had first found her. Leaving her there he said, "Enough. This is as far as I will take you." And he whirled away. For a time Yellow Woman sat on the cool sandstone and watched as the whirlwind disappeared into the far distance.

At last with a sigh, she got up and began the trek back to the village and her sisters' house. Arriving there, she greeted them

and told them about the meat and clothing she had brought.
They were delighted. Their sister had not only been returned
safe and whole, but had come laden with gifts from her husband, in the proper manner.

Thus, long ago, Yellow Woman returned home, and now the
four sisters live there together.

A HOT TIME

This story I have read and heard as a kind of "little," or "grand-mother," story, that is, a humorous story for children and others on purely social occasions. Humor is an important part of Native American daily life. Without it, Indians could hardly have survived five hundred long years of occupation. Humor is also a major aspect of traditional spiritual life for many Native American communities, where the sacred and the amusing are often combined in worship.

I think that Grandmother Spider, who is awesome in so many of her aspects, is also seen as one of us. Certainly, all the stories about her willing intervention on behalf of youngsters in difficulties beyond their abilities, and her unfailing good humor lend themselves to a view of her as capable of fun as well as of miracles.

I have incorporated some joking references to the overseriousness with which the stories of the people are often treated by mythologists and literary specialists—a bit of fun at my own expense, you might say.

Long ago the people were in the dark, and they were tired of not knowing when to go to sleep and when to get up. They didn't have Six Killer to pray to in the mornings when they went to the water to greet Long Man and prepare for the new day. True, there was a place of greater heat during some hours, and the air around them was more gray than dark, but they didn't have much light by which to work and play.

They were also yearning for a cozy fire to sit next to when they told stories after the little ones went to sleep, after the daily activities ended. Besides, they knew that fire was very powerful, and they wanted the joy and growing that came to people who had fire to grace their lives.

They really liked to pass the time companionably, and the only reason they didn't do as much of it as they liked is that when the darkness got a little darker some of them insisted it was time to go to sleep. They believed that if they had fire and some regular daylight, they'd be able to spend even more time telling stories and gossiping and being together. Maybe they would even have new ceremonies to hold and go to.

The people learned about some other people in a distant country who had firelight. They heard that those people got to spend all day and all night telling stories, singing, dancing, and generally carousing till all hours.

Well, they thought about all this for a long time. They thought about what they needed and wanted. They thought about those rumors, and they even sent some men to see if they were true. They listened to each other's ideas about what they might do if they had some firelight, and they dreamed up all sorts of interesting activities. Even those who liked to sleep early got caught up in the goings on. They began to think that maybe they could sleep more in light time, when there was true light, so they could also enjoy the fire when it was very dark.

There were a few, of course, who had some reservations about the whole affair. But aside from mumbling a bit, mostly among themselves about possible dangers and hazards from such a volatile and untested force, especially when it was in the untrained hands of the would-be merrymakers, they kept their reservations to themselves. And this, of course, is how reservations first got started.

After a proper length of time planning and dreaming, discussing and surmising, mumbling and wondering had gone by, the people settled into the serious business of strategy. "How will we get some firelight," they asked. "The people over in that other country who have some won't give us some. We tried."

"H'mmm," they sighed. They stopped discussing for a long pause.

"I know," one of the people finally said. He was a tall skinny man who decorated himself magnificently with feathers. He was especially proud of his luxurious thick hair fashioned in a spiky style. He kept it in place with a nice sticky clay that came from the nearby clay bed. His name was Buzzard.

Buzzard uncoiled his lanky form and stood. "Maybe someone

will take a little jaunt over there long after it gets dark, maybe just before light, and try to snag some," he intoned sonorously.

"Yeah, you need practice snagging," someone hooted. The others laughed.

After the general merriment at Buzzard's expense subsided, it was agreed that Buzzard would go. When the first rays of light were just emerging over the saddleback rise near the village, Buzzard came limping in. He was definitely the worse for wear, his fine feathers matted and blackened. He sported a bald spot right at his crown. The hair there never did grow back. "I blew it," he said resignedly. "Maybe someone else should try."

Well, a couple of others went, but with the same result.

Everyone was feeling pretty glum about how matters stood. They were trying to reconcile themselves to doing without the exciting firelight—which meant adjusting their plans, dreams, and hopes to fit their accustomed circumstances. Most were disappointed, except for the few who were relieved. They went whistling and giggling about their tasks, relieved that nothing fearful and different was going to unsettle their equilibrium just yet.

But Spider got to thinking. She was always doing that. She couldn't help it, of course, any more than Buzzard could help swooping, strutting, and snagging. She spun out her thought and wove implications, extrapolations, and a few elegant daydreams into a satisfying pattern. Her Dreaming done, she joined the folks sitting dejectedly around the empty place where they could almost see the firelight snapping cheerily on the sticks and branches they had carefully laid out in such anticipation just a few days before.

"Well," Spider began softly. "Maybe someone might try to get some firelight," she said to no one in particular. She sat down carefully so as not to jar her fragile joints unduly. "It's true I'm old and slow," she continued. She paused again for a silence, breathing it in and out comfortingly.

No one looked at her. As was their way, they just kept on sitting as they had been, doing whatever they had been doing even if that was just brooding or wishing over their regrets. But of course, they were all attending carefully to what she said.

"It's true I'm a very small person and not very strong," she said at last. "But I think I could give it a try. My old body would appreciate some firelight at night sometimes. And I wouldn't mind having a little brightness to tend." They sat companionably in silence after that, some wandering off, some coming over to join the group from time to time.

So Spider set out, much earlier than Buzzard and the others had because she was much slower. Along her way she stopped off at the clay bed and dug up some smooth, damp clay. She took some time to shape it into a tiny pot with a lid that she kept separately so they wouldn't stick together while they were drying. Her Dreaming had told her that the firelight would dry them more quickly and more finely than Heat Giver in the sky could. She had seen some fine potteries in her Dream, and she was looking forward to making and firing them.

The last one of her folks watched her make her slow way across the rise beyond the saddleback on her way to the Fire People's land. Her tiny figure soon disappeared in the grayness that met the top of the rise and clung to it like a u'tinaatz, a woman's short, light cloak.

As the next day was well advanced, the people saw her returning. She had a round lamp on her back and looked a bit misshapen in the gray distance. Their hearts fell to the ground in dismay when they saw this. "Oh, no," they said. "It's one thing for Buzzard to get a new hairstyle, but if something so horrible has happened to Spider!"

They were too heartsick to finish the thought, but waited as calmly as they might, busying themselves with whatever came to hand as was their way when worried or anxious.

At long last Spider was close by, grinning a satisfied grin. "Well," she said, "looks like I got it." She reached up and took the clay pot from her back, revealing a change such as they had feared. For on her back pulsed a bright red-orange design that hadn't been there the day before. But it was a very handsome and wise design, one she had dreamed of herself, and it exactly matched the one her pot lid sported, and she seemed happy to wear it.

She set the tiny pot down in front of her, sighing a small sigh of satisfaction as she removed the lid to reveal the bright glowing ember she had carefully carried so far. "Look," she said. "Firelight."

And there was a hot time in the old town that night.

SACRED SHOES

When I was very small, my great-grandmother told me a version of this story about a very advanced medicine woman. (Or was she really a supernatural? But if she was, how could the story end that way?) I remembered pieces of it, especially the part about how she shakes out her moccasins, maybe because Grandma Gunn's gestures were graphic at that point. I can see her still, pointing to her shoe and shaking her hand as though holding it. Maybe it was her acting ability that led me to major in drama in high school and my first year of college.

Later I read a version of the story in Gunn's Schat Chen, *and I have leaned heavily on it for my rendition here, taking liberties as I feel befit and honor the story's sense within its home context, fitting it into the pattern of stories I'm telling here as it fits within the pattern of life the Lagunas live there.*

Long ago. The people suffered from a terrible sickness. It was a sickness that made them break out all over with sores, and many died. The head clan's eldest daughter, Yellow Woman, got the sickness, and the people were very frightened, for if she died, something terrible would happen to them. But their medicine didn't work to heal Yellow Woman any better than it worked to heal the rest of those who were ill.

They had heard about a great healer woman who lived to the southwest of them. Her name was Qiyo Kepe, and she lived far to the south of them in a house that had leaves for a roof. The people sent a runner to bring her to their village so she could cure Yellow Woman. The runner was dispatched, and after some time he found her home and persuaded her to return to the village with him.

At the edge of the first river they came to, one that flowed swift and deep, Qiyo Kepe took off one of her moccasins to shake the sand out of it, and herds of deer, antelope, buffalo, and all the other animals of the forests and plains sprang into life. This frightened the messenger, and he hurried the old woman along. They rushed across the river and traveled as fast as he could urge her until they came to another river. Again she removed her moccasin and shook it, and birds flew forth from the wind her shaking made, singing. The messenger became even more frightened.

Again, when they came to a third river, she took off her moccasin, and as she shook it reptiles of all kinds came forth, springing into life from the specks of sand that she shook from her shoe. At this sight the messenger was even more terrified, and more than that, he was enraged.

At the fourth river, Qiyo Kepe again shook out her moccasin, and this time insects of every kind buzzed forth. In a mindless panic, the messenger hurried with the terrifying woman to the village where Yellow Woman was waiting for death.

Qiyo Kepe set to work immediately, bathing the sores on Yellow Woman's body with pure water from the nearby spring. That was all she used, but she used a lot of it, continuously bathing the young woman, and in four days Yellow Woman was well. Qiyo Kepe then turned her attention to the others. She told the women what to do, and because of her knowledge, all who were alive when she arrived in the village were healed.

Meantime the village men had been talking. They were angry that this woman could heal with water when all their medicine and incantations had failed. The medicine men's society was especially angry. So they told the messenger to take her home, then to pretend he had returned to the village. But he was to go to the river nearest her home and bring back a party of men who would be waiting there. They would return to the old woman's house and kill her, because they believed that only in this way could their power and the people's confidence in them be restored.

So they did as planned, but when the party returned to Qiyo Kepe's house, she met them at the door and asked them to come in. They refused, but said they would come back in four days to kill her and all of her family.

Hearing this, Qiyo Kepe took up the broom that was leaning against the doorjamb and began to sweep. As she swept, she sang a chant that went "Qiyo Kepe is not like you. Qiyo Kepe is one who knows. Generations will come and generations will go, before your disease's scars no longer show, before you will return to faith, because you have murdered Qiyo Kepe."

When the fourth day had passed, the men returned to Qiyo Kepe's home. They murdered the old woman and her brother and all of their families.

And when Qiyo Kepe was dead, all the animals began to mourn: the birds dropped their wings and were silent, the herds slunk away into the brush and the forests and remained unseen, the bees and the other insects rasped their mourning, and all the reptiles crawled away and hid themselves.

WHAT IS WAKAN

Supernatural occurrences are frequent if not common upon the Plains, as in other parts of the Indian nations. Not all occurrences are the same; some have consequences for only a few people, maybe a single person or family, while others have far-reaching effects. The coming of White Buffalo Woman was one of the latter, for she brought with her the sacred pipe the Lakota cherish still, and with it she gave them the religion of the sacred pipe, laws by which the Lakota were to live an upright life in harmony with all that is.

They say that this gift from Taku Wakan (That Which Is Sacred or Mysterious) occurred in the dim past, when human beings conversed readily with the animal and nonphysical peoples of their homelands. For those who lived upon the Great Plains, and even in the far Rockies, the buffalo was the animal being closest to humans. Not only did human beings rely heavily upon the buffalo for sustenance, clothing, housing, and all sorts of implements and sundries that make running a household much easier, but the buffalo as a spiritual presence and companion figured largely in human prayers, dreams, visions, and arts.

The holy man Black Elk (Roger Black Elk) was reported to have said that the wakan woman came among the Lakota very long ago, maybe eight hundred years before, when they were still in the south.

Long ago. The people were gathered into one of the large encampments that they enjoyed in the summertime. There were over two hundred cone-shaped lodges pointing their peaked tips skyward. Each held several people—husband, wives, children, perhaps a visiting relative or friend or two. There was much bustling about day and night. Every hand was busy preparing food, gathering food, working on art objects, dancing, singing, practicing for a night's entertainment, teaching, or just looking after the young. All day the sound of voices raised in laughter and conversation, all night voices raised at various parts of the camp in song, drumming everywhere, dogs and children scampering. It was indeed a happy and prosperous time.

During the summer camps, many who did not see one another in the long winter months came together to exchange news, renew acquaintance, cement bonds formed at earlier summer encampments. Often a young man would find his true love; and if he was mature enough to have made at least the beginnings of a reputation for himself as a good provider and an honorable person, he might propose and be accepted by her family. So the atmosphere around these large encampments was mostly warm, hopeful, and solid.

Of course, such a large population required a large supply of fresh meat, and hunters came and went constantly, sometimes in large parties, sometimes in small. One day two young men who were among those renewing a promising acquaintance of earlier summers set off together on a hunting expedition. They had heard that a small herd of buffalo had been sighted only a few miles from the encampment, and setting out before daylight they made their way toward the spot. As they walked, they chatted about this and that, trading hunting stories and bits of song, reminiscing about their past summers' weeks together, and planning their futures as young men have done since time immemorial.

One of the friends was a reserved young man, who, though fun-loving and a good hunter, was seen by many as having a serious and kindly nature. "He will be a great chief someday," some said, while others believed he would be a medicine man because he spent much time studying and helping one of the elders who possessed great learning in healing and other magical arts. But whatever they said, they were agreed on the character of the young man, who had gladdened many children's hearts by his willingness to play with them and teach them new skills. He seemed never too busy to stop and comfort a crying child, or to tell a story to a laughing bevy of young ones in the long evenings.

The other young man was not of so sterling a character. He was a somewhat dissolute youth, brave enough it is true, but impetuous and self-indulgent. During their walk, his conversation turned mainly on women and his many conquests. He was full of talk about how his prowess made him not only invincible on the hunt but among young women. According to him, even the most virtuous of the young ladies in his acquaintance pined for him.

His boastfulness did not unduly disturb his friend. Men were expected to brag, though they were expected to be truthful when recounting their triumphs; and as everyone was reasonably well known to the others, at least by reputation and peripheral acquaintance, it was no easy matter to get too far away from the facts. He did feel somewhat troubled at his friend's easy way with women's reputations. Real harm could befall them if his loose tales were believed by many. A girl's honor was precious, not because of questions of paternity, but because her right to participate before marriage in certain spiritual offices depended on her virginity. A woman who claimed the status falsely would be seriously chastised. More than that, she would cause harm to all the people. The buffalo might become angry and refuse to give of themselves for the people's well being, the sun might not give sufficient heat—or too much—the thunders might retreat to the edges of the world and refuse to come among them with rain. He chided his friend quietly now and again, reminding him that the young women he was discussing were renowned for their shyness and virtue, but his friend waved his objections away, laughing and calling him an old man.

They made their way through the dawn-lit world, happy in their youth, strength, and companionship, in their lives that stretched out before them. They were secure in the knowledge that their lives would follow the orderly pattern of their parents' and grandparents' lives, for had it not always been so?

At noon, when the sun was high overhead and the full heat of the day was upon the vast plain they trudged, they found small shade in some scrub pine near a quiet-flowing river. There they rested, eating pemmican and drinking deeply from the water. After eating, they waded into the water and splashed around, laughing with the zest of youth and high spirits. They were near the area where they thought the small herd of bison would be, so they were soon on their way. The sun would be up late, so they were certain they would have time to make their kill and get back to camp by moonrise.

As they topped the bluff that rose from the river bank, they could see for miles around. They saw a small herd of buffalo off in the northern distance. Glancing at each other, they grinned and began a slow trot toward them. When they were much closer to the bison, they would move slowly, crouching in the grass to avoid detection. Though reasonably seasoned, each young man could feel his pulse begin to beat more rapidly with the anticipation of a successful hunt.

They had run a few yards when the quieter of the two stopped. His friend slowed to a walk, looking back at his companion questioningly. He signaled him to stop, then gestured eastward. Looking where he was directed, the impulsive youth spied a figure moving rapidly toward them. What could it be?

He walked slowly back to his friend, asking what he thought it was. "I don't know," the other replied, "but I think we'd better wait here and see. Perhaps it's a buffalo alone. Maybe it wants to speak with us."

His friend snorted. "Oh, you don't really believe those old stories," he scoffed. "They're just old men's tales they tell us to keep themselves occupied. No one has talked to buffalo for a long time, if ever."

"Don't be so sure," his friend said in his quiet way. "You do not have your full years yet, so don't make light of others who have. Surely you know that a buffalo running alone is a strange enough occurrence."

Silenced by his friend's reasoning, the impulsive young man stood silently as they watched the buffalo—for so it proved to be—race across the broad plain toward them. Soon they realized that it was a white buffalo calf. Its coat shone like the sky just before sunrise. They glanced at each other. "Should we kill it?" the impetuous young man asked, already fitting his arrow into his bow.

His friend put his hand on the bow to stop him. "I think we'd better not do it," he said. "A white buffalo is wakan. It would be a bad thing to kill it." His friend lowered his bow reluctantly. "I suppose you're right," he said. His face showed his disappointment.

"Get down," his friend commanded quietly. Quickly they both secreted themselves in the tall grass, thinking the white buffalo would work itself past them. The wind was in their favor, and buffalo were known to be shortsighted.

They heard the steps of the buffalo draw near, then stop. It
became so quiet only the song of a distant bird could be heard;
even the wind had died into silence. After a time, they simultaneously raised their heads. The sight that met their astounded
eyes nearly drew all the breath from them. Standing before
them was the most beautiful woman either had ever seen.

She was dressed in skins so white they shone like snow on
the brightest morning, and so soft they draped softly over her
shapely arms and the thick white leggings that wrapped her
calves. Her moccasins were similarly made of white, soft leather,
and they, like the edge of her fringed dress, its sleeves, and
neckline were finely decorated with a porcupine-quill pattern
that spoke of her sacred mission and status. Worked with a
similar pattern a headband circled her head, holding her long
flowing hair in place. From her crown, two white plumes swirled
in the rising breeze.

The impudent young man, eyes alight with admiration,
stepped forward hastily, already preparing familiar compliments
and boasts that he believed would leave her as helpless with admiration as he. He could almost feel her strong, lovely body re-
laxing against his, and he was vividly imagining his first kiss
when she called to him. "Come here to me," she said, gazing
steadily at him. He all but sprang forward, and as he reached
her side made as if to embrace her. Just then a heavy fog swirled
in a whirlwind about them, hiding them from the sight of his
motionless friend, who stood nearby, filled with feelings that
hovered between exaltation and foreboding. In moments the
windcloud had vanished, and the woman stood again clearly
revealed in the afternoon sun, but the young man had disappeared. At the woman's feet lay a small pile of human bones.

Addressing the surviving young man, the wakan woman said,
"Your friend lacked balance and wisdom. He did not heed the
teachings of his elders, and he has suffered for his self-indulgence
and disrespect. It is right that men lust after women, but we
who are wakan, as are all women who walk in harmony with
all that is, are due the respect a wise person gives to everything
that lives. Your friend was ruled only by his passions, and before you lie the results of that foolish path.

"You are wiser by far, and because of this I am charging you
with a mission. You are to take this message to the encampment. In four days, I will come among you. You must tell the

wise ones what has transpired here and direct them to build a great lodge so that many can enter and hear my teachings. I will bring a message and an object of great importance to your people. Return to them now, as I have charged you."

The young man returned to the camp as quickly as he could, running most of the way. He went immediately to the large lodge of one of the elder men, a man honored by all for his integrity, intelligence, and kindness. By the time he arrived it was early evening, and the old man was eating his supper, reclining in his place outside his well-appointed lodge. He invited the young man to join him, and after a decent interval he listened to the young man's story. After he listened, he sat for a time quietly, reflecting on what he had heard. Having come to the proper understanding in his own mind, he thanked the young man and sent him back to his own lodge. His first wife sent some roasted meat for the young man's mother, along with her greetings.

The old man retired to a certain tipi where a number of elders gathered of an evening, and seating himself he smoked quietly until all were assembled. After a time given to reflection, he told of the young man's encounter with the wakan woman, and of her directions. After they had reflected on the matter and discussed it to their satisfaction, the men sent for several of the elder women and told them of the day's strange events. The women directed the erection of a lodge that was made of four large tipis yoked together, providing ample space for most of the people in the encampment. They decorated it and swept it carefully, arranging certain seats near the opening and along the sides as was proper. Meanwhile the men sent a party out to recover the bones of the foolish young man, thus confirming part of the story.

On the appointed day, a large throng of people gathered at the large tipi early, waiting anxiously for the wakan woman to make her appearance. They waited for several hours, excitement and impatience growing as the day grew hot. Suddenly those within the tipi heard a commotion outside. Children were shouting and running, yelling, "A calf! A calf!" Some people near the door of the tipi looked out and saw a small white buffalo calf trotting toward the east-facing opening. As it reached the door, it suddenly transformed into a lovely young woman carrying a bundle on her back. As she entered the tipi she sang and, walking slowly, acknowledged the elders. Then she stepped to the center of the lodge, where in accordance with custom, a special area had been covered with sweet grass, scented herbs, and sage blessed by medicine people.

Stooping down, she deposited her bundle, then carefully unwrapped it. She held it up so the bowl rested in one palm, the handle in the other. The people could see a pipe. The bowl was made of a deep red stone, its stem was of wood, and from the joint where they met hung twelve perfect feathers, tied to it with the grass that never dies. From the bowl the holy woman took a round stone, telling the people that it represented the earth and all that the earth, their mother, bore. "Respect her always," she instructed them. "Then you will prosper."

Next she placed a pinch of red willow bark in the bowl and lit it. She offered the pipe to the Great Mystery, then in brief prayers she offered it to the four horizontal directions, to the above and to the below, telling them that these were the sacred directions, to be honored each time they prayed with the pipe. Next she carried the pipe to the honored ones who had organized the gathering and offered each a smoke from it. She gave it into the keeping of the wise man who had first been consulted by her young messenger.

For four days she remained with the people, instructing them in a number of rites and proper ways of living. She cautioned them often concerning the proper attitude toward all living things, reminding them to respect the females of each of their relatives, and to protect the young. She made it clear that only from an attitude of humility, concern for all living things, and respect for their mother and all the great spirit beings could they prosper.

At the end of her teaching, she was escorted to the eastern door from which she had entered, and she walked a short way from the gathering place. Then she changed again, becoming a young, white calf. She ran a little ways in that form, then transformed again, this time into a yearling cow. Shortly afterward, she transformed once more, becoming a buffalo cow in full maturity. As she reached the bluff at the edge of the camp, the people saw her change a final time into a bony, aged beast who could barely shamble a few steps before she disappeared. They say that her transformations were a final teaching about the necessary transformations that all that live go through. As earth goes through her seasons, humans and other creatures go through theirs. Thus the balance is kept, and the flow of life proceeds in an orderly manner.

They say that sometimes the pipe grows long, and when it does times are lean. But when it becomes short, the people prosper.

MAY IT BE BEAUTIFUL
ALL AROUND

Some say that Beautyway is the mother chantway of the great Navajo healing system. Its sister ceremony, sometimes called Mountain Way, sometimes Mountain Chant, contains the beautiful healing prayer "House Made of Dawn." The complex chantway system composed of numerous chantways such as Enemy Way, Shooting Way, Blessing Way, Mothway, Upward Moving Way, Prostitution Way, and Emergence Way combines prayers of astonishing beauty, narrative, movement, gesture, and sandpainting to heal the sick, restore captives, and harmonize diverse energies.

These chantways were given to the people by the holy people or supernaturals, and Older Sister and Younger Sister were the agents of that gift. Beautyway and Mountain Chant are the chantways given by the sisters, and their story culminates when the transformed women return to the people and teach them the chants. I wonder what happened for them after.

In writing this rendition, I relied on Sheila Moon (1984) and an account recorded by Father Bernard Haile (1981), who recorded many of the chantways, as well as on details of the country from visits there and fragments of the story I have heard.

During the centuries-long war with the Pueblos, the Navajo, Diné—which means "the people" in the language of the bilagáana, the white man—two young women were separated from their family. There had been a retaliatory raid on their tiny settlement, and in the fray the young women had run into a deep box canyon to escape pursuit.

The rest of their family had also scattered, and the young women went to look for them after the fighting died down.

They had fled with no provisions, and the part of the country through which they wandered offered little by way of food or drink. They didn't miss the food, having dined well on a breakfast of corn soup and roast meat early that morning, but after a few hours they grew thirsty.

Seeing that they were in the foothills, with low mountain peaks not far off, they made their way in search of their people and a spring. These young women were strong and able. They had participated in the puberty ceremony of their people earlier that year and had demonstrated their strength and endurance. Both had run for hours, fasted for days, danced at night, and lived up to the greatest hopes of their family. To the Diné, strength in women was of even greater importance than strength in men, for women were the mothers of the people, and only strong women could take the rigors of pregnancy and child rearing without damage to themselves or the children. Upon the strength of the women depended the strength of the people, they said.

Each of the young women had been betrothed to a man she didn't love. There had been an earlier foray against the Pueblos in which the hands of the two maidens who were of superior strength and prowess were pledged to the warriors who brought back two Pueblo scalps. These two young women, sisters, had outshone all the other maidens, and so they became the choice of the successful warriors.

But the warriors who brought back the scalps, Bear Man and Snake Man, were old and unattractive to the two young sisters. They had dreamed of husbands who were slim and strong, with sweet young flesh tight and full with the juices of youth. These stringy old men whose skins hung loosely about their bones were not what they had in mind.

The raid excited as well as frightened them. Perhaps they hoped that in some way they would not have to honor the pledge. Maybe something would happen that would make it no longer necessary to do so, and they could return to their maidenly dreams of youthful lovers to marry.

The sisters climbed further and further into the canyon, checking below whenever they reached a vantage point for any sign of either their pursuers or their family. They saw no one until they were quite high up, then Older Sister, the maiden who

was pledged to Bear Man, thought she saw movement far below. "Look," she called to her sister, "I think we are being
followed."

Younger Sister joined her in looking over the steep cliff and
also made out two figures far below, climbing over the rocks
and boulders and coming in their direction. As they watched,
they saw one of them look up, almost directly at them. Ducking
quickly, they sat down to contemplate their situation.

"Do you think they are after us?" Older Sister asked.

"I can't be sure," her sister responded, "but they may well be.
We had better try and get through this pass and find some help."

That seemed wise to her sister, so they set off once more,
climbing swiftly out of the defile and scrambling up rock faces
that looked almost unscalable. Soon they had left the canyon
they had been ascending far behind, and they felt safer. They
could detect no sign that they had been spotted by their pursuers, so they sat in the shade of a scrub piñon to reconsider
their course. They sat for quite a while, but finally Younger Sister, the young woman pledged to the old man called Snake
Man, got reluctantly to her feet. "We had better go," she said to
her sister.

Just as Older Sister was rising to her feet, they heard the
sound of small rocks hitting the ground not more than a few
feet away. Both heads turned as one in the direction of the
sound, and they saw two handsome young men emerge from
some rocks above them and jump lightly to the lower ground
where the girls stood. Though one was taller and one shorter
and more stocky, both were handsome. Their perfect teeth
gleamed against their deeply tanned skin, their well greased
hair shone in the sun, as did their muscled arms and legs.

"We are trying to find our family," Younger Sister said.

"And there are two Pueblo men after us, or so it seemed,"
Older Sister chimed in.

"Eh, that is so," the taller of the young men replied. "That is
why we have come for you, to take you back to your family and
keep you from the men who pursue you."

"We will have to go the long way around," the other youth
said. "Don't worry. Though it will take some time, and it is already late, there are some old Anasazi ruins along our way. We
can spend the night in them safely enough." The men gave

Older Sister and Younger Sister water to drink, and then they started on their journey.

The young women followed the two men. They held their faces carefully impassive, but their eyes were bright. They walked and climbed for another hour or so, glancing at each other slyly from time to time, as the light slanted long and threw purple and blue shadows over the land.

As the shadows grew around them, they rounded a prominence and saw before them some ruined Pueblo dwellings. "Let us go up there and prepare for the night," the shorter man said.

"It is late enough," his companion agreed. So they ascended the rising canyon floor to the ruins and made the climb up decaying ladders into one of the higher of the dwellings.

"This will be a good place to stay tonight," the tall youth said. "We can sleep safely here."

The men had some dried meat and cornmeal with them, so the sisters made a tiny fire out of tinder wood they had brought up with them, and soon all were fed and settled in for the night. Soon Older Sister felt someone creep next to her in the dark, felt a smooth, muscled arm encircle her. She sighed quietly, and welcomed the man into her arms.

Not much later, Younger Sister also had a visitor, and she welcomed him as happily as her sister had welcomed hers. After a time, the only noise was the even breathing of four satisfied sleepers.

When the young women awoke, thin sunlight was filtering through chinks in the roof and the roof opening of the small cavelike room they had slept in. The room, which had seemed peaceful and clean the evening before was heaped with debris. They found themselves lying amid animal droppings and chips of wood, dead branches and bits of bone. Gasping, they sat up. As she did, Younger Sister saw several rattlesnakes slither away from the heap in which she had been lying, except for a very large one that lay, slightly coiled, near her hand.

On her part, Older Sister saw small heaps of bear claws and teeth in the debris scattered around her. The pungent smell of bear scat filled her nostrils. She turned toward her sister, and as she did she caught sight of a shambling furred figure near the ladder they had descended to enter the room. She pulled her manta about her tightly with one hand, reaching for her belt to

close it with the other. "Aaiii," she said in a frightened tone,
"where have we come to?"

Younger Sister stumbled to her and clung to her. She was
trembling so hard her teeth were clicking. "What shall we
do?" she asked in a whisper against clenched teeth. Her sister
held her hands tightly, hoping to soothe their trembling. When
Younger Sister grew calmer they looked around. The room was
again clean and peaceful, and the two handsome young men
were just stirring from sleep. The women looked at each other
silently, then Older Sister stood and said, "I will make a fire and
boil some cornmeal. Gather some wood, Younger Sister."

Quickly Younger Sister scrambled to her feet and up the ladder, relieved to emerge into the clean morning air. As she
was gathering some sticks on the roof just below the one onto
which she had emerged, she saw a shadow fall over her path. It
was her young man, tall and slender in the sunlight.

"Come," he said. "Let us get away from them for a while. I
know where there's a small spring. We can get some water." He
drew her behind him and they climbed down from the pueblo
and soon were out of sight behind the curving canyon wall.

As they walked, she saw many snakes sunning themselves
on the rocks or slithering down the rock walls that surrounded
them. When they got to the spring, her escort tapped one of the
rocks four times, and it swung inward, revealing a land extending
before them. "Come," he said. "I will take you to my mother."

After a short hike she saw a hogan in the near distance. A
woman stood outside, watching them. "Here is my wife," the
young man said to his mother, and he turned and walked away.

The woman took Younger Sister inside and after feeding her
gave her instructions about the work she was to do that day.
"Watch the kettle and see that it doesn't go over," she said.
"And make sure nothing burns." She said she was going to look
for some sheep that had wandered away and would not be back
until night.

Hours went by. Younger Sister watched the kettle, adding
water from time to time and keeping the flame burning steadily. But she grew tired of the task and went out. She wandered
around for a time, seeking a way back to her land, but she could
not find the door, though she tapped four times on a number of
rocks as she had seen her husband do.

She returned to the hogan to find her mother-in-law, and the fire had gone out—but not before the kettle's contents had burned. Her mother-in-law said nothing but set Younger Sister to scrubbing the kettle.

In the morning, the mother-in-law again went out, leaving Younger Sister to card wool. "Be attentive to your work," the older woman had said. "I must be gone, but you should have a fine heap of wool carded by the time I return. Take care that the wool you card does not get matted or scattered about."

But although Younger Sister tried to do as she was bid, having been reared to helpfulness and cooperation, and knowing her duty to her mother-in-law, she tired of her task and once again wandered around the land near the hogan, attempting to find her way home. When she returned to the hogan, the wool she had carded had matted badly. She had left it lying in a heap near the door, but somehow a flat rock had fallen on it and it was almost useless. Again her mother-in-law said nothing but began to card more wool she had prepared sometime during the day.

The third and fourth days were the same, though the tasks differed. However firm her resolve to please her mother-in-law, Younger Sister found herself searching the countryside for a way out. She could not concentrate on her task, despite her good intentions.

Having failed at each task, she was downcast. But on the fifth morning, her husband came to her and told her he wished to instruct her in a ceremony that she would take back to her people. She was to teach it to her brother. "I am Snake Man," he said. "My mother has told me of your work and she says you are ready for this instruction."

For four days, Younger Sister labored to learn the ceremony. It entailed prodigious feats of memorization, for there were many parts to it, many words to learn, many sandpaintings to memorize, many movements to practice. But at last she was proficient in its details. Telling her to return to her family, Snake Man, no longer young and handsome but old, his skin hanging in crepy folds from his limbs and his legs bowed and very thin, took her through his lands quickly and led her through a short tunnel that rose to emerge just beyond her mother's hogan.

Her people were glad to see her. They greeted her and brought her inside, offering her food and a place of honor to sit. She told them of her adventures and was surprised to learn that months had passed while she was gone. As they sat and exchanged their news, a clamor was heard in the yard. Rushing out to see what the commotion was, they saw Older Sister walking toward them. Joyously, the sisters greeted one another.

Older Sister had been taken to the land of the Bear People where she lived with Bear Man's mother and underwent trials and instruction just as her sister had. The ceremony she brought was called Mountain Way, and Younger Sister's was called Beautyway.

The young women taught their ceremonies to their brothers as they had been instructed. When the arduous process was completed to their satisfaction, they left the hogan one morning and made their way back to the hills. The last anyone saw of them were their shadowy bodies moving up the slopes, small in the distance.

It is said that they returned to live with their husbands, and that because of their continuing thought the ceremonies continue to have the power to heal.

THE ADVENTURERS

In the movement from gynocentrism to male dominance, the Goddess becomes grandmother of the Twins, or Triplets, and their mother, who in some stories is Yellow Woman, in others is unnamed, disappears, marries Wind or Sun, is killed, or reappears in other myths because she takes on a role in various rituals.

This anishinabeg (Algonquian) story begins with a tale reminiscent of the Iroquois myth of Sky Woman. They both display features found in the Cherokee myth of Sutalidihi, and no doubt parallels can be found widely scattered about the continent. The story contains an adventure among the star people (known as the "star husband motif" to ethnologists, as it is a frequently found element in oral traditions across the world). It is one of my favorite themes—and from a time before space travel seemed a likely topic for conversations from the collective unconscious. Maybe there's more to those tales (contemporary and traditional) than meets the psychoanalytical eye!

In some regards, Matchikwewis and Oshkikwe are archetypes, who in their sisterhood and powers resemble such pairs among the Pueblo, the Navajo, the Aztec, the Nootsac/Lummi, the Karok, and a multitude of other nations. There is some reference in the scholarship to the preexistence of female twins in Southwestern lore, and this story lends support to that idea, though Matchikwewis and Oshkikwe are the daughters of Nanabozho (or Wenebojo, as he is known in an Algonquian language close to Ojibwa), a brother of Stone Boy (Flint in the Haudinoshone myth), and thus are great-granddaughters of the Goddess. It is said that they are half-human, half-immortal or god, and they thus provide material for writers who would like to trace the history of half-breeds or mixed bloods to their mythological origins.

These demigoddesses are analogs of White Shell Woman and Changing Woman, Nau'ts'ity and Ic'sts'ity, Coatlicue and Cihuacoatl, just as their father and his siblings—some accounts give Nanabozho one, some two, some three brothers—find parallels in the Little War Twins

Masewe and Oyoyowe, Monster Slayer and Child of Water, Wild Boy and his brother, Flint and Sapling (or Bud and Sapling, depending on the account), Hunahpú and Xbalanque and their sons One Hunahpú and Seven Hunahpú, and Morning Star and Evening Star. I think the principle here is the idea of twinning, of complementarity, of duality that is not the same as opposition.

The concept is related to the social structural principle of inside-outside, and the Twins who in historical times have been religious functionaries—who are always men, or so the record would have us believe—are intelligences that guide the force of polarity, seasonality, ascent, and descent. Thus the division of society into its inside and out-side parts (the domestic and the foreign, the nagual and the tonal, the inner spirit and the outer spirits) reflects a central spiritual issue that is resolved by enactment in ceremony and myth.

Oshkikwe and Matchikwewis are the sacred beings who figure in women's stories among the Chippewa/Ojibwa/anishinabeg people. They are the heroines in stories women tell to women for their instruc-tion and spiritual development. The stories tell them who they are and instruct them in the ritual way of women.

It may be that there are always two lines, the male and the female, and that the choice of which will figure in a given ritual depends on the nature and purpose of the rite as much as upon the gender of the offi-ciants and participants.

Long ago, in a place much like this earth we live on, but still not the same as this place, dwelt two immortal beings or goddesses. These two, a woman and her daughter, lived alone. There were no others anywhere except plants. Every day they would gather plant offerings for their daily needs, making clothing, housing, implements, storage containers, perfumes, ornaments, and all sorts of ointments and salves for the care of skin and hair, eyes and teeth. Together they lived happily. The daughter particu-larly liked to go about the hills and gather flowers and fruit. She would dry the flowers for sachets and ointments, or use them for dyes, often incorporating their curving and angling shapes into her needlework. The fruit provided tasty meals alone and in combination with other foods and was useful as preserva-tives, cosmetics, and dyes.

One day while she was busy about her favorite occupation, a

strong gust of wind blew between her legs, raising her dress high. She couldn't lower it, so strong was the gust, and stood helpless, her slim body almost bowled over by the blast. As suddenly as it came, the wind stopped, and all was still. The girl looked around her but saw nothing. The plant she had been leaning over a few moments before appeared unchanged. She could see no sign of the violent wind anywhere around. Shrugging her shoulders and smoothing down her hair, she continued with her task, forgetting the episode.

Sometime later her mother grew concerned by something in her daughter's manner—perhaps her color was subtly altered, perhaps her gait changed ever so slightly, perhaps her sleeping was different than usual. In any case, something alerted the mother, who asked her if she was all right. "Of course I am," the daughter replied, but her mother didn't feel any easier in her mind. Again, she asked her daughter if she felt all right, and added, "Have you seen anyone out there, anyone at all?"

But again the daughter demurred. She felt fine, and she had seen no one. A few days later her mother again queried her, and again the daughter demurred, but her mother's persistence jogged her memory. She remembered the odd incident with the wind gust, though she didn't mention it to her mother until later. One day she realized that she wasn't feeling like herself, that something strange was happening with her body. This time when her mother asked her how she was feeling, she admitted to feeling strange, and told her mother about the wind.

"That's it!" her mother exclaimed. "I knew it." And explaining little more, she helped her daughter prepare for her first birth. Truthfully, the old woman was looking forward to grandchildren. She had become lonely, wandering alone with only her daughter for company upon Turtle Island. She felt a renewed lightness to her step as she busied herself with cleaning the house and storing herbs and special foods for her daughter and the coming child.

One day in the early autumn, a day when the sky was deep blue and the earth was full in color and ripeness, a day when a stiff breeze blew making everything fresh and clean, the daughter gave birth. Her firstborn, Nanabozho, was a lovely boy child, who cried satisfactorily then promptly fell asleep in his grandma's arms. At his birth, his mother had heard someone say, "Put him down on the ground at once," but she had handed him instead to her mother. As he fell asleep in his grandmother's cradling arms, his mother again heard the voice calling her to task for her disobedience. It wailed sorrowfully, "Had you listened to me, all human children would have walked right after birth as animals do. But now they will have to wait nearly twelve months before they will be able to do so." She knew it was so, for as things began, so they continued forever after, and as she was of the beginning, she made whatever would be so.

The second child, Half Boy, was humanlike in form but somehow indistinct. He was nearly formless, as though in his creation the thought of him had stopped half-formed. But he was as much spirit, manido, as his brother.

Some say that a third child was also born, and he was Flint or Stone Boy. He never moved or talked, but stayed near his mother's lodge until his wild eldest brother, Nanabozho, murdered him in revenge for the murder of their mother.

These three godlings took no time to grow to maturity, for they were manido and their laws of life are not the same as ours. The brothers had many adventures together, though their antics, especially those of Nanabozho, caused their grandmother many anxious moments. Early on, Stone Boy and Half Boy were killed by Nanabozho's brotherly hand. During all this time, the earth became more and more solid, more like it is now, and what Nanabozho did became part of the order of life on Turtle Island.

In time, Nanabozho (who was renowned for his sexual escapades) courted and won the heart of a human woman, who gave birth to two daughters by him. The woman also had a son, her sister's child, thus, in the Indian way, also hers. His name was Madjikiwis.

Matchikwewis was the sister born first, a year or so before Oshkikwe, and from the start she was very like her windson father. She blew hot and cold. She was excitable, changeable, subject to sudden bursts of gaiety or curiosity, and to as sudden bursts of anger.

Oshkikwe couldn't have been more different from her sister. Those who knew them often remarked on the difference, wondering at how they had been born to the same family. Where her sister was boisterous or seductive, Oshkikwe was reserved and modest. She was steady in her affections and loyalties, clear in her taste and purpose, calm and self-contained in her demeanor, and altogether of a reasonable and practical turn of mind. She provided the grounding both her mercurial sister and mother needed.

After they reached maturity, Matchikwewis and Oshkikwe had many adventures. You might say they were the marrying kind, for in those times, before the Europeans came, women married anyone they liked. Even though a woman might marry someone because her brother asked her to—because sisters didn't like to disappoint their brothers or bring them the shame of a broken promise to a friend—she could leave that husband and find another if she so chose. Or not. She could do without a husband if she wanted to.

Once Oshkikwe was living deep in the forestlands with her brother. Madjikiwis didn't have a wife and needed someone to help with all the chores that piled up while he was out hunting. Lacking a woman, he would have to do without proper attire, his snowshoes and other equipment would fall into disrepair, his house would begin to sag and leak. So Oshkikwe went to stay with Madjikiwis, and they worked together happily enough. The young man had gained a reputation as a lucky hunter. He had a whistle that he always kept with him, and he could blow it and turkeys would come from many directions; so they had plenty of turkey to eat and feathers for numerous uses.

After several months of laboring, the young man told his sister he was going to look for a wife. There was a village upriver where a woman he'd seen sometimes lived, and he thought he'd see if she would marry him.

Oshkikwe sent him off well provisioned for the journey. After traveling all day, he came to a house set alone in a small clearing. He saw smoke coming from the chimney and went up to the dwelling. An old woman met him at the door and invited him in. "You must be hungry," she said. "Come, let me give you some supper."

She settled the tired traveler near the fire, then hung a tiny pot over the flame to boil. She placed a tiny amount of rice into it and, after it had boiled a time, added some berries. When the meal was ready, she gave Madjikiwis a serving on a plate as

small as a child's toy dish. He ate politely, and he soon noticed
that each time he scooped up one mouthful, another appeared
on the plate. He ate until he was satisfied. Taking his plate, the
grandmother said, "You thought there was too little food, didn't
you, grandson," and she smiled, satisfied with herself.

In the morning before he set out, the grandmother told Madjikiwis that he would come to two more houses where grandmothers like herself would feed him. Indeed, each of the next
two nights he ate his evening meal comfortably warm at an old
woman's fire. Each of the women served his supper from a tiny
pot of rice, and each night he ate his fill as his tiny plate refilled
itself as soon as it was emptied. As he left the third grandmother's house to set out on the last day of his journey, she cautioned him to be watchful of someone who would follow him
and try to speak to him. "Don't answer him, no matter what he
says," she warned. "His name is Bebukowe, and he is all twisted
in his back. He looks like an insect, a grasshopper, maybe, or a
praying mantis. Be careful of him," she cautioned.

The young man set out. He had traveled for some hours
when he heard a voice hailing him. He didn't turn around but
quickened his pace, mindful of the grandmother's words. Still
the voice pursued him, sounding closer each time his pursuer
spoke. "Hey, Bozho, brother. Wait for me and we'll go together." Finally, annoyed, the young man turned and spoke to
the being that followed him. "Leave me be," he said irritably.
No sooner had he spoken, then to his dismay he realized he
was paralyzed.

The strange-looking person came right up to him. "Let us
sit," he said companionably, and to his astonishment the young
man found himself lowering himself to the ground. They sat
thus for some time, during which Bebukowe showed the young
man some tricks. The young man had some power of his own,
but though he could stave off some of the being's maneuvers, he
could not free himself from the paralysis that kept him prisoner
at Bebukowe's side.

At last he slept, and Bebukowe used his power to change appearances with the young traveler. Now he was tall and well-
formed while the comatose young man took on his humped-
back condition and insectlike features. When the youth awoke

in the morning, he saw the other dressed in his clothes and looking like him, and he realized Bebukowe had traded appearances with him.

The transformed man told him that the village he sought was just across the lake, and they found a small boat tied to some rice stalks and paddled across. Reaching the village, they were greeted by the headman, who welcomed Bebukowe in the form of the handsome young hunter. "We have heard of your luck as a hunter, and we welcome you to our village. I hope you will be willing to make your home among us, and maybe marry one of my daughters." The deceitful one nodded and looked honored, accepting the headman's offer graciously. But village youths set upon the true young hunter who had been transformed to look like a grasshopper and beat him severely, all but killing him. They threw his trampled body into a small creek that ran near the village.

Because of her power, Oshkikwe realized that her brother was in peril. She quickly journeyed to the village. Throwing a small square of buckskin she had a few feet in front of her, she was swiftly transported to the shore of the lake. She threw the skin once more and landed at the edge of the village near the creek where her brother's battered body lay. Gathering him up, she slung him across her back and trudged up the slope with him to her sister's house. Matchikwewis met her at the door surprised. When she saw Oshkikwe's burden she looked past his deformed appearance to his true form and exclaimed, "Oh, he is very handsome! Let's make him our husband!" Throwing her a glance, Oshkikwe replied shortly, "This is Madjikiwis, our brother. He's been hurt."

Chastised, Matchikwewis helped her sister lower Madjikiwis onto the sleeping mat then went outside. Oshkikwe took a hair from her head and trailed it across a stone she took from her bag. As she trailed it slowly across the rock, Madjikiwis sighed. She knew he would be restored. She built a tiny house, just large enough to hold his disfigured body, and within she built a small fire. She placed him within and poured a thick oil on the firestones. After she had laved them three times, she heard her brother say, "I think I'm coming back. Have you any more oil?" Hearing this, Matchikwewis rushed in saying, "I have some right here," but Oshkikwe had already poured some from her pot on the tiny stones that ringed the small house's fire.

When Madjikiwis was restored and rested, he went out and, taking his whistle, lured a large number of turkeys to him. Killing them swiftly, he returned to his sisters' house and held a feast for all the village. Bebukowe attended the gathering, but the gossips laughed and said that during the hunt he'd caught only a partridge. The people thought that strange for a man with the reputation he had. Madjikiwis called on Bebukowe to tell the truth about his identity, but Bebukowe refused. Again Madjikiwis asked, but Bebukowe remained adamant. So Madjikiwis told the gathering what had transpired; then to give proof to his words, he took the metal cane Bebukowe had used to transform himself and Madjikiwis and hit Bebukowe across the back. Immediately his back curved into its characteristic round lump, and his face changed its shape. He began to resemble a praying mantis or a grasshopper. Seeing himself unmasked, he shrieked, but Madjikiwis hit him again and from his hump a martin flew out, and his soul escaped into the afternoon sky.

As time went on, despite the many objects of beauty and usefulness that graced their lives, Matchikwewis and Oshkikwe became restless. Staying in the village was all very well, but they knew that life consisted of much more than rounds of cooking, gossiping, berrying, and rice-harvesting.

One night they lay on a hill beyond the village and watched the stars. "See that faint star there?" Matchikwewis asked her sister. "That's an old man. I bet he's very ugly and lacks any fire, if you know what I mean." She giggled. "And that one, the one that's so bright, do you see it? It's a young man. I'd like to marry that one," she said.

"Oh, I don't know," Oshkikwe said dreamily. "I wouldn't care if he was old. I'd just as well marry him."

"Well, there's no point in just lying around dreaming," Matchikwewis said, sitting up and facing her sister. Her face was alight with excitement. "Let's go up to where they live and see if they're wanting wives." Her excitement was contagious. Oshkikwe sat up too and regarded the stars for a time. She wondered what life was like there. What kind of people they were, what kind of customs they had. She remembered hearing stories about them and felt certain she would find them friendly enough. Most of all she wanted to travel, to change the pattern of her life for a time, to see how other people made their lives.

Oshkikwe and Matchikwewis talked for hours of their desire to travel to the star people's country. They talked until the stars were covered over with the mist that rose from the lake and covered the sky. At last they both slept, and while they slept each was visited by a star man. But neither woman got the one she'd hoped for. The younger one chose Oshkikwe, and the older chose Matchikwewis.

The next day, the sisters went about in a daze. They remembered the visits of the star men, but as though it had been a dream they had somehow dreamed together. The next night, they again took their robes to the hillside where they had previously spent the night, and again the star men visited them. This time, they took the sisters to their homes.

A long time passed. Oshkikwe gave birth to a son. He grew rapidly and soon could go about independently. She kept him supplied with bows and arrows and taught him the ways of her people, as well as those of her husband. The star people were kind, but they were strange to her, and after a time she longed to return to her village so far below. She confided her homesickness to her sister, and Matchikwewis confessed that she was also filled with longing for home.

That same night, one of the grandmothers in the village where they dwelt invited them to her lodge. When they entered the large, rounded room where she sat with her legs extended in front of her, they saw she was making twine by rolling a grasslike material on her thigh. She directed them to sit, then offered them food. She cooked by saying to the small pot that sat on the firestones, "What shall we fix for these guests?" Soon she served them some food on tiny plates. "Is this all she's going to give us," Matchikwewis whispered to her sister, nodding toward the bare spoonful of food in her dish. But like her brother, she soon discovered that as fast as she emptied the dish, it replenished itself.

Still making twine, the grandmother at length asked the sisters if they wanted to return to their homes. "I can help you, if you like. But you must follow my instructions carefully," she said.

The women admitted that they wished to return home and
agreed that they would obey her instructions. "Very well then,"
the grandmother said, making up her mind. She reached behind
her and revealed a very large ball of twine and a woven bag. She
instructed the women to enter the bag, cautioning them not to
look out of it until it had settled firmly to earth. Closing it
tightly, she began to lower it through the floor of her room, as
though it wasn't there, or was made of air.

The women felt themselves descending for a very long time.
At last Matchikwewis could endure the suspense no longer. She
raised herself above her sister and stuck her head out of the bag.
Immediately they began to descend precipitously, coming to
rest in the upper branches of a tall tree.

Eventually they were helped to the ground by a passing wolverine, to whom Matchikwewis called peremptorily, as was her
style: "Come get us down. I want to go first!" Of course he
took Oshkikwe first—there are some advantages to being modest. In her haste to descend, Matchikwewis overbalanced him
and he dropped her. She tumbled a considerable way to the
ground, breaking her ankle.

Wolverine was soon on his way, but Oshkikwe knew they
could not travel with Matchikwewis's broken ankle, so she built
a dwelling for them. The sisters settled down with Oshkikwe's
son, who had traveled unscathed with them from the stars but
who had returned to infancy with their return.

The women lived happily enough. Matchikwewis did much
of the cooking and sedentary work while her ankle healed, and
Oshkikwe gathered food and wood and played with her child.
One morning Matchikwewis told Oshkikwe over their morning meal that she had dreamed the night before. "There's a sorceress coming, and she's going to steal the baby. You must be
very careful," she stressed. "Don't leave him alone when you're
out gathering rice or cranberries. Or leave him in with me, and
I'll keep an eye on him."

Heeding her sister's warning, Oshkikwe was very careful. But
one morning Matchikwewis had gone down the trail to bathe,
and Oshkikwe needed a little wood for the fire. She stepped out
for only a second, thinking it would be safe enough and knowing that the little puppy they had taken in as companion to the
baby would bark if anyone entered the house. But when she returned, the place where her son's cradleboard hung was empty.

She looked rapidly around and found a corner of the cradle-board lying on the floor and just beyond it some deerhide.

Matchikwewis returned to find her sister hastily preparing to pursue her child and the sorceress. Rapidly she recounted what had transpired, and she told her sister she intended to follow them. "If I'm not back in ten days," she said, arranging her oiled hair hastily, "come after me." Matchikwewis agreed to the plan, first reminding Oshkikwe that where the sorceress was taking the child, he would mature very rapidly and would shortly be full-grown and not likely to remember them. Then she told Oshkikwe that she had better drain the milk from her breasts: "You won't have your boy or the puppy to nurse for some time, so you had better save yourself some pain." Indicating that she understood, Oshkikwe set out.

Soon she found tracks of a deer, a man, and a dog, and she knew that she was on their trail. The path she followed quickly became that other place, the place where the earth is not as solid as it seems to us, where it is more tenuous and obeys laws that differ from our own. Deep into that wilderness, she came upon the camp where her son was kept. She saw the puppy, now a small dog, sitting in the yard before the house.

Removing herself a ways, she sat down and thought about how she would retrieve her son. Fixing on a plan, she disarrayed her hair and dirtied her dress so that she'd look as though she had traveled a great distance and was destitute, then she went to the house.

As soon as she saw Oshkikwe, the sorceress ordered her away. "We don't want your kind around here!" she yelled. But Oshkikwe asked her for some bark to make a hut with, and under the laws of hospitality that are universal, the sorceress couldn't refuse. But she gave Oshkikwe bark that was half rotted, throwing it at her. The young man watched all this from the shadows of the house. When she returned, he asked the sorceress, who he believed to be his mother, why she had been so angry at the stranger.

"She's just an old sorceress," the woman replied. "I don't want any harm coming to us through her witchy doings. It would be best if she didn't hang around here."

"Well, that may be so, mother," the young man replied, "but I'm going to take her some better cuts of bark. It's a shame she should have only the rotten bits you gave her." And taking up

some well-shaped splits of bark, he made his way through the
trees to where Oshkikwe was erecting her small lodge. His dog
was already there, frisking around, happy to see her.

Oshkikwe was working with only her brief underskirt on,
leaving her breasts bare. When the young man saw them, he
felt as though he'd forgotten something, but he couldn't remember what. Seeing his look, Oshkikwe sat down, and leaning against one of the doorbeams she had just set in place, she
called the young dog to her and began to nurse it. Looking up at
her son, seemingly a grown man, she told him of his abduction
by the sorceress. She showed him the piece of his cradleboard,
hung with shiny shells and soft feathers, and she showed him
the piece of deerhide ripped from the sorceress's hindquarters
as she fled. "I guess your puppy did this, trying to protect you,"
she said.

She wanted him to return home with her right away, but he
demurred. He couldn't remember for himself any of what she
told him, and he wanted to be certain in his own mind before
he decided what to do. Back in his "mother's" house that night,
he lay down in his bed and began to moan. The sorceress asked
him what was wrong, and he told her he was very ill. "The
only thing that will help," he said, "is if I could see my cradle-
board, from when I was a baby." The woman brought it to him,
and he saw that a corner of it was missing and that the shells
and feathers ornamenting it were the same as those on the corner Oshkikwe had shown him.

When the sorceress prepared for bed, the young man watched
carefully from behind half-closed eyes; and when she raised her
dress over her head, he saw a barely healed scar on her buttock.
Its shape matched the shape of the deerhide he had seen in
Oshkikwe's hand. He went to sleep quickly, settled in his mind
about his next move.

The next day, he told the sorceress he was going hunting and
wouldn't be back until late. Then he went to Oshkikwe's house,
and greeting her as his mother, he told her he would go home
with her. Oshkikwe lifted the wooden bar she had put in place
in her hut the preceding day, revealing a tunnel which she, the
young man, and the dog quickly entered. "You will get smaller
and smaller as we go down," she told her son, "and so will your
dog. Soon I will have to carry you."

Sure enough, the man and the dog rapidly grew younger and

smaller as they fled down the tunnel. As they ran, they heard a commotion behind them. The sorceress, not trusting her captive, had followed him and seen him with Oshkikwe and soon realized that he had escaped. She followed immediately, furious to have lost him. By this time the young man had reverted to the stature of a small child. Even so his mother said, "Quickly, before you become any smaller, use your arrowhead and make a deep cut in the side of the tunnel."

Hastily he did as she bid, gouging a deep cut just over their heads. When the cut was completed, the upper part separated from the lower, cleaving the two worlds. The sorceress was caught in her own world, with little possibility of catching up to them. When Oshkikwe and her baby returned to their house, she found Matchikwewis oiling her hair, dressed as for a hard journey. "I was just readying myself to come after you," she said when she saw her sister. "Is it lunch yet?" Oshkikwe replied.

The days passed and the seasons changed. One fall day, Oshkikwe was out gathering cranberries when a mouse came to her. "Oshkikwe," Mouse said, "there's something I have to tell you. Your sister Matchikwewis is acting rather strangely lately, have you noticed that?"

Oshkikwe reflected in silence a time, then responded that indeed she had noticed that Matchikwewis had not been her usual bright self. "Maybe she's sad because the boy went to live with his grandmother last week," Oshkikwe offered. "Maybe she's just lonely and bored."

"Maybe," Mouse Woman replied. "But I believe she's after you."

"After me!" Oshkikwe exclaimed. "Why would she be after me? What for?"

"She is lonely, as you say," Mouse Woman replied. "And she has strong feelings for you, as they say."

Oshkikwe was taken aback. She remembered now an odd event of a few weeks back when she had come upon Matchikwewis kneeling at a stump, rubbing her face against it. "Come, Oshkikwe," she had called. "Put your face against this soft porcupine fur. It feels so soft and wonderful." Of course, Oshkikwe had done no such thing, but instead had prevailed upon her sister to leave off her activity and join her at the river. Oshkikwe also remembered the many gifts Matchikwewis had taken to giving her lately, and the especially nice dinners she had taken to preparing. Matchikwewis hadn't been much on cooking for the past few years. On reflection, her sudden interest in the art seemed somewhat odd.

That evening Oshkikwe watched Matchikwewis surreptitiously, wondering if she would give some clear sign of her feelings. She noticed that indeed Matchikwewis was at once brighter and more reserved than was her habit. She took special pains to make Oshkikwe comfortable, filling her with the most delicate morsels in the pot, giving her the tenderest portions of turkey, tending to the fire so it burned steadily.

Later, when they were both wrapped warmly in their sleeping robes, Matchikwewis raised up and rested on her arm and called Oshkikwe's name softly. This wasn't in itself odd; she often wanted to gossip softly late into the night, but perhaps because of Mouse Woman's words, Oshkikwe felt her heart begin to race. A feeling of dread began to grow in her belly. "Oshkikwe," Matchikwewis said again, "are you sleeping?" Oshkikwe made her breath come in even rhythm, and soon she heard her sister sigh and settle back down in her coverings.

The next morning she took her axe, as if she were going for wood, and she went to a part of the forest distant from the house but close enough that the sound of chopping would be heard all day. She set the axe to chopping and fled, returning to her mother's home. Eventually, she sent word to her sister that she was at their mother's, and a few weeks later Matchikwewis joined them, bright and laughing, filled with whimsy and impetuousness as before. If she had harbored special feelings for her sister, she did not let on, but occasionally she would be caught standing pensively against the doorway or staring into the fire and heard to sigh softly.

One day, in a fit of restlessness that expressed itself by turns in joking and irritability, she announced that she was going to get a husband. "That's a really fine idea," her old mother crowed. "Go get that man down there, Whitefish, to marry you. I have been craving fish to eat, and he's the best fisherman in the whole territory."

"I don't want to marry that smelly old man," Matchikwewis

retorted. "He's disgusting! If you think he's so attractive, you marry him yourself. I'm going to marry his brother. Raccoon's much richer and smells much better than scummy Whitefish." And she stomped out of the house, taking her hair oil and nice dress with her.

"Oh, dear," Oshkikwe worried. "Now she's going to get into some trouble."

"Let her," her mother replied. "If she has no more respect for her mother's feelings than that, she can find all the trouble she likes. It might make her easier to get along with, having some excitement to occupy her. You know how she gets. I always knew she was a wind child." The old woman complained, "It really is too bad. I could do with some fine fish to eat."

Oshkikwe sighed again, but her mother's desire for fish and Matchikwewis's plan to end her restlessness by marrying had set her thinking. Perhaps she would marry Whitefish herself. That way her mother's taste for fish could be satisfied and she herself would be beyond any advances Matchikwewis might make toward her. Yes, she thought, that's a good plan. Thus satisfied, she began to make preparations to visit Whitefish.

That afternoon she approached his dwelling. No one was there, so she went inside. The place was littered with dead and decaying fish heads and skin; fish bones were heaped in piles about the room. The whole place gave off an odor that made Oshkikwe gag. Dismayed, she looked around her, holding her palm against her nose and mouth. After a time, she straightened her shoulders and set to work. She got rid of her nice dress and spent the afternoon clearing out the debris, sweeping, scrubbing, and straightening. She worked quickly and efficiently. By evening, when Whitefish came home, the house was clean and sweet smelling, Oshkikwe was dressed once again in her nicest garment, and a delightful stew was bubbling in the pot that hung over the fire.

Well pleased, Whitefish sat down to his meal, and from that time Oshkikwe was his wife. The next day she took a large supply of fish to her mother, and the old woman was so delighted with the fish and her daughter's marriage that she scurried about distractedly, now and again muttering random phrases and rushing about some more.

Hearing that Oshkikwe had married and that her husband had brought a large supply of fish to her mother, her mother's sister decided to pay a visit. When she approached her sister's house, she called out a greeting. Quick as a frog snaps a fly, the woman was out of her house with a large stick, which she brandished menacingly.

"Now, you get out of here, you hear?" she threatened. When her sister didn't move but came forward a few steps smiling, thinking it was some new joke, the distraught woman advanced on her and began flailing her with the stick. Frightened and scandalized, Oshkikwe's aunt took to her heels and fled.

Oshkikwe came out. "Mother," she said in astonishment. "What are you doing? Why did you send your sister away like that?"

"Oh, I know her," Oshkikwe's mother responded angrily. "She wants to take a good look at my new son-in-law. She has a couple of daughters she wants to marry off to a good-looking man who will provide her with delicacies like my son-in-law has given me. I won't have her around trying to get him to leave us and marry one of them!"

"Mother," Oshkikwe said softly. "She's your sister. Didn't you say that you and she promised that you would always take care of each other? Didn't you say she was the most important person in the world to you?"

Oshkikwe's mother sighed and sat down near the fire, her mood changed at her daughter's words. "Yes," she sighed again, after a silence. "You're right. She's my dearest sister, and I don't want any harm to come to her. Of course you're right. I must make it up to her any way I can."

So saying, she got up and dressed her hair. Taking a carrying case, she laid in a fine supply of fresh fish, then hurried to her sister's place. Entering the house, she found her sister lying down, her worried daughters hovering over her.

"Oh, mother," they greeted her respectfully. "Here's your sister, and she's so very ill. What happened?"

"Never mind that," Oshkikwe's mother said, and kneeling by her sister's side, she offered her the fish and invited her to her own house as soon as she was feeling better.

"I'll never feel better," Oshkikwe's aunt protested. "I am so very ill from your attack on me. Did you forget the vow we made when we were young? No, I am too ill now to go to your house."

"What can I do to help you?" Oshkikwe's mother asked.

"Nothing will make me feel better," said Oshkikwe's aunt, "but the death of your son-in-law, Whitefish. Only a soup made with his meat will make me better."

"Very well, my sister," Oshkikwe's mother replied. "Then I will see to it."

With a heavy heart, the woman returned to her house, where she told Oshkikwe and Whitefish what had transpired. Oshkikwe protested furiously, but her husband quieted her. "Do as they say," he said to her. "But be watchful and save all of my bones. Don't worry. I'll come back to you if you do as I tell you."

Finally, Oshkikwe assented. Oshkikwe's mother set a large pot to boiling, and they put Whitefish into it. They boiled him until the flesh fell from the bones, then carefully took the stew to Oshkikwe's aunt. Everyone ate, and Oshkikwe carefully saved all the bones, wrapping them carefully in broad leaves and storing them in a heavy bag. Sadly she stole away to stash them in the crook of a tree near the lakeside, as he had directed her. It had been a frightening, dreadful day. She was surprised at the strength of her feelings. After all, she had only married him for distraction and to make things easier for her mother. But she found that she cared deeply for him and hoped he would indeed be restored to her.

After she had secured the bag of bones high in the tree, she returned home, heavy with sadness. On the path to her mother's house, she realized she could not sleep there. She made her way instead to her sister's home. Matchikwewis and her husband, who was Whitefish's brother, welcomed the sorrowing woman and comforted her.

"Don't be sad," they said. "It will work out. Be patient a time, that's all."

So Oshkikwe took heart and settled down to wait the ten days Whitefish had specified in his instructions. During that time, she and Matchikwewis spoke of their earlier life together, and of the vow they had made as children never to be parted. Oshkikwe told her sister of Mouse's words to her, and asked Matchikwewis if Mouse Woman's suspicions had been accurate.

"Yes, she spoke the truth," Matchikwewis admitted. "I know you very well, and we have been through so much together. It's natural that I would be in love with you."

"But," Oshkikwe protested, "we're sisters!"

"Oh, don't be shocked, Oshkikwe," Matchikwewis said. "It's not as though we aren't Nanabozho's daughters!"

"I would rather be married to Whitefish," Oshkikwe said THE defensively.

"And so you are," Matchikwewis smiled. "And right now I am married to Raccoon. But we are very close, you and I. And that's how it will remain."

They talked long into the nights, recalling their sojourn among the star people, their fright when the sorceress had stolen the boy, the time they and their sister Makos had traveled to a far country and stolen the sun, the moon, and a magical horse from an old sorceress who had meant to kill them and serve them to her daughters for dinner. They had each won a fine mate from the grateful people for that adventure.

At length the appointed period of waiting was ended, and Oshkikwe made her way to the tree to recover Whitefish's bones. Coon waited by the fire for her return, while Matchikwewis accompanied her. They retrieved the bones and returned to the house with them. Through the use of rich oil, in a tiny house built complete with its own small fire, they restored Whitefish to life.

But when he was restored, he said he no longer wished to remain among human beings. "They have treated me badly, and I would rather return to my original state of being," he said.

"I didn't marry you and restore you only to lose you," Oshkikwe objected. "You can't do that!"

"Then come with me," Whitefish said.

His brother agreed to change with him, as he was also weary of human quarrels. They went outside into the glittering night and, raising their arms, soared skyward, becoming birds as they rose.

The sisters stood quietly for a time. Then, grinning broadly, Matchikwewis raised her arms and took to the air. "Come on up," she cried.

And together they flew into the night.

TRANSFORMATION TIME

The story of Komo Kulshan, translated as "White Shining Mountain" or "Great White Watcher," is about Mount Baker, the third highest peak in Washington. Renamed by Captain George Vancouver in honor of his lieutenant Joseph Baker, Komo Kulshan is one of the abodes of the immortals, a peak created by them when the change of worlds took place.

In far northern Washington, where Washington and British Columbia meet, west and a bit north of Okanogan lands, the Lummi and Nootsac reside. Mount Baker, the northernmost high peak of the Cascades, overlooks Puget Sound and Georgia Strait. Near it are three smaller mountains, Kulshan's children, and far to the south towers their mother Clear Sky, identified on maps as Mount Rainier, while west lies Fair Maiden and her daughter.

The story of Clear Sky, Fair Maiden, and Kulshan might seem to be an animistic narrative about geographic features when read by modern, secular people, but to those who see through spiritual rather than physical eyes, it is about a truth of planetary being, one that points to a reality that underlies and shapes physical geography. The story is concerned with love, marriage, loss, and the permanence of relationship. To the spiritualist's eye, mountains and islands are persons, immortals, supernaturals, infused with a consciousness measurably different from human consciousness, terribly alien from it in many ways, and inordinately more powerful. Yet as this story testifies, in certain fundamental characteristics the two consciousnesses are akin, as everything in the multiverse is akin.

Clear Sky and Fair Maiden were sisters. They were close, being born but a year apart and having played together daily during their childhood. Clear Sky, the eldest, was very beautiful, but she could be spiteful and impetuous when she was crossed. Fair Maiden, the younger sister, was not especially attractive, but she had a kind and generous nature and a quick sense of humor. She was willing enough to follow her sister's lead in most things, and so they got along well.

When Clear Sky decided to marry a man whose name was White Shining Mountain, Fair Maiden agreed to the match. It was the custom for a man to have more than one wife, and women who shared a man with a sister thought themselves very fortunate. White Shining Mountain came from a powerful family and was extremely handsome in the bargain. The sisters thought themselves lucky to have made such a match. It achieved their most prized girlhood fantasies—not that they were much more than girls when they married, but they knew their business and excelled at the arts and crafts that made a man look even better than he might be.

For years the three lived amiably. Clear Sky, because of her beauty, seldom worried at finding White Shining Mountain in her sister's bed. He seldom went there, and when he did it was more out of courtesy than passion, as Clear Sky was aware. Their companionship was prized among their people, so their camp was often filled with laughing guests who worked alongside the women or White Shining Mountain, enjoying laughter, lively conversation, and good food, which the women all prepared and to which the men all contributed.

In the first years, Clear Sky gave birth to three children, and her beauty burned more deeply in her flesh. She developed a strength and a powerful inner brilliance that drew people to her.

Childless, Fair Maiden helped her sister with the children, and she took on much of the household work while her sister nursed babies. She was content, and her unfailing kindness, peacefulness, and soothing gentleness exerted a drawing power of their own. As the years passed, White Shining Mountain found himself more and more at her side. He began to spend nights in her bed, soothed in his heart by her soft presence.

Clear Sky endured this change in their lives for a time, but she was not a patient woman and soon enough her patience came to an end. She began to drop not very subtle hints to her husband, which he ignored. She began to complain about Fair

Maiden: her stew wasn't tasty, the fish or game in it was stringy or too mealy, the clothing she made fell apart quickly with the slightest wear and tear.

Fair Maiden turned her complaints aside softly, offering Clear Sky the tastiest portions of a meal, mending her torn apparel, and quietly going about her business. It did not occur to her that her sister was jealous of her. She couldn't imagine such a thing, for she knew she did not have Clear Sky's beauty, magnetism, or wit.

At last Clear Sky was beyond patience. One late afternoon when Fair Maiden was down by the river cleaning fish, she lit into White Shining Mountain. "I'll have no more of this!" she scolded. "You ignore me at night and leave me alone in the day. You don't smile at me the way you once did, before the children. Because I've given you children, you think you can throw me away? Ignore me?" She was beside herself with rage. "You should love me more than her, and spend the nights with me. I am your children's mother!"

Stunned at her outburst, and not certain what to do to calm her, White Shining Mountain sat silently. He thought to say, "She is also my wife," but he also thought the better of it. He remained silent, angering Clear Sky even more.

In a fit of anger, wanting him to show that he valued her more than Fair Maiden, Clear Sky said, "I'm going to go away, then. See if you like living without me!"

White Shining Mountain wanted very much for her to stay, but he didn't think she'd go very far. There were the children, he thought, and surely she wouldn't risk them to the wilderness or abandon them for long. "Let her go away," he thought. "Maybe it will help her find calm."

Seeing that White Shining Mountain wouldn't interfere or ask her to remain, that he wasn't going to tell her what she wanted to hear, Clear Sky turned on her heel and left their camp. When she was far away from their enclave, she turned to see the house and her family, but she couldn't make them out. Longing for another glimpse of her home, she stretched herself to see over the top of the brush that blocked her view. Still she couldn't see it well, and though she yearned for her home and family, she was still very angry. "Maybe he will come after me tonight," she comforted herself, and she continued her trek away from White Shining Mountain.

Later, she stopped again to look back. But she couldn't see the house because the trees were in her way. Even though she stood on her toes and made herself as tall as she could, she could only just make out the tips of the trees that ranged behind their encampment.

As evening was nearing, she stopped again and turned in the direction of the home she had left. She was still determined not to retrace her steps, but she wanted to see her children. Still she hoped to see White Shining Mountain coming behind her, moving through the valleys and mountainsides along her track. She stretched herself again, up as high as she could, and because she had stretched so many times she had become much taller, so at last she could clearly see the house, her children in the front playing a rowdy game. She could also see White Shining Mountain, sitting near the door watching them. The smoke from the house let her know that Fair Maiden worked within, probably preparing the evening meal.

Clear Sky was very sad, seeing them. She knew that White Shining Mountain would not come after her, so she decided she would not return. She made her camp there where she could see her family easily, and she began to cull seeds and plantlings, some she had carried with her as was her wont and others she had gathered, until she had plants sturdily growing for miles around her.

In time, Fair Maiden conceived, and one day she told White Shining Mountain that she wished to go visit her mother. "How can you go there," he protested. "She's out on that island far from here, and the way is difficult and trackless."

"I don't know," said Fair Maiden. "I am pregnant and I need to be with my mother now that Clear Sky is gone. You'll just have to help me find a way."

After giving the matter some thought, White Shining Mountain called together many of the animals. All those who could dig agreed to make a large ditch into which White Shining Mountain drew all the waters from the surrounding mountains, creating a river deep enough for a canoe to pass. He and his friends built a sturdy boat for Fair Maiden, and they loaded it with the many provisions she and her friends had made ready.

Bidding her husband good-bye, Fair Maiden climbed into the canoe and headed west down the newly created river. She soon left the mainland and was navigating among the many islands that dot the shore in that part of the country. At each island she chose for her night's stay, she left some seeds, roots, or shellfish. These proliferated in time, and the islands are named for the kind of edibles plentiful on it: camas, clams, berries.

She traveled on and on, but she could not find her mother's island. Coming to a high point, she climbed up it and stood, her tall figure creating wind eddies that spun outward from her body and formed vortices into which people and other creatures were drawn. They were carried away on the winds and killed. Oblivious, she stood, a tall figure against the sky, searching for her mother's island, which she knew to be nearby.

At last Changer, feeling concerned for those who were spinning to their deaths, called to her. "Maybe you need to rest, granddaughter," he said. "Why don't you just lie down for a while."

Realizing that she was indeed tired, Fair Maiden did as Changer bid, and fell asleep. While she slept, he transformed her into a long, low island, now known as Speiden Island. When her child was born, it too became an island—Sentinel Island, which is in the same shape as its mother.

Alone in the north with his three children, White Shining Mountain longed to see his wives. He kept stretching and stretching himself, hoping to catch a glimpse of them. Following his example, the children stretched themselves also. The three became taller and taller until they became high mountains, one a little east of Mount Baker, as Komo Kulshan is known in English, and the others, the mountains known as Twin Sisters, a little to the southeast of Kulshan. Far to the south, their mother Clear Sky, who whites know as Mount Rainier, dominates the plain. The plants she sowed grow richly along her lower slopes, and sometimes even yet she puts on a brilliant dress of pure white and looks northward for her family.

MYTH, MAGIC, AND MEDICINE IN THE MODERN WORLD

For tribal traditions in the New World (new compared to what? new to whom?), the modern era begins with Christopher Columbus five hundred years ago. Christ-bearing Dove, as his name goes in English, brought the four horsemen of the Apocalypse west along with Satan, the Cross, and the Inquisition. After sojourning on the island he named Española (Santo Domingo) on the eastern edge of the Caribbean, he abducted some local people and returned whence he came to get reinforcements. Within a handful of years, the thriving population of the New Eden he had stumbled upon was reduced by many millions. They did not succumb to supe-rior European war technology, nor to superior force of faith, but to superior disease (Brandon 1974, 97).

Over the years, the ritual tradition has undergone a num-ber of transformations, not all of them bad. A living thing changes as energies within it change, and inner energies change as external conditions (another way of talking about energies) change.

With the arrival of the Europeans, certain shifts in the tradi-tions that had been occurring over the preceding three or four centuries became pronounced, setting off a flurry of adjust-ments and readjustments over two continents. Central to the process of transformation was the slow shift from feminine or-derings to masculine arrangements within the traditions them-selves. The transformation of Ic'sts'ity (Uretsete) from a female to male supernatural, from mother to father of the Keres people; the shift of Xmucané and Xpiyacoc from female partners to elderly married couple among the Quiché Maya; the adaptation of Kanati the Hunter to husband of Selu, a seeming replacement of her polygynous relationships with him and Long Man; reifi-cation of the goddesses Cihuacoatl and Coatlicue—these are all evidence of the profound change in Native America resulting from its patriarchalization under Christian mercantilism.

A shift of such magnitude required a corresponding move-ment of all intelligences within the ritual system. They emerged in different forms and guises, around a reshaped focal point. It is to the most recent stages in the shift (one that is continuing) that the stories in this section speak.

By the time of the Aztecs, particularly in their last years, the old religion had entered a period of decline. The life-focused tradition of older civilizations had become death focused, and the form of ritual now far outweighed the spirit. This was not as morbid a tendency further north or to the east and south of Tenochtitlán, but it was occurring outside the capital in a muted degree.

Populations were on the move, ceremonial cities far to the north were abandoned, and some medicine elders say even the animals and plants were undergoing transformations. Certainly the climate was changing noticeably, reflecting (not causing) the great movements occurring in every other sphere. There was turmoil in the universe of power. The Great Mysteries wanted to tell and to hear another story.

At that time—one of beginnings as well as of ends—the great sister goddesses (there seem to have been a "blue million of them" as my mother would say) began to prepare the people for the great change. The old calendars kept track; it was no surprise that strange beasts were seen wandering the land, that odd crafts were sighted, that new gods appeared. That's what happens during a big ritual.

Lady Penance Grass, Malinalli, La Malinche, responding to her Elder Sisters' call, became the slave-diplomat who brought down the Aztec empire. The great speaker and his twin (or counterpart) the high priest of the goddess Serpent Skirt were killed. The gold that had adorned their lives—tons of it—began to trickle east, in a bizarre echo of Sun Woman's eastward journey a ritual age before. That gold, and the silver for which Mexico is famous, funded Anglo-European monarchies and the terrible wars they waged against each other for five hundred years. With the stolen riches, those monarchies became modern states that exert influence on world affairs far out of proportion to their numbers.

In another of those strange twists of ritual plot, not only precious metal went east. The idea of political freedom found its way aboard the slave ships, the gold ships, the ships filled with treasures and people of a plundered world. While the disease and disorder that came with Europeans wrought ruin, the freedom and faith they found in the new world created havoc in the old. In the universe of power, all transactions proceed in more directions than one.

That's how it is with big medicine—a phrase enshrined in

penny novels and early flicks. "Ugh! Heap Big Medicine!" the
native caricature says, his eyes wide with astonishment—or
narrow with guile. Well, heap big medicine indeed, a medicine
whose workings are still going on, affecting every nook and
cranny of modern planetary life.

The use of the word "medicine" to denote ritual magic is intriguing, its origins lost in the rush to take, settle, and forget.
But in early times—the colonial era, the westward movement,
the frontier days—native people often cured Anglo-European
newcomers of ailments. Presumably as a consequence of their
ministrations, practitioners who used native knowledge to di-
agnose and treat illness became known as "medicine men" or
"medicine women." In some regions, such as the northern California coastal area, shamans are still called "doctors," and their
ritual practice is known as "doctoring," although their healings
are unaccompanied by Western medical apparatus. The midewewin, an organization as well as occult discipline among the
Ojibwa/Chippewa Algonquians, is called the "medicine dance"
in English, and the structure where the rites take place is called
a "medicine lodge," though healing is not the primary purpose
of the rites, nor is it but one of many outcomes.

Over time, the term "medicine" has come to signify American Indian ritual magic, a use that distinguishes it from the for-
mal Western metaphysical tradition as the term "witchcraft"
distinguishes a number of old tribal earth religions from the
mystical rites practiced by the Roman-descended elite. Interestingly, African practitioners are known to the English—and thus
to Americans—as "witch doctors," a term which combines
Anglo attitudes toward both European and Native American sacred practice. "Medicine" or "doctoring" do not bear the implications of evil that "witch" or "witchcraft" carry, but there is
a class distinction operating in the use of the term "medicine."
My *Random House Unabridged Dictionary* (1966) gives the following racist definition: "any object or practice regarded by
savages as of medical efficacy whether for good or evil." This
implies that "savages" came up with the term and commonly
use it—which may indeed be the case, since English-speaking
white travelers to native communities coined it. According to
another story, it was coined by French travelers in Indian country. My dictionary also says the word "medicine" is "from

L(atin), the fem(inine) form of *medicinus*, pertaining to physicians," and instructs "see *medic.*" "Medic" is given as "*med(era)* (to) heal." Most recently, "medicine" has come to mean the sacred or spiritual practice of American Indian occultists, and perhaps this definition returns the term to its Graeco-Roman antecedents, albeit with feathers.

In her autobiography, the medicine woman María Sabina comments that disease is a spiritual disorder. "The spirit is what gets sick," she says, mirroring traditional native assumptions about the nature of disease. (Estrada 1981, 56) A flow chart of the sacred etiology of illness would reveal the pattern and thus dictate the treatment: spiritual disorder to astral reflection of the disorder to etheric or "energy" body to physical body. What must be contacted and reconnected with universal harmony is the spirit of the ailing person. To this end, a number of ploys are used. The first thing the healer must do is get a diagnosis. This may be effected several ways: by interviewing the patient and those close to her or him; by divination, prayer, and meditation in which guiding spirits inform the practitioner of the source and treatment for the ailment; or, as in the case of María Sabina, through the help of an "ally" (to use Carlos Castenedaʼs term), which Sabina calls "the children" or "the saint children."

According to a large number of medicine traditions, the cause of the spiritual disharmony that has led to disease is a violation of some taboo. If, for instance, one abuses plants, a disharmony is created in the psychesphere which must be played out in some way until harmony is restored. Certain illnesses can be traced to mistreatment of a plant community, and treatment can be undertaken to restore harmony within the patient and within the plant community that has suffered.

It is the loss of harmony, an inner-world imbalance, that reveals itself in physical or psychological ailment. It also plays itself out in social ailments, war, dictatorship, elitism, classism, sexism, and homophobia. This chain of action-consequence ensues because balance and harmony are fundamental laws of the cosmos. Disorder brings about a series of adjustments whose purpose is to reestablish harmony.

While the person or community suffering the ailment is often guilty of violating a spiritual law (taboo), just as often the entire state of disharmony nation- or worldwide works its way out in disease among the populace. Thus debilitating and devastating illnesses sweep through the population as the encompassing psychesphere attempts to regain its equilibrium. When a community is out of balance for whatever nearest reason, its most sensitive members are most likely to suffer in their bodies and minds. Thus oftentimes the most advanced medicine people suffer a number of compensatory ailments, often having to do with immune system dysfunctions such as rheumatoid arthritis, diabetes, cancer, lupus, chronic immunodeficiency syndrome (CIDS or CFIDS), and acquired immunodeficiency syndrome (AIDS). Their very sensitivity on psychic and spiritual levels makes them lightning rods, drawing the disharmony to themselves and grounding it, rendering it far less harmful to the larger community.

The notion of taboo violation as causative of illness may seem strange to modern minds, but it is no stranger than avoidance of radioactivity, toxic chemicals, or disease-bearing environments of all sorts. If one violates any of these strictures, disease is likely to ensue. In a similar fashion, traditionals know that it is unwise and unsafe to show disrespect for spirits, do violence to other life forms, engage in selfish behavior, or to abuse oneself or others. The exact forms of the disrespectful actions may vary, but by and large they are clear. Pretty Shield wasn't allowed to throw things at the chickadees because doing so was disrespectful of them. Her disrespect could have had grave consequences, so her grandmother hastened to clarify her situation with the birds and to admonish Pretty Shield strongly against repetition of her behavior.

This argument is not a case of "blaming the victim"—an accusation easy to make and difficult to dispute when the politics of our situation is so dreadfully confused and diseased. We native people are certain that disease is a symptom of spiritual disorder, but whether that disorder is the fault of the sufferers is another matter entirely. Indeed, there are powerful arguments advanced in the Indian community that many of us suffer from a variety of immune system disorders and other chronic debilitations because we are earth's children, and as she endures monstrous patriarchal abuse, we suffer as well, sharing in her pain and disease and in that way ameliorating its devastation and bringing some respite to her.

Native people are also convinced that disharmonious actions toward plant and animal communities turn them against human health and life. They become poisonous, where, before being mistreated, they were nutritious and safe for human use and consumption. Another consequence of disharmony is that they quietly disappear.

When Nau'ts'ity and Ic'sts'ity decide to have children before the time is right, Grandmother Spider comes to them and notes their decision. Saying that they have done this though they knew it was the wrong time (harmony is connected to what time it is, always), she advises them that she is going away. Clearly they do not care to follow her guidance, so she leaves them to follow their own devices, an action that is appropriate to the circumstances and thus restores at least some harmony in the cosmos. By and large, Indian people follow this track, seeing that the other intelligences around them act in that manner. Rather than confrontation or war, they engage in passive resistance, and if that fails they simply remove themselves physically or socially from the scene.

Right now, countless numbers of animal and plant species are following Grandmother's trail. They are leaving us to our own devices, rendering the planet more and more bleak and empty. Traditionals say that so long as modern people continue in their depredations of the planet, spewing negative thinking, disharmony, and disrespect for all that lives, famine, drought, and the loss of vast numbers of life-forms will continue to accelerate. Even the air is leaving. Violating taboos is very dangerous to all life, and while most Americans can blithely avoid the immediate consequences of disrespect, the human community over most of the world pays a very high price for our violations.

ROSES, ROSES

Tonantzin, as she is named in her mostly recent aspect, is our grand-
mother and mother. She is a healing goddess and incorporates in her
being the nurturing aspects of nature. She was revered among the
Aztecs as the goddess who was present at their own beginnings as
a people in their homeland, Aztlan. There is a depiction of her upon a
mountain there that reads "Our Mother stood here." She was seen
as the patroness of weaving, spinning, sweatbaths, and curing, and
mother of two divine sons: Maize and its obverse, Frost. In the first
view she is akin to Thinking Woman and Xmucané, and in the second
resembles Selu and Sky Woman.

In her guise as Our Lady of Guadalupe, the image she somehow
transferred to the cloth which hangs above the altar of her church re-
minds us that she is actual, real, and by extension, so are the other
deities. The nation of Mexico is under her care, formally dedicated to
her by the Roman Catholic Church. One thing about the supernatu-
rals: you can't fault their sense of humor.

Tonantzin, our Holy Mother, Cihuatzin, Revered Lady, Toci or
Tozi, Our Grandmother, Llama, Old Woman, Tocennan, All
Mother, Teteoinnan, Mother of the Gods, Tonan is the mother
of all and everything. She comes in many forms and guises all
over the Americas, and she is as much Sky as Earth, as much
Galaxy as Universe, as much Day as Night. The stars and the
planets are her children, and they are gods. The flowers and
fruits, the grain and animals, the rocks and mountains, the
oceans and rivers, the clouds and winds are all her children, and
they are gods, they are supernaturals, they are spirits, they are
the intelligence that graces every climate, every land, every
habitation, and they are her children. We are all her children,

and she is mother of us all. Together we share her bounty, share her pain, share her beauty, share her thought. Together we are one great cloak of her being, like the hundreds of feathers in the cloak the high priest Tlacaelel wore when carrying out her behests and giving her honor. In her guise as Teteoinnan, she was the gynarchic apotheosis, revealing her authority as highest divinity. Teteoinnan was pictured wearing a star skirt, a belted skirt made of leather straps that were studded with shells. When she danced, you could hear their rattling, a sure sign of her presence. Then she was the Great Goddess, the mother of all, mother of the gods, gynarch of the universe. In this guise she was huntress, archer, Goddess of the Deer.

Tonan was revered everywhere in the Land between the Waters, Mexico, except in the great imperial capital Tenochtitlán, where she was allowed only a wooden platform on the southern end of the great city. There unattended, she gazed out at that corner of the world, with no priesthood to honor her and no temple of her own. The Mexica had little use for her since they had fled their enslavement among the Culhua and raised their own empire over the land. In Calhuacán they had worshiped her under the name Toci, Our Grandmother, but in Tenochtitlán only in one of her guises was she a satisfactory goddess—as grandmother of Huitzilopochtli, as Yaocihuatl, Enemy Woman. But outside their city-state, she was widely and solemnly revered.

As Toci, Our Grandmother, she was depicted as a warrior woman who held a shield in one hand and a broom in the other, a foreshadowing of her granddaughters, the Adelitas, who many years in the future would fight for and help win the independence of Mexico after centuries of thralldom.

Her name, Tonan, was a Nahuatl name given to many mountains, for mountains were seen as coalescences of Earth Woman, places where her power rose to its heights, where the emanation of her spiritual energy was greatest. She was seen as extremely powerful, for her movements caused great earthquakes. Mountains had reared suddenly in flat pastures when she turned or raised her head.

All the efforts of the Catholics, all the coercion of the Inquisition could not eradicate her name, her worship, or her presence from the people's minds. They have never forgotten Tonan, nor has she forgotten them. All over Mexico you can see depictions of her, and throughout the American Southwest, in the Midwest, the West, in the Latino quarters in the East, you can see her, clothed in medieval European garb. Her dress of salmon pink is covered by a cloak of blue, which is dotted with stars. Around her head and body writhe serpent fires. Tonantzin is called Our Lady of Guadalupe, Nuestra Señora de Guadalupe. Even today, nearly five hundred years after the new order came to Mexico, her star-studded skirt, her brown skin, the flames that surround her remind us of who she is. I have her picture always with me, and I gaze at it as I write now.

On a wintry day in northern Mexico, in the year 1659 C.E., an impoverished Indian man whose Spanish name was Juan Diego was trudging cross-country on an errand. The Spaniards had long ago taken Mexico as their own. It had been one hundred forty years since Quetzalcoatl the Precious Twin had returned. As Diego approached a small hill, he heard a woman's voice calling his name.

Puzzled, he looked around. He had seen no one for some time, so the voice came out of nowhere, or so he thought. At the crest of the rise, he saw the figure of a woman, and she was beckoning to him. She was dressed in the peasant fashion of the day, her body modestly covered in a long-sleeved gown, her head and shoulders hidden beneath a long cloak.

Slowly, he went toward her. When he was within a few feet of her he stopped, and taking off his sombrero, he looked shyly groundward. He had seen that she was not one of the village women, no one he knew, and her presence made him feel at once safe and awed. He stood thus, not speaking. His deep sense of courtesy restrained him, and his rearing in soft-mannered ways led him to await her words patiently.

"I have a message I want you to take to the city, to the archbishop," she said calmly. Her voice, though soft, was warm and clear.

"But, Lady," he objected softly. "It is far, and I am but an Indian. The archbishop will not have reason to see me."

"Go, and do as I say. Tell him that I wish to have a church built here, in my honor. Tell him to dedicate it to me." She smiled gently at Juan Diego.

"But, Lady," he said again. "I have no shoes. I do not speak their language very well. Surely the archbishop will not have time for the likes of me."

"It will be well," she said.

So, hesitatingly, he walked away from her. He felt certain that no one would see him in the capital, but he was willing to try. He had a sense that the Lady was not like them, not an Indian, certainly not a Spaniard. Something about her, her presence, made him recognize he must do as she directed him.

But, as he thought, the archbishop would not see him. He managed to tell his story to one of the priests at the cathedral, and the man said he would carry the message to His Excellency. After many hours, he returned and took the barefoot man in to see the archbishop.

Juan Diego told his story, but the archbishop did not believe him. After listening to him carefully, he sent him away with words of blessing.

Juan Diego began the long trek back to where he'd seen the Lady. When he arrived at the small hill, she stood waiting for him. It was deep winter, and very cold. The stiff grass was brown and dry, and a bleak wind scudded clouds across the afternoon sky.

He told her what had happened at the cathedral, and awaited her response.

"Take off your tilpa," she instructed him. He made a move to obey her, and as he did he saw to his astonishment that the ground at her feet was suddenly thick in riotous roses. He gasped, taking a step backward.

"Don't be frightened," the Lady said. "Fill your tilpa with blossoms and carry it carefully back to the city. Ask again to see the archbishop, and when you do, open it and show him the roses."

Awed, Juan Diego leaned down and plucked an armload of the flowers. Filling his tilpa and wrapping its ends loosely around them so they wouldn't be crushed, he lifted the bundle carefully into his arms.

Back in the city, he hastened to the cathedral as soon as it was light. The sacristan let him in, and he stood in the drafty church entry gazing at the lighted candles, smelling the incense from early Mass. He went further in, stopping at the carved basin just inside the chancel. Dipping his hand in the icy water,

he blessed himself quickly and knelt down on one knee briefly.
Then clutching his bundle, he started for the front of the cathedral, following the sacristan. He was led to a room off the cathedral where the archbishop was sitting down to a meal. Juan
Diego had not eaten in many hours, and walking so far with no
food had left him weak.

Still, he did not give in to the small urge to gaze hungrily at
the food. Instead he told the archbishop that the Lady had instructed him to show what he carried to him. As he spoke, he
let the ends of the tilpa drop so that the roses could fall to the
floor. He heard the archbishop's sharp intake of breath and
glanced up. His Excellency's fair skin had turned some shades
lighter, and his eyes were round as a child's. His gaze was fixed
on the tilpa that hung from Juan Diego's upraised hands.

"A miracle," the archbishop whispered. His monsignor nodded and fell to his knees.

After a time, Juan Diego lowered his arms so he could look
over them at his tilpa. He saw that no roses had fallen to the
floor, for it was quite bare of blossoms. Then, turning his gaze
to the woven cloth he held, he saw what had set the other men
reeling. Somehow an image of the Lady had become imprinted
on the cloak.

Ah, he thought, Tonantzin, Our Mother, has returned. Like
the others, he sank to his knees, still clutching the worn wrap
in both hands.

Recovering himself, the archbishop took the cloak from Juan
Diego and spread it reverently upon the table, pushing aside the
breakfast things and the food. He gazed at it in silence for a
time, then turned to the Indian and said, "Tell the Virgin Morena I will honor her request. I will build her church, and she
will become the Patroness of New Spain." Then he turned to
his aide and instructed him to feed Juan Diego and make sure
he had another tilpa to wrap himself in for the journey back to
deliver his message.

As Juan Diego was being led away, he heard the archbishop
call after him, "Thank you, and go with God."

A FISH OF ANOTHER HUE

The ixkareya, the immortals, lived long before the human beings. The Karok, like other Californian communities, know of their existence because some of them still speak with these elusive beings. Katimin was one of the towns where the gods went about making human beings—the five-fingered beings, as the Pueblo have it, the earth-surface people, as the Maya and Navajo call them.

In the Katimin neighborhood, there is a story about a woman chief who knew that the people would be visited by the whites, the strangers. After seeing to their continued well-being, she transformed herself to stone so she could keep watch over them through their transition time.

The world-renewal ceremony referred to in this story is a ritual that is occasionally performed. Its purpose is exactly what its name suggests: to renew or restabilize the world in the configurations of power (or energy) established at the time of the beginnings, the time when the mountains, rivers, weather, and creatures became what they have been since human history began. There is a fatawenan, or "priest," and two women who assist him, called ikiyawan, pikiawish women, or "priestesses."

This rendition is based on narratives recounted by Mary Ike and Georgia Orcutt. Details of dress I have taken from those I've seen worn at powwows or other gatherings by California Indian women.

Early in my residence in California in the 1970s, I attended a Native American dinner at which we ate acorn mush, a staple of Karok, Yurok, and other California Indians' diet. It is similar to cream of wheat, poi, or grits. Its making requires several washings, called "leaching," so that the toxic materials in acorns, which are poison to humans, are removed. For this purpose, the women would go to riverbeds, where the flat stone had been carved into both deep and shallow holes. Here they mashed and leached the acorns.

The animals were once people, but the ixkareya were the head of everything. When the arara, the Indians, came, the ixkareya became rocks, trees, rivers, mountains, and everything.

Not long after the time of the ixkareya, there was a young woman living at Katimin who was to be married. Her espoused was a boy she had her heart set on, and she was joyful at their impending nuptials.

But no, it was not to be. Shortly before the celebration of their union, the young man was killed in a boating accident. His death brought more than grief to the young girl. It brought determination.

She knew her lover was a very good sailor, and that he often led parties through the intricacies of the river and its falls. It seemed uncanny that he had died, and she believed deeply in the senselessness of his death. One so young, with so much life to live.

She wept for a time, but it was not enough. She refused to eat, intending to starve herself to death to join him.

She was a shaman, a pikiawish woman of the world-renewal ceremony when they fix the world in its place once again, and her training in the mysteries fitted her well for the plan she resolved upon. In the newness of time each annual cycle, the salmon returned to bring forth new life. In the newness of time each annual cycle, the people, the arara, swam up the mystic rivers, returning to their origins to bring forth new life, the new days of the coming year.

The maiden went to the dance ground. She swept it with a brush broom of herbs. She put on her skirt with the shells that adorned it, held at their tops with twine, their bases hanging loosely all around. She put on her necklaces of shell, her bracelets. She placed her woven star hat on her head, it fitted snug over her crown. She put on her anklets of shell, strands and strands of them. She made on her face the proper design. She marked her arms and chest.

She began to dance and sing. Striking two smooth pieces of hard wood together, she sang. She continued to dance and sing. Slowly, slowly, she moved, and the dignity of the song, the strength of her purpose, began to move her. She no longer moved. IT moved her.

She began to walk away from the ground, went walking a long way. She came to the Klamath River, where the women were working. She continued along it until she was in the land of the ixkareya, until there were many of them all around. She continued on, climbing to Asfam Karoom, and looked down. She saw where those ixkareya lived. She could smell the sea, see its great glittering body below. She went down.

There was an old woman sitting near the shore. Her house was there, near the high tide line. The girl went over to her and sat down. After a time, the old woman spoke. "Seems like I always hear it when an ikiyawan, a priestess, goes through Astuwise. Your ceremonial skirt always strikes the rocks of the Astuwise when you pass. I can hear the shells clacking against the rock way over here, in our country." She sat silently for a time. The girl said nothing.

At length, the old woman offered, "The one you seek is here, but you cannot see him or take him away."

Companionably, she asked the girl, "How is it in Katimin? Do you still have the pikiawish, the world-renewal dance? Is the old oak tree still there, the one where we used to put the wood when we went after it on the hill? Do you still prepare the acorns for the priest? Do you still leach them and make the tiny replica of the sacred mountain from sand you have soaked in the basin sunk in the flat stones?"

The girl answered the old woman carefully, but she was torn with the thought that she could not return with her lover nor see him there. Yes, they did the ceremony still. Yes, the oak tree still stood. It was ancient now and might not last much longer. Yes, there they stored the wood. Yes, they still fed the fatawenan, the priest. Yes, they still used the leaching water to wet the sand from which they fashioned the sacred mountain. Yes, the salmon returned.

"I was a pikiawish woman during my time in your country," the old woman said. "I was like you, a little bit, back on earth. Maybe you are a little bit like me." She gestured toward the north. "See there along the shore where it curves away from us? There your lover walks."

The young pikiawish woman looked in the direction the old woman indicated. She saw her lover, his lithe body so familiar and so dear, his skin just darker than the sand, seeming almost

rosy against its light tan. She wanted to run to him, but she
stayed seated, only a slight clinking of the shells on her skirt
and wrists betraying her desire.

"You must go," the old woman said. "You can't stay up here
because you haven't died. This place in the sky is for those who
have died, like me." She rose and went into her hut, returning
shortly with a large basket. She carried it to the girl and set it on
the sand beside her. The girl saw that it was full of spring
salmon.

"Take this salmon below with you," she said. "It is at least
part of what you seek. When someone dies, rub a little of the
salmon on the lips of the dead one. Don't put it on while life
remains, it won't work that way. Wait until death has come,
then rub it on. Then the dead will come to life again."

Sadly, the pikiawish girl took the basket. She lifted it to her
back, securing it around her forehead with the thong handle
woven into its sides.

When she returned to Katimin she discovered to her surprise
that she had been gone for a year. The people, the arara, had
searched for her, finally giving up, not knowing where to look
further. They knew how despondent she had been, and they
grieved. But at her return, they were again happy, particularly
as she had brought the salmon from the land of the dead.

After that no one died. The land of the arara became much
more densely populated. At last the basket of salmon was used
up and people began to die once more. The life of the arara became more normal, but it was also filled again with sorrow
sometimes, when someone died.

But the people had learned wisdom. They knew that death
brought grief, but it also brought new life, just as the pikiawish
ceremony did.

When the young pikiawish woman became very old, when
her skin was soft as buckskin with her years, then she died. She
went again to the land near the sea far from Katimin, and that
time there she remained.

THE HUNTER

The story I have titled "The Hunter" is the first story my great-grandmother, Mita Atseye Gunn, told me. I was very young, and it formed many fantasies I played out over my childhood. My mother and my great-grandmother were going to Albuquerque one day, and when we passed the road that used to lead north to Paguate from Old Laguna, Grandma Gunn pointed to the great rocks she said were the old giantess's head and body. She was right: they certainly looked like the petrified body parts of a huge and frightening being.

Again I have leaned on Uncle John Gunn's collection of Laguna stories in Schat Chen *(1977) for some particulars, details I had forgotten after so many years, as well as upon my own memory of the land that sometimes seems more than twelve hundred miles away and the memories of her own my mother has shared with me. Writing the story of the girl I have named Simana (it is spelled "Shimana," as "s" is pronounced "sh") was a journey home.*

Maatsiñe, paper bread, is a wonderful concoction made from thin blue cornmeal batter. The batter is spread on a griddle in a thin sheet (ideally the griddle is made of slate stone and heated over a wood fire), lifted off carefully, by hand, and stacked on another just like it. When a sufficiently high pile of the sheets has been stacked, the whole is folded into a bundle that is about the size of a thick business envelope. It is sweet and crisp, the thin flakes falling about you as you munch and melting deliciously on your tongue.

Shimana didn't have brothers or cousin-brothers, and on one of the winter days when all the boys used to go rabbit hunting, she got up very early and told her mother she was going rabbit hunting as well. "It's true I'm a girl," she said, "but I believe I can kill as many rabbits as any of the boys."

Her mother agreed, and fixed her a big breakfast of maatsiñe, warm blue corn drink, and some sweet, tender pinto beans that had simmered all night in the special bean pot her own aunt-mother had made.

After she ate, Shimana got her hunting stick and went out. She walked into the low hills and spent hours hunting rabbits. She killed many, and as the afternoon waned and some snow flurried down, she decided to rest for a while in a small cave on the north side of Timiya—that hill about three miles southwest of the village where we went a few years ago to get wood—and roast herself some rabbit because she was cold and hungry.

An old giant woman, one of those who used to live in the mountains around here, must have smelled Shimana's dinner cooking, because about the time Shimana was getting ready to eat she looked up and saw this enormous face peering down at her. The giant woman was so big, bigger than the hill Shimana's little shelter was in. Her mouth was wider than this room, maybe wider than this house.

Shimana was very frightened. She scampered back against the cave wall. She didn't know what to do. "Guwatsi, little girl," the giant woman said politely. "I'm wondering if there's someone eating around here. Maybe they could let someone have a little food. Someone has been hunting for two days with no success. You're a smart, brave girl, I can see, and you have great skill with your stick."

Shimana was too frightened to answer politely, as she should have. She just threw a rabbit out of the cave to the giant.

The giant swallowed the tiny creature with one gulp, and indicated she was still hungry. Shimana threw her another, then another. Soon all the rabbits Shimana had caught had disappeared down the huge throat of the giant woman. She had devoured them without even chewing. But she still wanted more.

Shimana began to throw her clothes out of the cave, hoping that the huge woman would be satisfied with them. But no, she wasn't satisfied even then. She began to move closer to the small cave where Shimana crouched. Shimana flattened herself along the back wall of the cave, just out of reach of the giant woman's fingers. Her hand was far too big to fit into the small opening.

"What shall I do?" Shimana wondered desperately. "I have no more to give her, and she's strong enough to tear this mesa apart if she wants to!"

Just then she saw a stick being poked through the opening. "Oh, no," she thought. "She's hunting me like a rabbit!"

Frightened, she began to call on the supernaturals to help her. She composed herself and thought as hard as she could, then sent a voice to those who live beyond human realms.

The stick was probing the cave. Once it almost touched her. She threw herself flat on the ground, tucking her prostrate body as far into the corner of the cave as she could.

Just then she heard a small voice calling her name. "Shimana," said the voice. "Look just over your nose."

Shimana opened her tight-squeezed eyes and looked where she was directed. There, just a couple of inches from her nose in a tiny crevice in the cave wall, was a small spider.

"Oh, grandmother," said Shimana. "Are you there?"

"Haa, yes, granddaughter," Spider answered. "I am here."

"Oh, grandmother," Shimana said. "There's a giant woman outside and she's hunting me."

"Eh, yes, granddaughter. That's why I called you. I can help you. Just do as I tell you."

"Alright, grandmother," Shimana said. "What should I do?"

"Here, take this," Old Spider said, handing the girl some white foamy substance. Rub this over the tip of your hunting stick, then poke it out of the cave opening. When the giant woman grasps it, twist it sharply around several times and hold it tightly. Then she won't be able to move. After she is still, take some pollen from your pouch and blow some over the opening.

Shimana did as she was told, and soon the monstrous fingers were tightly wrapped around the hunting stick and the giant woman was immobile.

"Now, call for my grandsons. They will come help you."

Again, Shimana did as she was bid. Soon Masewe and his brother Oyoyowe, who had been rabbit hunting in the Sipi Mountains east of the Rio Grande, heard her and decided to go to see what the trouble was.

They soon arrived at the place and found the old giant woman bent over the cave opening. One hand seemed to be caught at the opening, while in the other was a huge boulder with which she had been pounding the front of the recess, making marks that you can still see on the stone.

"Oh, grandsons," she said, "are you here?"

"Haa," they replied. "We are here, grandmother."

"What are you doing, grandsons?" the giantess asked, ingenuously.

"Oh, we are hunting rabbits," they answered.

"You certainly have nice hunting sticks," she said.

"Yes," said Masewe, and you can see them better if you stand up and turn your head a little to one side."

As she began to rise, they threw their sticks and she fell, causing earth tremors for miles around. The Little Twins killed the giant and cut her open, taking out the girl's clothes and returning them to her. Then they cut off the giant woman's head and threw it over to the southeast, where it now lies, turned to stone, on the north of the old trail that used to lead to Stchummuya, the Place Where Bees Live.

That stone is called Skoyo Kowowwe, the Giant's Face. The brothers threw her heart to the north. It is that hill northeast of the village. You know the one, it's on the way to Qischch, the town they call Paguate. That hill, you know, we call Ka'wash'ka, or Heart.

Then, when Shimana was dressed and ready, the brothers took her hunting with them for a while, and they caught many rabbits for her to take home to her family.

DEER WOMAN

Like the Pueblos and their cultural descendants the Navajo, the Cherokee tell stories featuring two men—sometimes brothers, sometimes
twins, sometimes half-brothers (as in the Six Killer story in this volume). I have followed that tradition in this account of a contemporary
encounter with Deer Woman and another who may be like her. While
I can find no explicit comment on the presence of more than one Deer
Woman, some old accounts specify that there are two or more such
supernatural beings.

While the old stories relate encounters with Deer Woman—one of
those ephemeral beings called the little people, Yunwitsansdi—among
the Cherokee in regions of the old Cherokee homelands in the southeastern part of the country, now known as Georgia and North Carolina, encounters with them in Oklahoma, where the majority of the
Cherokee now reside, are not uncommon. In her notes to the section
entitled "The Little People" in Friends of Thunder, Anna G. Kilpatrick, the Cherokee folklorist, comments that she and her husband
Jack F. Kilpatrick have collected "a sheaf of anecdotes relating to encounters with the Little People either by persons known to the narrator
or, in one case, by the narrator herself." She adds, "to the average
Cherokee with some degree of traditional upbringing, the existence of
the Little People is an indisputable fact" (1964, 79). According to
Kilpatrick, the Oklahoma Cherokee don't seem to feel that any danger
is associated with these encounters except "the danger of becoming
fascinated by them and following them off to unpredictable adventures" (79). Nor, it seems, are these encounters confined to Cherokee
people. Deer Woman has shown up at dances among Kiowa and
Chocktaws, or so some stories I've been told assert. Maybe she and
the other Yunwitsansdi moved to Oklahoma (which was to be Indian
territory "as long as the grass should grow," so the broken treaties
proclaimed) during the great removal period in the early nineteenth
century. At that time, almost all the nations and tribes of the American

Southeast, along with a number from the Prairies, were compelled to leave their own lands and take up residence hundreds of miles inland. In the latter part of the nineteenth century, many tribes and bands from the West and the Southwest were also forced to move to the region, by then part of eastern Oklahoma.

My rendition of the Deer Woman story is composed from a combination of stories I have read and been told by witnesses or friends of witnesses of encounters with Deer Woman. I have included some details in this account from my own encounters with the shadowy Yunwitsansdi, who are often described as being "three feet tall."

Two young men were out "snagging"—chasing girls—one afternoon. They rode around in their pickup, their Indian Cadillac, cruising up this road and down that one through steamy green countryside, stopping by friends' places here and there to lift a few. The day was sultry as summer days in Oklahoma get, hot as a sweat.

Long after dark, they stopped at a tavern twenty or thirty miles outside of Anadarko, and joined some skins gathered around several tables. After the muggy heat outside, the slowly turning fan inside felt cool. When they'd been there a while, one of the men at their table asked them if they were headed to the stomp dance. "Sure," they said, though truth to tell, they hadn't known there was a stomp dance that night. The three headed out to the pickup.

They drove for some distance along narrow country roads, turning occasionally at unmarked crossings, bumping across cattle guards, until at length they saw the light of the bonfire. Several unshaded lights hung from small huts that ringed the danceground, and headlights shone from a couple of parking cars.

They pulled into a spot in the midst of a new Winnebago, a Dodge van, two Toyotas, and a small herd of more battered models, and made their way to the danceground. The dance was going strong, and the sound of turtle shell and aluminum can rattles and singing, mixed with occasional laughter and bits of talk, reached their ears. "Alright!" exclaimed Ray, the taller and heavier of the two, slapping his buddy's raised hand in glee. "Yeah!" his pal Jackie responded, and they grinned at each other in the unsteady light. Slapping the man who'd ridden along with them on the back, the taller one said, "Man, let's go find us some snags!"

They hung out all night, occasionally starting a conversation with one good-looking woman or another, but though the brother who'd accompanied them soon disappeared with a long-legged beauty named Lurine, the two anxious friends didn't score. They were not the sort to feel disheartened, though. They kept up their spirits, dancing well and singing even better. They didn't really care so much about snagging. It simply gave them something to think about while they filled the day and night with interesting activity. They were among their own people, and they were satisfied with their lives and themselves.

Toward morning, though, Ray spotted two strikingly beautiful young women stepping onto the danceground. Their long hair flowed like black rivers down their backs. They were dressed in traditional clothes, and something about them—some elusive something—made Ray shiver with what felt almost like recognition and, at the same time, like dread. "Who are they?" he asked his friend, but the smaller man shrugged silently. Ray could see his eyes shining for a moment as the fire near them flared up suddenly.

At the same moment, they both saw the young women looking at them out of the corners of their eyes as they danced modestly and almost gravely past. Jackie nudged Ray and let out a long slow sigh. "Alright," he said in a low, almost reverent voice. "Alright!"

When the dance was ended, the young women made their way to where the two youths were standing. One of them said, "My friend and I need a ride to Anadarko, and they told us you were coming from there." As she said that, she gestured with her chin over her left shoulder toward a vaguely visible group standing on the other side of the danceground.

"What's your friend's name?" Ray countered.

"Linda," the other woman said. "Hers is Junella."

"My friend's name's Jackie," Ray said, grinning. "When do you want to take off?"

"We'll go whenever you do," Junella answered. She held his eyes with hers. "Where are you parked?"

They made their way to the pickup and got in. It was a tight

fit, but nobody seemed to mind. Ray drove, backing the pickup
carefully to thread among the haphazardly parked vehicles. As
he did, he glanced down for a second, and he thought he saw
the feet of both women as deer hooves. "Man," he thought, "I
gotta lay off the weed." He didn't remember he'd quit smoking
it months before, and he hadn't had even a beer since they'd left
the tavern hours before. The women tucked their feet under
their bags, and in the darkness he didn't see them anymore. Besides, he had more engaging things on his mind.

They drove companionably for some time, joking around,
telling a bit about themselves, their tastes in music, where
they'd gone to school, when they'd graduated. Linda kept fid-
dling with the dial, reaching across Junella to get to the knob.
Her taste seemed to run to either hard core country-and-western
or what Ray privately thought of as "space" music.

She and Junella occasionally lapsed into what seemed like a
private conversation or joke, Ray couldn't be sure which; then,
as though remembering themselves, they'd laugh and engage
the men in conversation again.

After they'd traveled for an hour or so, Linda suddenly pointed
to a road that intersected the one they were on. "Take a left,"
she said, and Ray complied. He didn't even think about it or
protest that they were on the road to Anadarko already. A few
hundred yards further she said, "Take a right." Again he complied, putting the brake on suddenly as he went into the turn,
spilling Junella hard against him. He finished shifting quickly and
put his arm around her. She leaned into him, saying nothing.

The road they had turned onto soon became gravel, and by
the time they'd gone less than a quarter mile turned into hard-
packed dirt. Ray could smell water nearby. He saw some trees
standing low on the horizon and realized it was coming light.

"Let's go to the water," Linda said. "Junella and I are traditional, and we try to wash in fresh running water every
morning."

"Yeah," Junella murmured. "We were raised by our mother's
grandmother, and the old lady was real strict about some things.
She always made sure we prayed to Long Man every day."
Jackie and Ray climbed out of the truck, the women following.
They made their way through the thickest of scrub oak and
bushes and clambered down the short bank to the stream, the

men leading the way. They stopped at the edge of the water, but the young women stepped right in, though still dressed in their dance clothes. They bent and splashed water on their faces, speaking the old tongue softly as they did so. The men removed their tennis shoes and followed suit, tucking their caps in the hip pockets of their jeans.

After a suitable silence, Junella pointed to the opposite bank with her uplifted chin. "See that path," she asked the men. "I think it goes to our old house. Let's go up there and see."

"Yes," Linda said, "I thought it felt familiar around here. I bet it is our old place." As the women didn't move to cross the shallow river and go up the path, the men took the lead again. Ray briefly wondered at his untypical pliability, but he banished the thought almost as it arose. He raised his head just as he reached the far bank and saw that the small trees and brush were backed by a stone bluff that rose steeply above them. As he tilted his head back to spot the top of the bluff, he had a flashing picture of the small round feet he'd thought he'd seen set against the floorboard of the truck. But as the image flashed into his mind, the sun blazed out over the bluff; the thought faded as quickly as it had come, leaving him with a slightly dazed feeling and a tingling that climbed rapidly up his spine. He put on his cap.

Jackie led the way through the thicket, walking as quickly as the low branches would allow, bending almost double in places. Ray followed him, and the women came after. Shortly they emerged from the trees onto a rocky area that ran along the foot of the bluff like a narrow path. When he reached it, Jackie stopped and waited while the others caught up. "Do you still think this is the old homestead?" he quipped. The women laughed sharply, then fell into animated conversation in the old language.

Neither Ray nor Jackie could speak it, so they stood waiting, admiring the beauty of the morning, feeling the cool dawn air on their cheeks and the water still making their jeans cling to their ankles. At least their feet were dry, and so were the tennies they'd replaced after leaving the river.

After a few animated exchanges, the women started up the path, the men following. "She says it's this way," Linda said over her shoulder. "It can't be far." They trudged along for what seemed a long time, following the line of the bluff that seemed to grow even higher. After a time, Junella turned into a narrow break in the rock and began to trudge up its gradual slope, which soon became a steep rise.

"I bet we're not going to grandma's house," Jackie said in quiet tones to his friend. "I didn't know this bluff was even here," Ray replied. "It's not much farther," Junella said cheerfully. "What's the matter, you dudes out of shape or something?"

"Well, I used to say I'd walk a mile for a Camel," Jackie said wryly, "but I didn't say anything about snags!" He and Ray laughed, perhaps more heartily than the joke warranted.

"This is the only time I've heard of Little Red Riding Hood leading the wolves to grandma's," Ray muttered. "Yah," Linda responded brightly. "And wait'll you see what I'm carrying in my basket of goodies." The women glanced at each other, amused, and Jackie laughed abashedly.

"Here's the little creek I was looking for," Junella said suddenly. "Let's walk in it for a while." Ray looked at Jackie quizzically.

"I don't want to walk in that," Jackie said quickly. "I just got dry from the last dip." The women were already in the water walking upstream. "Not to worry," Junella said. "It's not wet— it's the path to the old house."

"Yeah, right," Ray mumbled, stepping into the water with a sigh. Jackie followed him, falling suddenly silent. As they stepped into what they thought was a fast-running stream, their feet touched down on soft grass. "Hey!" Ray exlaimed. "What's happening?" He stopped abruptly, and Jackie ploughed into him. "Watch it, man," the smaller man said shortly. He brushed past Ray and made after the women, who were disappearing around a sharp turn. Ray stood rooted a moment, then hurried after him. "Wait up," he called. His voice sounded loudly against the cliff and came back to him with a crack.

As he turned the corner, he saw Linda reaching upward along the cliff where a tall rock slab leaned against it. She grasped the edge of the slab and pulled. To the men's astonishment, it swung open, for all the world like an ordinary door. The women stepped through.

Ray and Jackie regarded each other for long moments. Finally Ray shrugged, and Jackie gestured with his outspread arm at the opening in the cliff. They followed the women inside.

Within, they were greeted with an astonishing scene. Scores of people, upward of two hundred, stood or walked about a green land. Houses stood scattered in the near distance, and smoke arose from a few chimneys. There were tables spread under some large trees, sycamore or elm, Ray thought, and upon them food was spread in large quantities and tantalizing variety. Suddenly aware they hadn't eaten since early the day before, the men started forward. But before they'd taken more than a few steps, Linda and Junella took their arms and led them away from the feast toward the doorway of one of the houses.

There sat a man who seemed ancient to the young men. His age wasn't so much in his hair, though it hung in waist-long white strands. It wasn't even so much in his skin, wrinkled and weathered though his face was beneath the tall crowned hat he wore. It was just that he seemed to be age personified. He seemed to be older than the bluff, than the river, than even the sky.

Next to him lay two large mastiffs, their long, lean bodies relaxed, their heads raised, their eyes alert and full of intelligence. "So," the old one said to the women, "I see you've snagged two strong young men." He shot an amused glance in the young men's direction. "Go, get ready," he directed the women, and at his words they slipped into the house, closing the door softly behind them.

The young men stood uneasily beside the old one, who disregarded them completely, lost in his own thoughts as he gazed steadily at some point directly before him.

After half an hour or more had passed, the old man addressed the young men again. "It was a good thing that you did," he mused, "following my nieces here. I wonder that you didn't give up or get lost along the way." He chuckled quietly as at a private joke. "Maybe you two are intelligent men." He turned his head suddenly and gave them an appraising look. Each of the young men shifted under that knowing gaze uncomfortably. From somewhere, the ground, the sky, they didn't feel sure, they heard thunder rumbling. "I have told everybody that they did well for themselves by bringing you here."

Seeing the surprised look on their faces, he smiled. "Yes, you didn't hear me, I know. I guess we talk different here than you're

used to where you come from. Maybe you'll be here long enough
to get used to it," he added, "that is, if you like my nieces well
enough. We'll feed you soon," he said. "But first there are some
games I want you to join in." He pointed with pursed lips and
chin in the direction of a low hill that rose just beyond the farthest dwelling. Again the thunder rumbled, louder than before.

A moment later the women appeared. Their long, flowing
hair was gone, and their heads shone in the soft light that filled
the area, allowing distant features to recede into its haze. The
women wore soft clothing that completely covered their bodies, even their hands and feet. The bright, gleaming cloth reflected light at the same intensity as their bald heads. Their dark
eyes seemed huge and luminous against skin that gave off a soft
radiance. Seeing them, both men were nearly overcome with
fear. "They have no hair at all," Ray thought. "Where is this
place?" He glanced over at Jackie, whose face mirrored his own
unease. Jackie shook his head almost imperceptibly, slowly
moving it from side to side in a gesture that seemed mournful
and at the same time oddly resigned.

Linda and Junella moved to the young men, each taking one
by the hand and drawing him toward the central area nearby. In
a daze, Ray and Jackie allowed themselves to be led into the
center of the area ringed by heavily laden tables, barely aware
that the old man had risen from his place and with his dogs was
following behind them. They were joined by a number of other
young men, all wearing caps like the ones Ray and Jackie wore.
Two of the men carried bats, several wore gloves, and one was
tossing a baseball in the air as he walked. Slowly the throng
made their way past the tables and came to an open area where
Jackie and Ray saw familiar shapes. They were bases, and the
field that the soft light revealed to them was a baseball diamond.

The old man took his place behind home plate, and one of
the young men crouched before him as a loud peal of thunder
crashed around them. "Play ball!" the old man shouted, and the
men took up their places as the women retired to some benches
at the edge of the field.

The bewildered young men found their positions, and the
game was on. It was a hard-played game, lasting some time. At
length it reached a rowdy end, the team Jackie and Ray were on
barely edging out the opposition in spite of a couple of ques-

tionable calls the old man made against them. Their victory was due in no small measure to the wiry Jackie's superb pitching. He'd pitched two no hit innings, and that had won them the game.

As they walked with the players back toward the houses, the old man came up to them. Slapping each in turn on the back a couple of times, he told them he thought they were good players. "Maybe that means you'll be ready for tomorrow's games," he said, watching Jackie sharply. "They're not what you're used to, I imagine, but you'll do alright."

They reached the tables and were helped to several large portions of food by people whose faces never seemed to come quite into focus but whose goodwill seemed unquestionable. They ate amid much laughter and good-natured joshing, only belatedly realizing that neither Linda nor Junella was among the revelers. Ray made his way to Jackie and asked him if he'd seen either woman. Replying in the negative, Jackie offered to go look around for them.

They both agreed to make a quick search and to rendezvous at the large tree near the old man's house. But after a fruitless hour, Ray went to the front of the house and waited. His friend didn't come. At last, growing bored, he made his way back to the tables where a group had set up a drum and were singing lustily. A few of the younger people had formed a tight circle around the drummers and were slowly stepping round in it, their arms about each others' waists and shoulders. "Alright!" Ray thought, "49's!" He was cheered at the anticipation of the close social bond dancing, drumming and singing, the joking and relaxation the social signified. He joined the circle between two women he hadn't seen before who easily made way for him and smoothly closed about him, each wrapping an arm around his waist. He forgot all about his friend.

When Ray awoke, the sun was beating down on his head. He sat up and realized he was lying near the river's edge, his legs in the thicket, his head and half-turned face unshielded from the sun. It was about a third of the way up in a clear sky. As he looked groggily around, he discovered Junella sitting quietly a few yards away on a large stone. "Hey," she said, smiling.

"How'd I get here?" Ray asked. He stood and stretched, surreptitiously feeling to see if everything worked. His memory seemed hesitant to return, but he had half-formed impressions of a baseball game and eating and then the '49. He looked around. "Where's Jackie, and, uh—"

"Linda?" Junella supplied as he paused. "Yeah, Linda," he finished.

"Jackie is staying there," she told him calmly. She reached into her bag and brought out a man's wristwatch. "He said to give you this," she said, holding it out to him.

Ray felt suddenly dizzy. He swayed for a moment while strange images swept through him. Junella with no hair and that eerie light—that pale tan but with spots or a pattern of soft grey dots that sort of fuzzed out at the edges to blend into the tan. The old man.

He took a step in her direction. "Hey," he began. "What the hell's—" He broke off. The rock where she sat was empty. On the ground next to it lay Jackie's watch.

When he told me the story, about fifteen months afterward, Ray had heard that Jackie had showed up at his folks' place. They lived out in the country, a mile or so beyond one of the numerous small towns that dot the Oklahoma landscape. The woman who told him about Jackie's return, Jackie's cousin Ruth Ann, said he had come home with a strange woman who was a real fox. At thirteen, Ruth Ann had developed an eye for good looks and thought herself quite a judge of women's appearance. They hadn't stayed long, he'd heard. They packed up some of Jackie's things and visited with his family. Ray had been in Tulsa and hadn't heard Jackie was back. None of their friends had seen him either. There had been a child with them, he said, maybe two or so, Ruth Ann had thought, because she could walk by herself.

"You know," he'd said thoughtfully, turning a Calistoga slowly between his big hands. The gesture made him seem very young and somehow vulnerable. "One of my grandma's brothers, old Jess, used to talk about the little people a lot. He used to tell stories about strange things happening around the countryside here. I never paid much attention. You know how it is, I just thought he was putting me on, or maybe he was pining away for the old days. He said Deer Woman would come to dances sometimes, and if you weren't careful she'd put her spell on you and take you inside the mountain to meet her uncle. He said her uncle was Thunder, one of the old gods or supernaturals, whatever the traditionals call them."

He finished his drink in a couple of swallows, pushing away from the table where we sat. "I dunno," and he gave me a look that I still haven't forgotten, a look somehow wounded and yet with a kind of wild hope mixed in. "Maybe those old guys know something, eh?"

It was a few years before I saw Ray again. Then I ran into him unexpectedly in San Francisco a couple of years ago. We talked for a while, standing on the street near the Mission BART station. He started to leave when my curiosity got the better of my manners. I asked if he'd ever found out what happened to Jackie.

Well, he said that he'd heard that Jackie came home off and on, but the woman—probably Linda, though he wasn't sure— was never with him. Then he'd heard that someone had run into him, or a guy they thought sure was him, up in Seattle. He'd gone alcoholic. They'd heard he'd died. "But the weird thing is that he'd evidently been telling someone all about that time inside the mountain, and that he'd married her, and about some other stuff, stuff I guess he wasn't supposed to tell." Another guy down on his luck, he guessed. "Remember how I was telling you about my crazy uncle, the one who used to tell about Deer Woman? Until I heard about Jackie, I'd forgotten that the old man used to say that the ones who stayed there were never supposed to talk about it. If they did, they died in short order."

After that there didn't seem to be much more to say. Last time I saw Ray, he was heading down the steps to catch BART. He was on his way to a meeting, and he was running late.

SOMEDAY SOON

In 1986 two American men went to Belize (formerly British Honduras) to make a video travelogue to help Belize become better known to American tourists. One of the men was Native American. The other, a spiritual seeker of Middle Eastern Christian descent was curious about what had happened to the Maya; he was also interested in finding the lost continent of Atlantis, which he thought might be beneath the Caribbean Sea, as many seekers have believed. In the process of making their film, they became acquainted with a Maya who took them to the Maya homelands in Belize. What transpired over the next two or three years is recorded in "Someday Soon."

The Mopán Maya, among whom the two men moved for many months in that and following years, are said to be the oldest of the various Maya groups. Scholars are coming to believe that they are the original Maya, from whom the others derived. The Crystal Skull, the amazing crystallized remains of the immortal I have called Crystal Woman, was found in Mopán country early this century. Studied by archaeologists, visited by seekers, and filmed by the men who quested among the Maya and discovered the Skull in the process, this being (I can't call her an artifact!) is a powerful and beautiful presence. I was honored to have channeled information from her when I visited her home in Canada in the summer of 1987. Much of what she told me is included in this story.

The events as they have unfolded to this time are uncannily parallel to events described in traditional myths and legends of the Maya and other Native Americans. This account is offered as a demonstration that the immortals are still among us, even among people who rely on high-tech equipment, jet planes, and hotel accommodations during their quests.

The Mopán Maya of Belize say that the new age will begin in 2012, when an era of harmony, peace, and renewal will be ushered in.

Long ago, Crystal Woman. Before the human beings, before the five-fingered beings. She standing there in the southwest. In the southeast, standing. In the mountains on the edge of the world, before the world became as we know it, there she stood. There she waited for the time to be ripe.

She was a priestess, a shaman, a medicine woman. She was an adept trained in the seven arts and the thirteen ways. In the ways of the immortals one of whom she was. It was in the time of the end, of the transformation from this, that she was, to another thing. It was their work, the work of the thirteen of them, to become all that was possible to become, to know all it was possible to know. To put that knowledge into their being-bodies. To infuse their cell and bone with all they knew. Only thus could they be sabías, women of knowledge. There were twelve who were younger, and an old woman who was wise in the ways of the sacred. She they called Mother, and she would in later days be called Mother of the Gods.

There in the Cave of Knowing they practiced their art. There they became all they knew. There in the cave in the west where the crystals now grow. The place reached by river, by boat, by crawling on hands and knees and slithering like serpents, under the mountain, they were. They entered. And so they became. Over many days, they became. Over centuries, thirteen times fifty-two bundles of years, they became. And then they were very old. The Ancient of Days they were known then. The Women of Wisdom. The Crones.

Scores of them had come to their place of learning from the east. In the east they had begun. With the dawn they had touched land, from the waters of the void, from the waters of emptiness, they had come forth and there they had remained. The waters returned in a rush, and the lands they had left were drowned.

There they remained for many years. Then they were young and shaken by the cataclysm, but they persevered. They there grew in age and wisdom. They had been priestesses in the days before. The days before their land had failed, the seas had drawn away from their shores, the depths of the waters had stood empty around them.

Then they had seen that the time of their youth was at an end. That they must leave the island of their childhood and find their way to a new land. Then they had gone west, and emerged as dawn touched the eastern shore from the dry ocean bed of their journey. Then they had slept, and the waters had been restored.

When they had gone to the west, their sisters had gone to the east. Thus they say that the lost sister will return. For the sisters will be united and their knowing will be whole in the ripeness of completion.

Long they had stayed there, learning the ways of the spirit and the mystery. Long they had stayed, waiting for Huracán, Gucumatz, to tell them their way. Long they tended the land they had entered, making it full of life, of plants and birds, of beasts and reptiles, of insects and beings so small they cannot be seen. There they planted corn. There they planted tobacco. There they stayed, learning and growing, making the world in the ways it would need to be.

In the fullness of time, the thirteen removed themselves to the west. They raised the mountains there to cover their abode. They hollowed out caves where they could live undisturbed over ages, to do the work it was given them to do next.

In that time, they infused their cells, all their flesh and bone, with the knowing. In that time, those periods, they danced and chanted, chanted and danced; they entered the heart of heaven, the heart of earth, the greenness of the fire that flickers between this world and the other one. In those long years, they perfected their skills and made into flesh every word they said.

And then at last it was finished, all but the sacrifice was done. They lay still and deep within their bodies, quiet and at rest within their sacred flesh. They lay as though sleeping, without thought, without movement, without breath. Long they lay there, unmoving. Long they lay at rest.

And as they lay there, their flesh became stone. It became hardened and rigid. Each cell became mineral, became hard, was petrified. They slowly over this time abstracted their being, their consciousness, from their flesh. They entered another kind of being that mortals call air, fire, spirit. They entered the world that surrounds this world, the world that interpenetrates this world. In this time, as the old stories say, they left the world and went to another world, the world of the spirits, the world of the supernaturals, the world of the immortals, the world of the gods. The immortals they became. The spirits they became. The supernaturals they became. The holy people they became. The gods they became.

And the stone they flew from like birds. Rising as heat from the fire, they retained all they knew, all they took with them, all they had left behind. Saying, when it is time, when it is time, when it is time, they shall come, the human beings, and take these crystallizations to their homes. There they shall smoke them, they shall sing them, they shall dance them into gleaming purity, translucence, clarity. Then they shall polish them, court them, honor them. Then they shall use them to speak to us in our place of abiding. Thus they shall learn the ways of the universe, the dance of the stars, the beginning and end of all things.

In later times, long after the gods had gone away, the priestesses and the shamans came to the hills. They entered the channel to the place of the crystals beneath the peaks. They moved along the river, they crawled on their knees, they slithered like serpents, until they entered the cave of being and found the thirteen bodies made of stone laid out perfectly, their limbs ordered in alignment, their heads to the west.

In that place where thousands of crystals grew, some as large as boulders, some tiny and new, the priestesses found the fire of life burning. Behind it grew the ten-branched tree of life. Upon each branch hung a disk, and each disk was made of gold.

Carefully they removed one body. Carefully they wrapped it in skins and softened bark. Gently they moved it from the cave of its sleeping to the place of becoming. The citadel they had made for the work they would do. The room cleansed by sacred smoke. The place cleansed by clear, pure flame. The place cleansed by water. The place made of stone, whose floor was of packed earth. Into this place they brought the stone woman, and in this place they removed her head.

And for generations after, unceasingly night after night, they sang and smoked the head until all traces of flesh had vanished, leaving only image of bone, until all smokiness within was banished, and the mineral was clear as pure water, sweet as spring. Women and men, they smoked her. Women and men, they sang. The priests all sang, and all bathed the head in the sacred mist, the smoke infused with life.

The head only they made sacred. Two rounded eye sockets,

below it the bony ridge of the nose and wide grinning mouth,
upper and lower jaw filled each with its row of perfect teeth.
The lower jaw was separated from the skull in the final period,
for a priest of the last generations to sing her into crystal grasped
it and tore it from the head, though the two fit snugly when
matched together. In this way, he thought to compel the goddess within to answer whenever they had need. Her head only
they made sacred, wrapping the rest of the figure in leaves, skin,
and bark, they reserved them.

For generations, they used what they had prepared to gain
knowledge and to see to the needs of the people. For generations, they walked the path the immortals had set for them and
left sleeping beneath the mountains until the people were ripe.

In time, they fell into conflict. In time, the world was much
changed. In time, they began to walk by themselves. Halting,
stumbling, they took their first steps alone, along the path
marked by a soft, clear, glowing green light.

In time, as the days wheeled and turned, the temples fell and
were buried beneath the proliferation of green. In time, the
priests and priestesses faded into the forests, the writings fell to
the fires, the statues were stolen, the people continued to survive. In the forests they lived. In the paths of the holy ones they
lived. In the shadow of the immortals, they lived. And all the
knowing seemed to sleep.

The skull lay hidden in the deep rubble of its house. From
time to time, a wise one would come to her, take her for a time,
restore the link between the world of the immortals and the
world of the human beings. And time sunk deeper into the
green.

And then one day, more than seventy years ago, a maiden was
out walking. This maiden had no parents, or they had died. She
did not know. Her father who adopted her was from a land far
away from the jungle, far, far away from the green. But he knew
of the old ones, the Ancient of Days. He had come to the forest,
seeking, and had left his daughter behind to be raised by the
Indians while he sought further, sought the green, sought the
teachings, sought the way that seemed lost to him long before.

On the day she was wandering, he had been gone for seven
years and then had returned. There was much activity around
the old temples. The lost cities of the lost tribes. The Indians

were hired to do the digging. They were not asked much, they did not say much. And on the day she went walking, the child, whose name means Daughter of Dawn Light, or Daughter of Corn, looked down. From among the vines that grew thick and tangled over the stones of the ruined temple, she saw a small but unmistakable flash of light.

She went to her father and told him. He went to see for himself, but the light did not beckon him with its brightness. He saw only vines and rubble. He saw only darkness within the interstices. He saw only holes.

But this chief was a wise man, wise enough to follow a maiden, his adopted child. He ordered the men to clear away the stones, to make an opening sufficiently large that they could climb down into the room below.

After many weeks, the floor was uncovered. An opening large enough was cleared, and enough rock moved so that there was no danger. Then he called his daughter, Dawn Light Girl, and said, "You found it. You go down and bring it up."

So Dawn Light Girl entered the cave they had made together, the builders of the old times and the workers of the new, and she brought the skull out of the room and gave it to her father. Only the head was there. The lower jaw was found later, lying a few feet away from the place where the skull had lain.

It is said the Indians were joyful. They danced and sang for days. They erected a brush shelter and for miles around they came to pay homage. "Our Grandmother is restored to us," they said.

It is said they were unhappy, stricken that their crystal was thus exposed, that they came for days to bid her good-bye.

In time the headman from far away left the region. He took his daughter and the skull away. It is said the people tried to keep it, but the white man refused. "I must take it for safekeeping," he told them.

It is also said the headman said to the people, "I cannot take this with me. You must keep it because it is yours." But the people demurred, saying, "No. It was found by your daughter, Sun Woman. It must stay with her." And so saying, they parted, the man, his daughter, and the immortal woman's bones went north, went east. The people, the forests, and the fallen temples stayed.

Years passed. In the year 1987, C.E., two men made their way south to the coastal city a few hundred miles to the north of the place where the skull had been found. By then the world was changing. It was the days of the beginning. It was the days of the end. They went to seek answers to an old, old question: Where were the Mayas? Where was the lost world? Did anyone know of the calendar that told the end of the days? Like the heroes of old, they were seeking. Like the old heroes, they had traveled great distances in short time.

They were led by a wise one into the forest, and there bemused by the green light the foliage and the sun together cast upon them, they climbed the old temples and sat in the house of the gods, looking out at the forest below. Many days they spent in the wilderness, learning the ways of the people, the ways of the forest, the ways of the gods.

In the fullness of time, they found the place where the skull had come to light, and after a time they discovered its present home. They made their way far to the north, to the crisp, suburban home of Sun Woman, Daughter of Light. She and her companion, both old women now, greeted them warmly and asked them in.

In the weeks and months that followed, they strengthened their bonds with the people to the south and the women in the north. Over that time, Sun Woman entrusted them more and more with the crystal. Over time the wise men in the south taught them the old ways, the dances, and the ascent of the tree of life. They took the men to the place of the beginnings, and they remembered the old times for the two men's sakes.

As was proper, the two men brought gifts and food to the south on their journeys, taking care of the people as the people took care of them. As was proper, the two men paid their respects to Old Sun Woman and her companion, and aided them as they could.

It is said that at the time of the beginning, the Goddess will return in the fullness of her being. It is said that the Mother of All and Everything, the Grandmother of the Sun and the Dawn, will return to her children and with her will come harmony, peace, and the healing of the world. It is said that time is coming. Soon.

POSTSCRIPT

CULTURAL DIMENSIONS,
GE-OLOGICAL LOCATIONS,
AND HERSTORICAL CIRCUMSTANCES
OF THE GODDESSES, THE PEOPLE,
AND THE RITUAL TRADITION

One of the articles of faith among people who write about and study Native Americans is their diversity. "There's no such thing as an Indian," I was taught to say as a young instructor of Native American studies. At San Diego State, where I taught in the early 1970s, I was cautioned against grouping native peoples under the rubric "Indian" because pan-Indianism was not popular among our various peoples. Certainly it is true that there are Indians and there are Indians, as I had known from earliest childhood, so I accepted the pronouncements. But my studies over the past two decades have suggested, indeed, confirmed, that while the distinctions among native communities are many and, linguistically at least, the differences are vast, the similarities are far greater and much more profound.

I have believed for some time that the similarities in world view and spiritual understanding are marked because the supernaturals who live on this continent with us possess marked similarities among themselves, and so their teachings to us are similar, varying because of locale and because of the language and histories of the various peoples they instruct. Perhaps differences exist because different landscapes give rise to different spirits or supernaturals. But only recently did it occur to me to wonder where the idea of vast distinctions among Native Americans had originated. I mentioned my query to an Indian friend, who looked at me with a grin and quipped, "From the anthros."

To many native people, anthropologists represent a number of things, including colonialism. Many native people see them as a sort of contemporary colonial front, following in a line that descends from soldiers and missionaries through Indian agents and traders to academics, anthropologists, folklorists, and most recently, literary specialists like myself. This front operates analogously to the other arms of the colonizer, coming in and taking human remains along with spiritual and aesthetic treasures as the others have helped themselves to economic and geographical ones.

It has been in the interests of the settlers to view us as distinct and to educate us to view ourselves as distinct. There is an old American adage that implies, "United we conquer, divided we fall." Until my conversation with my friend about distinctions among Indians, I didn't realize that the adage need be only slightly modified to remind us that it also means "Divided *they* fall, united *they* resist conquest." The idea of a unified Red Nation must even yet pose a grave threat to Western hegemony, else why should they emphasize our differences more than our commonalities?

There are many features of Indianism, *indianismo,* as the psychological, cultural, and spiritual attitude common to the people of the tribes is eloquently termed in Spanish. Concourse with the immortals is one; the knowledge that the planet and all that dwell upon it—including rocks, bodies of water, meteorological phenomena, and geographical features—are alive is another. Powerful kinship bonding and the notion of mutual respect and interchange among spirits, animals, humans, and gods are also definitive. There is a fifth aspect of *indianismo* that bears mentioning, and that is the sense of fate or destiny.

The peoples whose stories are included in this collection deserve to be recognized. Their histories—both mundane and spiritual—their environs, and some details of their spiritual life and ritual traditions bear mentioning. While these summaries are necessarily brief, what follows concerns each specific tribal group; and while their stories are organized along lines determined by their position in an overall philosophic scheme, the following remarks are simply in alphabetical order by tribal or national name.

ANISHINABEG (CHIPPEWA/OJIBWA)

The anishinabeg, one of numerous Algonquian groups, have a body of stories that reflect their mysterious experience. They say they came to their lands in and around the Great Lakes from the East, following a white stone called a "megis." The story reminds me of the sacred stone of Islam, enshrined in the Kaabah, circumambulated in prayer to Allah for so many centuries that its original translucent pearl white has gone dark, or so I have been told. I am also reminded of the Hopi migration account in which they follow a star by night and a cloud by day, which has obvious biblical parallels—both Old and New Testament.

I don't know whether the megis is dark now after centuries of

use or whether it survives, but it seems amazing to me that
this magical stone, pronounced something like "magi," should
have a similar function to the star the wise men followed to
Bethlehem, to the pillar of fire and pillar of cloud that led the
Hebrews out of Egypt, and to the stone of the Kaabah. Syn-
chronicity, or something more? Speculation is on the surface
useless at this point in our recovery of the Way, but perhaps it is
also a kind of megis that if followed persistently, perseveringly,
will bring us to our proper land of consciousness, where the
world will again live in harmony with the planet, the Beloved
Woman Earth.

The anishinabeg enjoy a ceremony or spiritual discipline, the
midewewin, or "medicine dance," that to my mind resembles
fabled mystery schools of the Mediterranean region, where es-
oteric disciplines yielded direct perception of the divine.

It seems that a human being can, through devoted application of the discipline, attain the state of a manido, that of a spirit
or immortal, and live increasingly longer spans of times, even
millennia. Mystery schools are thus not repositories of mystical
disciplines known only to the Old World, but are part of the
spiritual life of this continent as well. The midewewin is composed of four steps, initiations, or "lodges," as they are usually
termed, although it is rumored that another three levels are possible to attain.

There is a persistent notion—difficult to trace in the literature—that the midewewin was a sacred school whose chief
practitioners and teachers were women. A Yurok woman once
told me that the only spiritual practitioners she had met among
her people were women. Not that, as she hastened to add, men
could not be doctors, as adepts are called in California, but only
that she had never known or heard of any who were.

Fragments, tantalizing fragments, hints about a mystical congress of women adepts haunt the continent, always just on the
brink of revelation, always just over the next rise. Victor Barnouw, editor of *Wisconsin Chippewa Myths and Tales* (1977), is of
the opinion that the midewewin is male dominated, and that
the spiritual discipline of fasting and dreaming is of particular
significance to adolescent males. However, being himself a man,
there exists the possibility that what he hears is tailored to

match his expectations; or perhaps his information comes as a consequence of particular questions that themselves elicit gender-biased responses.

Of the Chippewa, William Brandon writes in his wide-ranging history *The Last Americans:*

> The Ojibwa made up one of the largest nations north of Mexico, with a wild-guess population of 25,000 or more—very probably more. The last syllable of Ojibwa is pronounced "way"; the name refers to the peculiar puckered seam of their moccasins; Europeans garbled it into Chippeway and stuck to it so persistently that many Ojibwas today call themselves Chippewa; but some Ojibwas today prefer another more ancient name for themselves, Anishinabeg or Anishinaubag, meaning "we people." North of the Ojibwa an almost identical people known as the Cree controlled the enormous spruce-fir country that ran all the way up to Hudson bay. At the eastern end of Lake Superior, at the present Sault Ste. Marie, the Ojibwa joined with the Ottawa and Potawatomi in a loose confederacy known to white traders as the Three Fires. In the traditions of all three of these tribes they were originally one, and that not too many centuries ago. (1974, 185)

For centuries, the anishinabeg people have harvested wild rice on the lake shores, fished, hunted, gathered a large variety of greens, roots, and berries, and drawn maple syrup to sweeten lives once sweet in other ways. In those earlier, seemingly more happy, times, women decided who would eat and when, and what would be worn, owned, used to store and carry things, even who would live where. A lot of power for the frailer vessel, or so the Jesuits who came among them believed. The black-robed worthies hastened to put an end to that foolishness, along with what they regarded as the foolishness of indulging children by failure to beat, chain, humiliate, and terrorize them on frequent occasion. Catholicism soon changed matters, creating as many native families in its own patriarchal image as possible. It seems that patriarchy had taken hold in Amerikka, the land of the four winds, during the eighteenth and nineteenth centuries. But life is long—lakes, forests, rice plants, fish, stars, and

people survive—and patriarchy's history on this continent is
brief indeed. What's five hundred years in the sweep of a people's
tenancy that goes back at least hundreds of thousands?

According to Victor Barnouw in *Wisconsin Chippewa Myths and Tales,* from which I adapted the story of Oshkikwe and Matchikwewis, the Chippewa are individualistic people who value their privacy. Their houses are often built far from the nearest neighbor. In *Ojibway Woman,* Ruth Landes conveys a similar impression. From her study one also gets a clear sense of the suspicion of practitioners of the mystic arts. She records stories that feature the abduction of women by lascivious sorcerers whose powers are so great that the women cannot resist and their families cannot save them. I've met more than one such in my time.

Certainly the spiritual life of the anishinabeg is rich and in some particulars frightening, as are the spiritual lives of all those who engage in exchanges with the supernaturals, who may or may not be given to indulging the needs and whims of mortals, and who have their own agendas, their own purposes, and their own ways. Supernaturals are treated with enormous respect and approached with great caution and reverence because they are not controllable by humans, whose powers are always less than theirs. Western neo-Pagans, generally unaware of the perils of exchanges with the spirit people, take real risks courting their attention.

Fortunately for them, courting and winning are usually very different kettles of fish. Securing the beneficence of a spirit teacher does not just come for the wishing. Great discipline, devotion, and knowledge, as well as luck, are required, which is why native people depend not only on institutionalized systems of study but on everyday activities, customs, and teachings to reduce the peril greatly; it is also why gambling is universally engaged in among them.

What Pretty Shield and her sisters have told us about these matters in their autobiographies is significant. From their hints, we can see what is required of women who would walk the path of the mysteries: a great deal of service; a willingness to earn the power or "medicine" of the powerful by doing them favors; the ability to fast, to dream, to trust the supernatural workings of luck and ignore the opinions of others; the possession of a powerful sense of fun and an unswerving self-discipline that often means foregoing for a lifetime certain foods and activities safely enjoyed by others.

AZTEC

There is a Keres story about a strange people who came through Keres country long ago. It is said that they carried long dry sticks, like wands rather than walking sticks, and they could cause flowers to bloom from those sticks on command. The Keres say that the strangers remained among them for a while, then moved south. It is thought that they became the Aztecs.

However the Aztec people came into being—their own various stories do not include a stopover among northern Pueblos—it is safe to say that they are among the native peoples best known to Americans, even though, compared to the Keres, they are relatively new people. Perhaps their brilliant lifestyle, the spectacular destruction of their wealthiest branch, the Mexica of Tenochtitlán–Mexico City by Cortés in the early sixteenth century, the great wealth that went from their lands to fund the family quarrels of European monarchs, account for their fame. Or perhaps the tendency of the conquering people to maximize the villainy of those they have destroyed explains the notoriety of the Aztecs, as it does our familiarity of the "warrior" people of the American plains.

The fall of Moctezuma—Montezuma as he is best known, or in some scholarly texts Moctezoma or Mocteuzoma—enthralls schoolchildren in the Southwest. It is one of the stories I heard or read so long ago I hardly remember a time I didn't know it, but it was certainly in Catholic school that its message was drilled into us. I was told the Indian people thought the Spaniards were gods and that they fell down and adored them, willingly giving them entry to the wealth of Mexico. While that isn't exactly how the events transpired, it is close enough to the truth to suffice. Important to the tale, and all but left out of my earliest instructions, was the woman Malinalli, or Doña Marina, who led the Spaniards into Tenochtitlán and, through her linguistic and diplomatic skills, instigated the downfall of the Aztec empire.

I first saw Malinalli, called La Malinche, which means Woman Chief, dancing with Cortés in the Matachine dances held on New Year's Day in my native Chicano village of Cubero, New Mexico, when I was twelve. My father was majordomo that year, and he decided to reinstitute the Matachines, fallen into disuse in previous years, for Cubero's Fiesta de Nuestra Señora de la Luz, Feast of Our Lady of Light. Rehearsals were held in our front yard, where the dancers learned their steps on the cold, hard clay. I spent hours watching them, wishing I could dance too. But except for La Malinche, danced by a girl child who had just made her first communion, the dancers were all men.

The day of the fiesta the whole village attended Mass, then gathered around the ground in front of our small adobe church in the cold wind to await the Matachines. The musicos, musicians, whose instruments were an accordion, a violin, and a guitar, began to play, and soon the matachines came: two lines of spirit people (young men wearing miterlike hats hung with brightly colored silk scarves behind and before, covering their faces so that only their eyes showed). Each of these dancers carried a strange branching mirrored wand in one hand and a rattle in the other. Around and among them danced the sacred clowns, three old men whose shuffling, shambling steps still haunt me. I was so fascinated by the clowns that it was difficult to attend to the rest of the action.

But I do remember a tall man, wearing a black suit and hat in the style of the Spanish colonial period. On his arm he led a young girl, her long black hair, loose under her communion veil, flowed down the back of her white communion dress. The couple danced between the dancing lines of supernaturals, going slowly from the top where they entered to the bottom (or so it seemed to me) to face the Bull, a man who wore a large, horned bull's head made of wood and black cloth.

Always confined between the lines of masked men, the pair danced toward the Bull who, I was told, signified death, and then they danced away. Back and forth the couple went, always in the soft cadenced step of the dance, sometimes pursued by the Bull, sometimes pushing it back toward the end of the line where it had entered. The clowns shuffled in and around the dancers, in perfect time, but always with markedly odd step.

I asked what the dance was about, and my parents said that it was about Cortés and the Malinche dancing to end the reign of death. Cortés danced with the Malinche because her purity and innocence gave him the power to best the Bull, they said.

Today the Aztec dances are performed throughout Mexico and the American Southwest. Among the Pueblos, dances often feature the Flag of Moctezuma, a long, slender golden banner raised upon a high pole and carried among the drummers. A contingent of Aztec dancers usually come to display their amazing art at the Annual Ceremonial Fair in Gallup, New Mexico.

The Aztecs who, perforce, welcomed the Spaniards and who lost their empire to them became the Mexicans, and their land, called New Spain by the conquistadores, was renamed Mexico after the revolution—Mexico, the country of the Mexica, one of the mightiest tribes in the Americas not so long ago. The fact that Mexico is an impoverished country today is, of course, a result of that conquest. Her wealth was exported, and the monarchies that prospered from it became bloody empires in their turn.

CHEROKEE

According to James Mooney, the Cherokee were the mountain people of the South,

> holding the entire Allegheny region from the interlocking head-streams of the Kanawha and the Tennessee southward almost to the site of Atlanta, and from the Blue Ridge on the east to the Cumberland range on the west, a territory comprising an area of about 40,000 square miles, now included in the states of Virginia, Tennessee, North Carolina, South Carolina, Georgia and Alabama. . . . Itsâti, or Echota, on the south bank of the Little Tennessee, a few miles above the mouth of Tellico River was commonly considered the capital of the Cherokee Nation. (Mooney 1982, 14)

It is said that the Cherokee were descended from the mound builders of that area, which would put them in the vicinity since time immemorial. They were part of what is referred to as

Iroquoian people, and around the fifteenth and sixteenth centuries were as expansionist along the southern Atlantic seaboard as their cousins were along the northern. Together these tribes were bent upon taking as much land as they could from the predominantly Algonquian peoples along the Atlantic seaboard and across the Alleghenies in the north, and from the Chickasaw, Choctaw, Creek, and other southern tribes. While they were expanding their holdings, they were also at war with one another, and according to tradition, every Haudinashone (Iroquois) boy longed for the time when he would be old enough to meet a Cherokee in battle.

The homelands of the Eastern Cherokee, as those survivors of American politics have come to be called, are largely settled in North Carolina and nearby states. The Smoky Mountains rise softly in their background, and the land of many lakes and gentle slopes mists into the mountain fastnesses that were their homes. Early in the first U.S. administration, President Washington called for discussion of the "Indian problem," and while he favored war to rid the colonies of this unwanted obstacle to the Anglo-American dominance he envisioned, other statesmen called for their removal to the interior where they were to be resettled.

Not much came of these early discussions as the infant nation was faced with more pressing threats from the French, the English, the Spanish, and the New England whiskey brewers, but within ten or fifteen years of the formation of the federation, John C. Calhoun came forward with the plan he had earlier suggested. At this time Andrew Jackson, "president of the people"—that is, the white people—thought that Calhoun had a champion plan, which he determined to implement. By the 1820s native people from all over the Southeast and Prairie regions were being marched to a small area in the southern portion of the Louisiana Purchase, recently added to the lands held by the United States by Thomas Jefferson, an early proponent of Indian removal.

However the Cherokee, steadfast and recalcitrant as mountain people usually are, refused to go. Instead they went to the United States Congress, lobbying it unceasingly, and to the United States Supreme Court, where they won a judgment that prohibited the president from forcing them off their lands. They had earlier formed a constitutional government of their own, fashioned after that of the United States. This constitution disenfranchised women and black Cherokee, making the Cherokee Nation resemble more closely the white nation they were attempting to placate. To this end they became heavily Christianized, or more accurately, the upper classes among them did, the men often marrying daughters of white missionaries who helped them in their appeals to the American government. The same upper-class Cherokee also joined with the rest of what they thought of as their southern brethren in buying and selling African people as slaves, and in general they felt themselves to be a model of white-style civilization.

Their efforts gained for them, along with other southern Indian confederacies, the title "Civilized Tribe." Aside from that honor, their appeals fell upon deaf ears. In the 1830s they were sent marching westward, arriving in Indian Territory (now eastern Oklahoma) impoverished, their numbers greatly reduced by starvation, execution, disease, and exposure. The Oklahoma Cherokee still remember that march in an annual enactment, the Trail of Tears Pageant held at their capital, Talequah, each summer.

The Cherokee paid heavily for their legalistic, institutional, and above all passive resistance to removal (which nearly a hundred years later Emily Pankhurst and Mahatma Gandhi would both emulate), and for their alliance with the South in the American Civil War. The Cherokee were a long time in rebuilding their traditional strength, though their level of literacy, medical care, housing, and economic development was high before the Allotment Act and the Homestead Acts combined to deprive them of much of their new landholdings. Today they are emerging from a long and difficult passage under the able leadership of Wilma Mankiller, a woman whose name and renown make me wonder if she is under the direct tutelage of Sutalidihi, Six Killer, the major deity of the Cherokee pantheon.

I have rendered four Cherokee stories in this book. I feel almost as close to the Cherokee as to my own people, probably because both of my sons are of Cherokee descent, making me an "in-law." As their mother I am responsible for teaching them something of Cherokee beliefs and ways.

There is an abundance of information about this popular tribe, both in its historical and spiritual dimensions. James Mooney (1982) collected hundreds of Cherokee stories and chants, and notebooks of conjurors' information about their use of plants for healing and other sorts of spells. Along with this, he recorded useful information about the people he talked to, giving us a view into their lives in the reservation period of American Indian life. But he was only one of many who have published in this specialty. The Cherokee themselves were literate (at about 98 percent) before the Civil War, and had devised a syllabary, a writing system not based on phonics but on symbols that stand for certain sounds. The Cherokee syllabary made them literate in their own language. In the period before and after removal they published a newspaper, the *Cherokee Phoenix,* which circulated throughout Cherokee country and contained all sorts of news and information.

The literacy of the people led conjurors to write down chants, spells, and data, and these notebooks provide detailed information both to other Cherokee and—by way of the works of Mooney, Jack and Anna Kilpatrick, and others—to non-Cherokees interested in their ways. Much of this material has not been printed, of course, but rests in hiding places in tree stumps, attics, ceilings, and trunks, or is being used by present-day conjurors, as they call the adewehi, the shamans, among them.

The story of the Ani Kutani, the clan of magicians and adepts who are said to have lived among the Cherokee in times gone by, is intriguingly similar to some stories of the Druids, who, it is said, exerted great influence over the people, taking women who appealed to their fancy whether they wished to be taken or not, and living off the labor of the rest who supported their studies. It is also reminiscent of the Aztec nobles and their priestly brothers and sisters or of the anishinabeg's uneasy relationship to the mide who were often seen as threateningly powerful, able to overcome those who lacked their magical skill. Perhaps priesthoods everywhere become arrogant and must be constrained. Perhaps the story of the people's uprising against the Ani Kutani is the story of the first American revolution.

The sacred fire was central to the Cherokee spiritual system, thus the placement of Six Killer, Sutalidihi, as the primary goddess. It is possible that in her origins she was Grandmother of the Light, a function that becomes the province of Spider

Woman, as well as Sun Woman (Six Killer). Her connections to fire are not clear, but as she was the supreme being, and the sacred fire was central to Cherokee religion, the connection seems evident. There is again a curious connection here to the old religion as practiced in northern Scotland, where the lighting of New Fire played a central role in worship. Among the Druids who may not have extended their influence as far north as the Scottish Highlands, the lighting of the New Fire may have involved human sacrifice. This ritual, particularly in its gorier aspects, clearly has parallels to the Aztec system, which itself derives from earlier Mesoamerican spiritual practice, making the link between Xmucané, the goddess of the Quiché Maya, and Sutalidihi likely.

There is much evidence that the primacy of the sacred fire was also recognized by the Pueblo in the Classic era, around the twelfth century. Given this, one can argue that these societies are remnants of what was a vast Gulf of Mexico civilization all but vanished long before the coming of the white man.

Among the people of the central region of North America, the rituals connected with fire seem to have focused on the Sun Dance, a major spiritual rite that spread across the Plains in the nineteenth century. This ceremony involves self-sacrifice rather than the sacrifice of others. One offers oneself by dancing for days in the brutal glare of the July sun, without water or food. The dancer is tied to the Sun Dance tree by thongs attached to a small piece of wood and inserted beneath the pectorals, suggesting the ceremony's derivation from an earlier rite that concerned itself with fire and blood sacrifice. The Way of the Tree and the Way of Sacrifice are thus combined, as they are combined in Christian ritual, and the proper relation between the human and the divine is made evident.

NAVAJO (DINÉ)

The Navajo, or Diné, as they call themselves, came to the American Southwest millennia after the various Pueblos were established there. Their language, a variety of Athabascan, which is one of the major native languages spoken in Alaska, puts their origins far to the north of their present homelands. Perhaps they

were originally the people beloved by anthropologists who
trekked across the great Bering Straits. They came into the Southwest in the twelfth century, about the time the Mayan and Pueblo civilizations—along with numerous other Mayan-derived societies along the Mississippi Delta and Florida—were in decline.

The Navajo themselves insist that they are descendants—and
enemies—of the Anazazi, the old Pueblo people whose villages
are still to be seen in the cliffs of Navajo country, and they are
no doubt accurate in their perspective. Certainly their myths
and stories are largely variants of stories current among the
Pueblo and Maya, as are many of their pre-European practices
and accoutrements. But their cosmogony, akin to that of the
Keres, offers numerous differences, thus supporting both traditions of their origin. War with the Pueblos figures as largely in
their spiritual history as do typically Pueblo goddesses, holy
people, and heroes. Undoubtedly there was much intermarry-
ing between the newcomers and the locals, so that after centuries a people who are neither Pueblo nor northerner came
into being, and these are the Diné, the Navajo.

Their lands stretch westward away from Keres country—
though there is a small Navajo reservation nestled on the edges
of the Laguna reservation and mostly surrounded by it—far
into what is now Arizona. A hardy and expanding people, the
Diné live in diverse high plateau country, where lovely forests
and arid plains, flat-topped mesas and breathtakingly beautiful
canyons, enormous skies whose sunsets and sunrises offer all
the colored splendor any human heart can bear to see; a realm
wherein tumultuous electric storms and whirling dustdevils
make it clear that human life is held in the hands of the gods.

Today the Diné live in diverse accommodations—traditional
hogans and brush shelter kitchens squat next to fine mobile
homes and suburban-style houses. While many on the Navajo
reservation must truck water fifty or sixty miles and travel a
like distance for Western medical assistance, great powerline
towers march westward to Los Angeles and San Diego. Those
towers look like Yei, holy people. Perhaps they are there to remind those of us who miss the message in the rocks and skies
that the Yei do indeed exist, as actual as you or I.

But within the interstices of modern life—trucks, cars, radio
stations where Navajo-speaking DJ's play American music

(mostly country and western) and run their ads in Navajo—even in the modern tumult of tribal politics centered in the fine administration buildings and council hall at Window Rock—the old traditions remain, hardy and persistent as the desert grass that grows in the driest places. There, way out there, far, far away from the turbulence of modernism, the Sings are held, the dances go on.

Top a rise on a star-studded night in the high desert and descend its slope. Hear the drum pounding, its song coming up from the ground beneath your feet. See the beautiful women swaying in the Squaw Dance. Notice the land, the vastness around you, and say there are no goddesses, no gods. Say that the holy people are imaginary substitutes for hidden human instinctual drives. Go on, I dare you. Say it.

FLATHEAD AND OKANOGAN

The many native communities of the Northern Rockies are a diverse group who share some cultural features with the peoples usually designated as "Plains Indians" by ethnographers, who divide the communities into regional groups based as much on their material culture as on their geographical location. But while the material culture of the people of the Northern Rockies differs in many particulars from that of the Plains complex, they shared other features and often traded, intermixed, and fought. On the other hand, the Northern Rockies Salishan Flathead are quite different from another cluster of people designated Salish. A friend in Washington who was raised in and near the communities that she says are "true" Salish tells me that the Flathead tribes who live in the Northern Rockies are not Salish in the way that the people around the Seattle area are. Presumably, the two groups are academically classified under the same generic name for linguistic reasons; but the Flathead, like the Northwest Okanogan, are as closely allied culturally with Plains groups as they are with coastal peoples, largely because of where they live, along the eastern slopes of the Rockies and its lower slopes in Montana.

Among the Skokomish, a Salishan group who live along Hood Canal in Washington, there is a story of a great flood. The story, reported to Ella E. Clark by Mrs. Rose Purdy, can be found in Clark's *Indian Legends of the Pacific Northwest* (1953). As Mrs. Purdy tells it, the Skokomish tied their canoes together and were raised higher and higher in the Olympic Mountains with the rising waters. Some canoes broke loose from the chain and went "down, down, down." Those who were lost to the south finally came to dry land and became known as the Flatheads. "That is why the Skokomish and the Flatheads speak the same language," Mrs. Purdy says (Clark 1953, 44).

The Flatheads claim that they invited the Blackrobes (Jesuit priests) into their mountain fastnesses in the eighteenth century because the power the Jesuits represented seemed to them to be responsible for the greater prowess in war their traditional opponents, the Blackfeet—a Plains-cultured community—had suddenly developed. At great personal cost, a party of several Flathead men crossed the greater part of the continent in search of missionaries who would return with them to the Rockies. Eventually their quest was rewarded when Blackrobes did indeed enter their communities to baptize and instruct them in the ways of Christendom. I don't think it helped much in their battles with the Blackfeet or other Rocky Mountain and Plains opponents, for before another century had passed the need to best the Blackfeet had lost its urgency. After the United States annexed much of Mexico at the close of the Mexican-American War in 1848, the influx of Anglo-Americans into the Northwest via the Great Plains virtually put an end to Indian lifeways. The exigencies of survival dramatically changed the identity of the enemy, transforming the lifestyles and languages of all the parties to earlier combats.

In this large complex of interdependent Plains and mountain peoples, all relied to a greater or lesser extent on buffalo as a source of food and foundation of religion. Among the native people of the Plains and those myriad related communities farther north—the Salish, the Nootsac, the Flathead, the Kutenai, the Nootka, the Lummi, and many more in Montana, Oregon, Washington, and British Columbia—stories of interchanges with immortals, sky people, and Thunder abound. The recorded stories feature male protagonists and gods with greater frequency than female protagonists. There are a number of reasons for this, among them the prohibition that forbade the telling of women's stories to men. As the whites gathering the stories were usually male, and the people they gathered them from were male, there was also the tendency to report only those stories that were asked about as well as those deemed suitable for white ears. Taken together, the paucity of women's stories, stories dealing with female gods, immortals, or protagonists, is readily explained.

But the rarity of stories about the Goddess or other female immortals may reflect the decay of gynarchies throughout the Americas as much as it reflects the local customs. The story of Scomalt told here may be a reference to an earlier gynocratic social scheme, pointing to gynocratic organization among the immortals. Whether these systems were falling into disuse before contact with the whites or have been suppressed or forgotten under pressure from the Christian patriarchy is a matter that needs exploring.

HAUDINASHONE (IROQUOIS)

Comprising a number of Iroquoian-speaking tribes, but populated by a large number of Algonquians from among the surrounding tribes with whom they were long at war, and from whom they secured a number of captives who became adoptees, the Haudinashone confederacy, at the time of contact with whites in the mid or late seventeenth century, was composed of the Five Fires (which became the Six Fires in the eighteenth century): the Seneca, the Mohawk, the Onondaga, the Tuscarora, the Cayuga, and the Oneida. Famous for their constitutional government designed, it is said, by the Pine Tree sachem, Deganiwideh, the Haudinashone live in the area of New York State and adjoining Ontario, Canada.

Haudinashone women held considerable political power through the Matrons, the female heads of the clans. Longhouses, which accommodated a number of families, were governed by an elder woman who had gained appropriate stature through her actions and demeanor as well as her clan's position in the community. These households were generated by marriage in a matrilocal system where the husband moved into his wife's mother's household, as was also the practice among the Keres and Navajo. Some Haudinashone Matrons held more social power than others, and these were the heads of villages or clusters of longhouses. The Matrons chose representatives to the village council from among those of their sons/nephews who possessed the proper abilities, and they selected those who served on the tribal councils and the council for the overall confederacy of the Six Fires. They also held the power of impeachment, as they were the custodians of the antler-headdresses that were the sign of office for councilmen. In matters of policy, the women devised and the men implemented. The men were custodians of public affairs and Speakers, while women were custodians of the private or domestic sphere and deciders.

In spiritual matters, one of the important spiritual methods was dream enactment, for traditional Haudinashone believe that dreams expressed the spirit's desires, which must be met. Dreamers' families and friends were responsible for helping them to enact the dream and fulfill its promise. They had a concept of orenda, or spiritual power—analogous to the Keres concept of iyanyi ("the corn, it goes this way")—that loosely translated means sacred or good, infused with a kind of nonphysical energy that is neither emotional nor mental but of the essence of spirit. Persons rich in orenda were sachems or wise ones, and villages or tribes possessed of orenda in good measure prospered.

With the American Revolution, decided as it was in favor of the colonists, the Haudinashone fell into decline. With Christianization and accommodation to white demands that they be more like whites—that is, more patriarchal and secular—the power of the Longhouse fell into decline and Haudinashone women lost much of the status they had hitherto held.

Deganiwideh, who brought the Law of the Great Peace to the Haudinashone confederacy, did not, I think, generate the idea of gynocracy among them. What he did conceive of was a way that they could expand their hegemony over the neighboring Algonquians (he was Algonquian by birth). By codifying their existing system and amalgamating it with his own dream-inspired one, he made it possible for the Haudinashone to gain ascendancy during the turbulent times of the early settlement of Anglo-Europeans on the Atlantic seaboard.

After the Revolution, a misogynist prophet named Handsome Lake, who despised the power held by "old women," obtained a vision in which women were disempowered. Marrying couples, urged to leave behind archaic customs, were told that the wife must cling to the husband and leave her mother and the Longhouse behind. The people were to develop the American custom of isolated nuclear family households, and the governing of the polities, along with economic power, was to be transferred to the hands of men.

Given the Haudinashone belief that dreams must be lived out one way or another (a symbolic enactment properly executed could suffice), the dreadful straits they were in after the triumphant American "patriots" entered their lands, burned many dwellings, and salted the fields so that food could no longer be grown there—this move toward patriarchalization went a long way toward breaking the power of women. The widespread demoralization that ensued resulted in severe depression, disorientation anomie, and alcoholism among women and men alike. It is not surprising that the controlling power of the Matrons was considerably weakened under these devastating circumstances.

In spite of these events, many among the Haudinashone still cling to their ancient creation myth that puts the beginning of the world in the hands of Sky Woman. Given this, one must suppose that the parts of their old religion that derive from and gain support from that myth surely must remain extant.

KAROK

Far to the north of the Pueblo-Aztec-Navajo complex, the Karok people speak a language that is related to the languages spoken in Anahuac, the Land between the Waters. Except for this, they are culturally all but indistinguishable from their near neighbors, the Yurok, whose language is "a remote western offshoot of the great Algonquian family, of which the bulk resided east of the Mississippi and even on the Atlantic coast," according to A. L. Kroeber in his classic *Handbook of the Indians of California.* He writes that the Karok are "one of the northernmost members of the scattered Hokan group which reaches south to Tehuantepec" (Kroeber 1980, 98–99).

The Anglo name "Karok" means "upriver" in Karok, and the
Karok have lived upriver from the Yurok along the Klamath in
northern California since "time immemorial." They have no
ethnic name for themselves, according to Kroeber, but refer to
themselves as Arara, people, as the Navajo call themselves
Diné, which also means people. Indeed, most native communities refer to themselves as "the people," not being as wrapped
up in the glories of nationalism as are their modern non-Indian
compatriots.

It isn't clear to me whether the Yurok became like the Karok,
or vice versa, but I surmise that they each became what they
were supposed to be, living where they did and being taught
the Way where they were, combining it with spiritual elements
they had carried into the region with them. Certainly the stories the Karok recount bear striking resemblances to Aztec or
Pueblo-Navajo stories; but then again, they bear marked resemblance to Algonquian traditions, for example, the story of
Matchikwewis and Oshkikwe.

Grace Buzalijko, who compiled the Karok myths gathered by
Kroeber and E. W. Gifford, in her foreword to *Karok Myths*,
writes:

> At the Karok center of the world, Katimin, and at Weit-
> spus, the Yurok center, . . . Creator Gods [*sic*] set about
> and completed the creation of their respective worlds.
> When the ground was planted with trees and flowering
> plants, the air and marshes stocked with birds, the
> streams with fish, the land with animals, they made the
> people. Upon the emergence of the people into their
> world, these same Gods taught them the Way they were
> to follow, the rules and the customs and beliefs by which
> the Way should be forever maintained. (1980, xxiv)

This, she says, is a summation of the creation myths of the
two peoples as related to her by Robert Spott, a Yurok Indian,
in the 1940s.

The Karok and Yurok say that there were people who came
before the humans. These immortals—the ixkareya or wogé,
depending on which group names them—are usually distin-

guished from gods in some sense and are always characterized as creatively potent non-human beings, "supernaturals," in a precise understanding of the word. In this the Karok and Yurok are saying something that all native peoples are saying, something that has been attributed to "primitive consciousness" or a systemic way of articulating and sublimating powerful instinctual drives. The something they are saying, though, might be better thought of as factual. In so doing, the apparent puzzle of how the Karok-Hokan people and the Yurok-Algonquian people wind up living the same Way and telling stories about the same immortals is resolved.

As far as the Karok-Yurok and the others who live in the region are concerned, there are beings who are not human and who possess powers far beyond human power. They use these powers to create humans, deities, and geographical features. In short, they bioengineer and terraform. And while these concepts in their mythic, spiritual dimensions have been largely relegated to the "woo-woo" bin of contemporary Western thought, fit only for science fiction and fantasy, modern science points toward rationalist acceptance of both bioengineering and terraforming as reasonable, rational, mechanical operations, well within the purview of postmodern technology. The major difference the Indians have with the scientists in all of this is the spiritual dimension they find in their interactions with the immortals, whoever they might be and however they go about performing their miracles.

The coming of the Spaniards to Anahuac meant not simply the return of Quetzalcoatl. It meant that the native peoples of that region had met their destiny. The fatalism that is so vivid in the story of the fall of the Aztecs permeates much of Native American thought. That idea is central to the stories in this collection, highlighted in the Karok story I have rendered.

The native people of the Pacific Coast were decimated after the coming of the Americans in the late nineteenth and early twentieth centuries. The conquest of California after the treaty with Mexico forms one of the bloodiest annals in American history, and one of the least known. The conquest of the Pacific Northwest, equally obscure though more recent, taking place mostly in the twentieth century, is one of devastation and loss.

Children were taken away from their villages and herded into
Indian schools where they died by the thousands of Anglo-
European diseases. Their deaths were hastened by lowered resistance brought on by loss of cultural identity, economic hard-
ship occasioned by laws passed against their right to lands and
resources they formerly relied on, and disintegration of their
communities as they were moved, re-moved, and required to
obey white laws, customs, and dictates.

KERES

The Keres are an ancient people, settled in their homelands
long before the "dawn of history," as it is phrased in Western
terms, though of course not long before the Keres "dawn,"
which was far in the distant past.

The Keres say that long ago they lived in the beautiful white
village, Kush Ka-tret, where two of the stories rendered here are
set. Many things happened there, but finally the area was
drowned. An old story, recorded by John M. Gunn (1977), reports that some men had gone fishing far out from the large island named Shipap, where they originally lived. They were
gone for quite a while, and when they returned the island had
vanished. All that they could see was a giant animal, maybe a
whale, swimming around where their homelands had been.

Gunn believed that they were referring to the lost continent
of Atlantis, a much-sought mythical land in his time. Others of
his generation, scholars and amateur classicists working and re-
searching in the latter nineteenth and early twentieth centuries,
believed that the Maya or the Egyptians came from Atlantis, or
even that they both did, one branch heading westward and scat-
tering from there and the other going to the east.

In our time, many still hunt for the lost continent, believing
that the ancients had their origins there and in Lemuria or perhaps Mu. In *Maya/Atlantis: Queen Móo and the Egyptian Sphinx*
(1973), August LePlongeon proposes the intriguing possibility
that Mu was the name of one of the last queens of Mayaland,
and that she fled to her relatives' domains in Egypt. His evidence, like Gunn's, revolves around the similarities in the two

civilizations in architecture, language, and lore. There is, to my mind, more to be said for their ideas than for those of modern scholars who insist that the native peoples of the Americas migrated here by way of the Bering Straits, following the herds of mastodons well over twenty thousand years ago during the last ice age. That theory is odd because the mastodons, along with the horse, originated in the Americas, not Asia; and for the Bering Straits land bridge to rise above water, glaciation had to extend far to the south. A migration from Asia to the Americas would require covering some ten thousand miles of glacial land to arrive south of the ice. On 1 January 1991, CNN's Headline News reported an odd item: it seems that several researchers—paleontologists, I think—have discovered the fossil remains of quarter-sized heads of mice. They said that their discovery suggests that human life began some fifteen million years earlier than previously supposed, and raises serious questions about the theory that the human race had its origins in Asia or Africa. Maybe it began in America, they said.

Imagine the consequences to the Western version of history that civilization spread from Mesopotamia via Egypt to Greece, to Europe and Britain, thence to white America, should alternative theorists such as Gunn and LePlongeon be correct. What if civilization went as much from here to there as vice versa?

As to the Keres, their tenure in the Southwest, whence they may have come from Florida by way of Ohio, is of thousands of years' standing. Their present lands are in western and central New Mexico, extending westward from Albuquerque to the foothills of the Cibola National Forest, which encompasses Mount Taylor, and extend northward along the Rio Grande. Their tribal designations today include Laguna and Acoma to the west and Cochiti, Santa Ana, Sía, and San Filipé along the river.

The lands of the Western Keres, as the Acoma and Laguna are called, are my homelands, and Laguna is my mother village—I was raised just a few miles away. The shocking power, expanse, and angularity of the high plateau there is marked by tabletop mountains, mesas, that march in geometric pattern toward the horizon. The region is full of huge sandstone and volcanic formations and cliffs, deep arroyos and canyons, box canyons, lava beds, and miles of plain that only recently has begun to carry noticeable greenery old timers say characterized it a century ago. It is a land of huge skies, often filled with looming

thunderheads, enormous cloud formations that tower above
the mountains and mesas and send forth lightning bolts and
fast, hard rain. If one thinks of the land as female, then the female image I was raised to is huge, stony, wondrous, soaring,
challenging, magnificent, and intense, and only in tiny, transi-
tory ways is she fragile, gentle, delicate.

The Woman veiled in Clouds, Tse'pina—Mount Taylor as she
is styled in English (after some white male adventurer)—grows
out of the plain some 14,000 feet above sea level, or around
7,500 feet above the plain. She is a lovely woman mountain
whose head rises powerful and bare above timberline.

Acoma, the westernmost Keres pueblo, is perched atop a rock
mesa, all but inaccessible until late this century, when they
built a ramp up one side to allow motor vehicles to ascend it.
There are two main Acoma communities in the flats, twenty or
thirty miles from the mother village: Acomita and McCartys.
The main pueblo of Acoma (Acu) was established long before
the coming of the Spaniards, who were able to conquer it only
after a long siege. Its defenses were impregnable, but its water
supply was limited. Its large stone cisterns were dependent on
rainfall for replenishment, and when it didn't rain, water had to
be carried up the rough, narrow stone staircase that wound its
way up a cleft in the mesa's side. It was carried in ollas, huge
water jars, on the heads of the admittedly tiny but astonish-
ingly strong Acoma women.

Laguna, a few miles southeast of Acoma, was established in
the eighteenth century by a coalition of predominantly Keres-
speaking refugees and protective Spaniards. The Pueblos had
evicted the Spanish invaders in the sixteenth century, but after
devastating struggles with the mounted Navajo, Apache, Sho-
shone, Ute, and occasionally Comanche, they sent south to
New Spain requesting the Crown to send military aid. By then
their numbers had been reduced by as much as 80 percent by
war, starvation that came in its wake, and sickness. Whole
pueblos, such as Pecos, the easternmost of the group, populated
by some 20,000 souls in Coronado's time, and La Cienega, a
Northern Keres pueblo, were obliterated.

Growing up, I thought there were four varieties of Indians:
Pueblo, Navajo, Apache, and Comanche. I thought all Indians
east of the Pueblos were the latter, except the Haudinashone,
who figured largely in my Catholic schools' indoctrination lore,

and the Sioux (Lakota), from whom I was descended through my mother's father.

Laguna Pueblo was established near the shores of what was then a large lake, hence the name. The lake had dried up by the time I was married in the late 1950s, but I remember driving along it in my youth. Uranium mining, a thirty-year drought, and postwar population growth in the state were all factors, I suppose. But I have heard Lagunas say that the main factor has been the influx of Anglos, white people, who do not know how to "think good thoughts" and so the rain people won't come, and the lake spirits remove to more congenial environs.

In time the pueblo grew, and other villages were established. They include Old Laguna, Encinal, Casa Blanca, Seama, Paraje, Paguate, Mesita, New York, and Philadelphia. Cubero, my hometown, which is predominantly Chicano, might also have been a Laguna village, founded it is said by a maverick couple, a Mexican man and a Laguna woman who married and found it diplomatic to settle outside Laguna. But Cubero became a Spanish-Mexican village rather than a Laguna satellite. Paguate, founded similarly, went the other way.

The houses around Laguna and Acoma, at least before the advent of HUD monstrosities in the sixties, are of native stone. Good stone masons could erect a wall of stones so perfectly fitted that they would stand a hundred years or more. The walls were plastered on the outside with mud mixed with straw. The inside, plastered with a finer variety of clay, was "whitewashed" with a fine white clay found only in special locations and carried to the site. The roofs were spanned with logs from which the bark had been peeled, over which a lattice of small branches was laid, the whole covered with a thick layer of mud that baked in the sun, keeping out most of the rain and all of the wind.

Since the coming of the Spaniards over four hundred years ago, the Keres have been both Catholic and Keres, though the Presbyterians made sizeable inroads in the early twentieth century. Until the latter half of this century, many spoke Spanish as well as Keres. Today most speak English, many exclusively. The median education level at Laguna is very high, ranging from post-secondary vocational training in fields such as electronics and mechanics through doctorates. Many younger Lagunas hold at least a baccalaureate.

In this setting, Keres peoples pursue ancient ways and modern ones. In this setting, Thought Woman spins her web of dreams, thinks us into existence, dances us into being. And as she thinks, so we are.

LAKOTA

As renowned in American lore as the Karok, Flathead, Okanogan, Nootsac, and Lummi are obscure, and even more familiar to Americans than the Aztecs, the Lakota live on the northern Plains. One of the many Siouian peoples, the Lakota originated in the South, from the same area as the Cherokee and their sister people, the Haudinashone. That was several hundred years ago, and they moved north, entering the eastern edge of the Plains, settling along the upper reaches of the Missouri, where their lifestyle took on the rhythms and style of woodland people. They lived in wigwams, large houses made of bark-covered poles and shaped like somewhat rounded Quonset huts. Within these dwellings, more than one family lived, each having an area designated as its own. In this they resembled the Haudinashone rather than the anishinabeg, who were more inclined to single-family dwellings of the same general type.

In the late eighteenth century, the Lakota moved across the Missouri and came to the Plains, where their material culture and general way of life changed dramatically. Historians say that they had attempted to cross the Missouri for some time, but were held back by the Arikara until a dreadful smallpox epidemic devastated that tribe, leaving the road clear for the Lakota to head west.

While peoples far to the east of the present homelands of the Lakota in South Dakota depended upon the buffalo for food, the concept of the buffalo as centrally sacred to their way of life seems to have particularly marked the spiritual thought of the Plains.

With the buffalo—said to have numbered some 160,000,000 in the nineteenth century—and the Sun Dance, the people of the Great Plains (once termed the Great American Desert by American writers) developed the culture of tipi, feathered headdress, pipe, mounted warfare, and resistance to white encroachment that characterizes, in the American mind, the Indian way. From plains country comes the myth of the dying warrior—as well as the supporting cast of "braves," "chiefs," "squaws," and "papooses"—that enlivens much of American literature and entertainment of the twentieth century.

The conquest of the Plains was as dreadful as the decimation of other native peoples, though their resistance to conquest may have been greater. Accustomed to fighting—albeit not the kind of fighting they were faced with when the American cavalry went after them with all the military might and fervor it had generated during the Civil War—the Plains people were able to mount resistances that still speak vividly to the hearts of many Americans. The end, when it came, was at Wounded Knee in 1892. With that final massacre of scores of starving, unarmed men, women, and children by the U.S. Army, "the tribes were wiped out, the history books censored," as singer-songwriter Buffy Saint Marie, a Cree Indian herself, has written.

In the general bloodletting of that era, one wonders how many goddesses, rituals, and myths fell into obscurity even among native people who, perforce, were patriarchalized in the aftermath of war.

LUMMI/NOOTSAC

The peoples who live in the far northwest portion of the United States and Canada are blessed with lands that are abundant in fish, game, timber, plants, and rainfall. The towering, magnificent peaks, the lush rain forests where one can be helplessly lost less than twenty feet from a road, the icy blue bays and sounds, and the thundering pine forests that sweep down into the water require real humility on the part of humans who visit or dwell there.

Like the Southwest, the Northwest demands acquiescence to the will of the Goddess. The vastness and mysteriousness of the surroundings evoke in any who are spiritually alive a sense of awe that is overwhelming.

I think some of the most impressive experiences I have had with the land have been in the Pacific Northwest, where the Nootsac and Lummi live. The sight indelibly imprinted on my brain is of the piled blue peaks of the Cascades marching ever upward in the distance from our vantage point, peaks upon peaks reaching toward the sky. This massive range, capped by snow, though it was late summer when I saw it, ascends to its crown, which is known in English as Mount Rainier.

The Lummi and Nootsac live near Puget Sound, on what is now the Washington–British Columbia border, near Okanogan territory. From their villages, on clear days, you can see the towering peaks of the Cascades. They lived by fishing, hunting, gathering, praying, and being together, their houses of wood and generally commodious, their society ordered and satisfying.

In the aftermath of the Bay Area/Santa Cruz earthquake of 1989, a number of earthquake stories were aired. One reported that there was a great quake near Lummi/Nootsac country in the late seventeenth century, around 1680, that shattered the rockbeds of the region and raised a mountain. While it is au courant to argue that native people sit around and make up stories about gods and goddesses because they don't know the scientific truth of planetary matters, the report gives me pause: perhaps goddesses really do make themselves into mountains and islands. There is seismographic evidence to bear out the Indian people's assertions.

MAYA

The most singular of all peoples on the planet, and one of the most enigmatic, the Maya ruled over an area about the size of modern Italy and even richer in artistic and architectural treasures. The classic age of the Maya lasted longer than the entire life of the Roman Empire, so William Brandon writes, and Mayan ceremonial cities numbered well over one hundred (Brandon 1974, 47). They had a calendar that told the time more accurately than any in the world until the advent of the sidereal calendar of modern Western astronomy. Nor does the Mayan calendar confine itself to the day, month, and year, but it designates what time it is, ceremonially, spiritually, in the locale and in the universe. The Maya developed the concept of zero, a feat only matched later by the Arabs, and they had a mathematical system that is eerily similar to that used by computers.

The Maya had a unique system of writing that combined hieroglyphs and phonetics, enabling them both to connote and denote significance and convey exact shades of meaning. For all their accomplishments, they weren't much on empire building. The idea of expansion and conquest seemed to bore them.

Despite their mathematical, spiritual, and aesthetic advancements, or perhaps because of them, the Maya economic system remained simple; farming was done by individual families who tended "milpas," small plots of land cleared by chopping and burning growth that would interfere with growing foodstuffs. Land thus prepared was planted, and while it was gestating and burgeoning, another milpa was prepared. While this method seems primitive to people raised to agri-business modes of food production, it had the remarkably civilized virtue of protecting the environment from overuse, thus keeping a solid resource base available for the support of two or so million people in a relatively small area.

The Maya are said to have reached the height of their civilization around a thousand years ago, though early ceremonial centers date to 1200 B.C., more than three thousand years ago. (Contemporary digs are likely to recast the whole scholarship on a people who during an earlier heyday were probably gynocratic.) Their land area dominated all of the rainforest of central Guatemala, the Yucatán Peninsula and the dry brush country of northern Yucatán. At its height, Mayaland included territory that is presently located in Honduras, El Salvador, Guatemala, Belize, and the Mexican states of Quintana Roo, Yucatán, Campeche, Tabasco, and Chiapas. Maya people still live in many of these regions.

Of abiding interest to spiritual seekers from North America is the question of the Maya who built the ceremonial centers. It is rumored that the people were ruled by a race of mental, rather than physical, giants who, for obscure reasons, one day up and vanished sometime after the invasion from Spain. I first heard the tale in my junior or senior religion class at Saint Vincent's Academy in Albuquerque, where our teacher, Sister Conrad, imparted it to her breathless (or bored) charges. Naturally, I was among the breathless, happy indeed to be considering more exciting matters than the papal *Encyclicals*.

Sister Conrad told us that the Maya had vanished, and that

nearly five centuries after their disappearance a cave filled with hundreds of mummified bodies was discovered. No one knew how they had gotten there, but Sister Conrad, as I recall hazily, suggested that nonhuman forces—was it something about flying saucers? this was around 1956—were involved.

The puzzle of what happened to the Maya is readily enough solved, of course. They are where they've always been. What seems to have disappeared are the noble-priest classes, who abandoned the ceremonial cities for the forests and either fled to an unknown destination or blended into the general population around the milpas. What also vanished, though not half so mysteriously, were the many books they possessed that recorded their knowledge and history. These were quite deliberately burned by a Spanish bishop named Landa.

This worthy did not believe in peaceful coexistence, yet for some reason he invented a kind of alphabetical written language that combined basic Maya hieroglyph-words with sounds in Spanish, which he taught to some of his Christianized captives. Using the system he devised, his pupils recorded some of the old books, evidently from memory. While white scholars don't know exactly what sources were used in the Landa-inspired work, some early translations of it have survived. The most popular of the "alphabetic substitutes for hieroglyphic books," as Dennis Tedlock has it, are the Chilam Balam, or "Jaguar Priest," books of Yucatán and the Popul Vuh (Council Book) of the Quiché Maya of Guatemala (Tedlock 1985, 28). Other material pertaining to the ancients has been preserved on the stelae—great stones covered with hieroglyphs and phonetic-based "words," which have only in this century yielded at all to translation— and on pottery, jewelry, and probably of most significance, in the religion and stories of the Maya survivors themselves.

Based on their sacred calendar, Maya prophecies testify that quite soon this world will take a turn in its long spiral path around the center of the galaxy returning us to our more usual place (or psychic space) in the cosmos. By the mid twenty-first century we will be more and more aware of the presence of the supernaturals among us. I hope that this volume will aid in the process of return, enabling women to recover our ancient medicine ways and once again establish our ongoing relation to the Great Mystery. Nos vemos.

GLOSSARY

AMOTKEN (SMOTKEN) Okanogan/Flathead. Washington State, British Columbia, Montana. The goddess Scomalt's son; a god.

BUD See Flint Boy.

CHANGER Nootsac/Lummi. Washington State, British Columbia. The personage (gender unspecified) who can transform beings into geological forms; a great wizard and a deity.

CHANGING WOMAN Diné (Navajo). Arizona and New Mexico. The major goddess figure among the Diné, particularly connected to puberty ceremonies and healing.

CHILD OF WATER Navajo (Diné). Arizona and New Mexico. White Shell Woman's son, helps Monster Slayer destroy the alien monsters who inhabited the fourth world to make it safe for earth-surface people (human beings). Rain is his father.

CIHUACOATL See Serpent Woman. Also title of her major priest.

CLEAR SKY Nootsac/Lummi. Washington State, British Columbia. The co-wife of Komo Kulshan who transforms herself into a mountain.

COATLICUE See Serpent Skirt.

CRYSTAL WOMAN Mopán Maya. Southern Belize (Toledo District). Popularly known as the Crystal Skull, and called Gentian (or so she told me), this supernatural being functions as a transmitter between the world of the supernaturals and humans, particularly medicine people. The skull is of one who was originally an earth dweller (but nonhuman) and was "magically" transformed by exhaustive ritual and, I suppose, technological skill that seems very magical to those at our limited stage of development. The process begun by Gentian and her cohorts was completed over generations by Maya people long before white contact.

DEER WOMAN   Cherokee, Choctaw. North Carolina, Mississippi, Arkansas, Georgia, Tennessee, and Oklahoma. A supernatural who appears as a human woman and as a doe by turns. She is said to bewitch men and women and eventually cause their deaths or descent into prostitution.

FAIR MAIDEN   Nootsac/Lummi. Washington State, British Columbia. Clear Sky's co-wife and sister, Fair Maiden is transformed into the feature now called Speiden Island on English-language maps.

FLINT BOY   Haudinashone (Iroquois). New York State, Ontario. Grandson of Sky Woman. A somewhat misshapen, deceitful, self-centered, spiritually backward god who can't do anything right. In trying to outdo his brother, Sapling, he creates alien monsters and makes life difficult for humans. Sky Woman's favorite.

GRANDMOTHER SPIDER (SPIDER WOMAN; OLD SPIDER)   Cherokee, Keres, Diné. Southeastern United States, Oklahoma, New Mexico, Arizona. The goddess who brings the light. In some stories she is the origin of corn, the grandmother of the sun, the power of creative (magically empowered) thought. Often depicted as a spider with a four-direction symbol on her back.

GUADALUPE, OUR LADY OF   See Tonan.

HUNAHPÚ   Quiché Maya. Guatemala Highlands, northern Belize. Grandson of Xmucané, son of Xquic (Blood Woman). One of the set of twin brothers said to have received Xmucané's creative and ritual power when the Maya gynarchy changed to a male-centered system.

IC'STS'ITY (IC'TS'ITY)   Keres Pueblo. New Mexico. Co-creatrix of the universe. In her many aspects she becomes Iyatiku, mother of the Keres Pueblos, and simultaneously Uretsete, father of the Keres.

IYATIKU (NAIYA IYATIKU, BEAUTIFUL CORN WOMAN) Keres Pueblo. New Mexico. A major goddess, peaceful, harmonious, she governs the traditional and spiritual affairs of the Keres people from her present home in Shipap, the place where the four rivers meet.

KOCHINNENAKO See Yellow Woman.

LA VIRGIN MORENA See Tonan.

LITTLE WAR TWINS See Masewe and Oyoyowe.

LONG MAN Cherokee. Georgia, Tennessee, North Carolina, Arkansas, Mississippi, Oklahoma. A god, Six Killer's consort and father of their son Wild Boy (Blood Boy). Intelligence-being of rivers.

MALINALLI (MALINAL, LADY MARINA, LA MALINCHE) Aztec. Mexico. Leader of the revolt against the Aztec patriarchy. Her name means "penance grass," associated with the gentler self-sacrificing spiritual path of the god Quetzalcoatl.

MASEWE Keres Pueblo. New Mexico. One of the Little War Twins, grandsons of Grandmother Spider. Hero in many tales, now a prominent feature of the Sandia Mountains east of Albuquerque.

MATCHIKWEWIS Anishinabeg (Ojibwa/Chippewa). Wisconsin, Minnesota, Michigan, Ontario, Manitoba, Ohio, Indiana, Illinois, Iowa, North Dakota, Montana, Saskatchewan. Demigoddess (Half goddess, half-human (?), maybe half-non-human magical being). Major figure in anishinabeg oral tradition, model of witchy-womanhood and ritual competence.

MONSTER SLAYER Diné (Navajo). Arizona and New Mexico. Changing Woman's son and lead destroyer of alien monsters who plague her and her people. Sun is his father.

NAIYA IYATIKU See Iyatiku. Naiya means "our dear mother."

NANABOZHO (NANABOZO, WENEBOZO, NANABUSH) Anishinabeg (Ojibwa/Chippewa). Great Lakes regions and throughout northern regions along U.S.–Canadian border. Trickster god, one of five brothers (or four, three, or two, depending on the narrative and narrator). A manido (manidoo, manidou) or spirit with vast creative power. Father of Matchikwewis and Oshkikwe.

NAU'TS'ITY (NAU'TS'STSITY, NAOSETE, NAOTSETE) Keres Pueblo. New Mexico. Sun Woman. Co-creatrix of the universe. She has gone to the east, and is to return to her sister's side in times to come. Some around Laguna say those times have come, and that she has returned in the guise of the atomic/hydrogen "suns," which were built mainly in her original lands where the uranium used to create the superhuman detonations were mined and milled.

OLDER SISTER Diné (Navajo). Arizona and New Mexico. The human woman who becomes a supernatural after being abducted by a spirit man (a supernatural) along with her younger sister.

ONE HUNAHPÚ Quiché Maya. Guatemala Highlands, northern Belize. One of Xmucané and Xpiyacoc's twin sons.

OSHKIKWE Sister of Matchikwewis, more frequently the semi-divine heroine of women's ritual narratives than her sister.

OYOYOWE Keres Pueblo. New Mexico. One of the Little War Twins, grandson of Grandmother Spider. A god, also a prominent feature of the western slope of the Sandia Mountains east of Albuquerque.

PIKIAWISH WOMAN Karok. California. Pikiawish means something like priestess or sorceress. A female shaman and practitioner of world-renewal rites.

QIYO KEPE Keres Pueblo. New Mexico. The extraordinarily powerful sorceress who cures the clan uncle's daughter using only water and empties her shoes to give life to all the animal people.

QUETZALCOATL (PRECIOUS TWIN, MORNING STAR) Aztec. Mexico. The Maya believed he was to return on Ce Acatl, One Reed, which coincided with the date Cortés set foot on the Yucatán Peninsula from Cuba. His next return (Ce Acatl) is imminent. Sometimes identified as Evening Star, his twin.

SAPLING Haudinashone (Iroquois). New York State, Ontario. The grandson of Sky Woman who she has made an outcast. The creative principle, green and nourishing. The spirit of nurturance and model for what makes a real man, a real chief, or sachem (Pine Tree).

SCOMALT (SKOMELTEM) Okanogan/Flathead. Washington, Oregon, British Columbia, Montana. Giantess, goddess, and head of state of a giant white-skinned race. Enormous powers.

SELU Cherokee. Oklahoma, North Carolina, Georgia, Tennessee, Mississippi, Arkansas. Corn Woman, goddess of corn, mother of the Thunder Twins, lover of Long Man and Kanati.

SERPENT SKIRT (COATLICUE) Aztec. Mexico. Horrifying major deity (rivaled in importance only by Serpent Woman) who accepted human sacrifices in the fire said to be the spirit of her son, Smoking Mirror. Her major priest was uelatoani (emperor) or tlatoani (great speaker), also known as Quetzalcoatl (another deity consumed in flame). It was the tlatoani Moctezuma and the goddess's reign of human sacrifice that Malinalli helped Cortés overthrow.

SERPENT WOMAN (CIHUACOATL, SNAKE WOMAN) Aztec. Mexico. Grisly major deity whose priest Tlacaelel was also called cihuacoatl. She presided over the feeding of the gods and goddesses as the responsible deity tending to their needs.

SEVEN HUNAHPÚ (SEVEN JAGUAR, SEVEN HUNTER) Quiché Maya. Guatemala Highlands, northern Belize. One of the twin sons of Xmucané and Xpiyacoc.

SIX KILLER (SUTALIDIHI) Cherokee. Georgia, North Carolina, Mississippi, Tennessee, Arkansas, and Oklahoma. Major deity of the Cherokee, radioactive fire, powerful and sometimes vengeful. The Great Measurer or Apportioner.

SKY WOMAN Haudinashone (Iroquois). New York State, Ontario. Major deity of the Haudinashone. She falls through the void of space and creates the human universe(s). Grandmother of the god-twins, Sapling and Flint Boy.

SMOKING MIRROR/HUITZILOPOCHTLI (BLUE HUMMINGBIRD ON THE LEFT, TEZCATLIPOCA) Aztec. Mexico. Coatlicue's son, associated with the sun. Also called Heart of Coatlicue (or Heart of Earth). Human beings (usually from non-Aztec, conquered peoples) were burned in the fire at the goddess's feet to feed her so she would bring prosperity to the Aztecs.

SMOTKEN See Amotken.

S'TS'TSI'NAKU See Grandmother Spider.

SUTALIDIHI See Six Killer.

THINKING WOMAN (THOUGHT WOMAN) Keres Pueblo. New Mexico. See Grandmother Spider.

TONAN Aztec. Mexico. A primary goddess, creative principle, gentle, peaceful, powerful, full, and ripe. Seen as a mountain or the spirit that informs several Mexican mountains. She is transformed into Our Lady of Guadalupe (La Virgin de Guadalupe) after the Spaniards bring Catholicism into the region. Some of her other names are Tonantzin (Our Holy Mother), Cihuatzin (Reverend Lady), Toci (Our Grandmother), Llama (Old Woman), Tocennan (All Mother), Yaocihuatl (Enemy Woman), and Teteoinnan (Mother of the Gods). She is very like Iyatiku, Changing Woman, Scomalt, Spider Grandmother, Fair Maiden, and Sky Woman in the variety of her guises.

TONANTZIN See Tonan.

TS'ITS'NAKU See Grandmother Spider.

WHITE SHELL WOMAN Diné (Navajo). Arizona and New Mexico. The other creatrix-goddess of the Diné. Responsible (like Xmucané of the Quiché Maya) for creating earth-surface people from corn. Originally a stone being, or an Air Spirit captured in stone, she and her goddess-sister Changing Woman bear, in that sense, remarkable resemblance to Crystal Woman of the Mopán Maya. Mother of Child of Water.

XBALANQUE Quiché Maya. Guatemalan Highlands and northern Belize. Twin son of Xquic and twin grandson of Xmucané. Receives gynarchical power along with brother Hunahpú, his twin. If "X" means "woman" then Xbalanque is the twin sister/daughter/granddaughter.

XMUCANÉ (GRANDMOTHER OF THE LIGHT) Quiché Maya. Guatemalan Highlands and northern Belize. Divine midwife and patroness of birth. Original power of day keeping, the ritual system used by Maya practitioners.

XPIYACOC (GRANDMOTHER OF THE SUN) Quiché Maya. Guatemalan Highlands and northern Belize. Keeper of Days, along with Xmucané his/her sister goddess, also the power that makes marriage possible, the divine matchmaker. It is believed that "he" was originally "she," and the "X," meaning "woman" attests to that idea.

XQUIC (BLOOD WOMAN) Quiché Maya. Guatemalan Highlands and northern Belize. Daughter-in-law of Xmucané and mother of Hunahpú and Xbalanque, the Little War Twins of the Mayan cosmogyny.

YELLOW WOMAN (KOCHINNENAKO) Keres Pueblo. New Mexico. A corn ear, sacred and infused with being. A figure in many narratives concerned with rituals related to wilderness and natural surroundings of the pueblo. A supernatural being, but not a goddess. Possessed of magical powers, particularly those connected with transformation and conferral of power from one moiety (socio-ritual division of the pueblo) to the other.

BIBLIOGRAPHY

Allen, Paula Gunn. 1986. *The Sacred Hoop: Recovering the Feminine in American Indian Traditions.* Boston: Beacon Press.

Barnouw, Victor, ed. 1977. *Wisconsin Chippewa Myths and Tales and Their Relation to Chippewa Life.* Madison: University of Wisconsin Press.

Benedict, Ruth. 1981. *Tales of the Cochiti Indians.* Albuquerque: University of New Mexico Press.

Boas, Franz. 1928. *Keresan Texts.* New York: Publications of the American Ethnological Society.

Brandon, William. 1974. *The Last Americans: The Indian in American Culture.* New York: McGraw-Hill Book Company.

Bruchac, Joseph. 1987. *Stone Giants and Flying Heads.* Santa Cruz: Crossing Press.

Brundage, Burr Cartwright. 1979. *The Fifth Sun: Aztec Gods, Aztec World.* Austin: University of Texas Press.

Burland, C. A. 1967. *The Gods of Mexico.* New York: G. P. Putnam's Sons.

Burland, C. A., and Werner Forman. 1975. *Feathered Serpent and Smoking Mirror.* New York: G. P. Putnam's Sons.

Clark, Ella E. 1953. *Indian Legends of the Pacific Northwest.* Berkeley: University of California Press.

————. 1966. *Indian Legends from the Northern Rockies.* Norman: University of Oklahoma Press.

"Creation Story: A Mohawk Account." 1982. *Akwesasne Notes Calendar.* Mohawk via Roosevelt Town, N.Y.: Akwesasne Notes.

Curtis, Natalie, ed. 1950. *The Indians' Book: Songs and Legends of the American Indians.* New York: Dover Publications.

DeMallie, Raymond J., ed. 1984. *The Sixth Grandfather: Black Elk's Teachings Given to John G. Neihardt.* Lincoln: University of Nebraska Press.

Edmonson, Munro S. 1971. *The Book of Counsel: The Popul Vuh of the Quiché Maya of Guatemala.* Middle American Research Institute, Publication 35. New Orleans: Tulane University.

Erdoes, Richard, and Alfonso Ortiz. 1984. *American Indian Myths and Legends.* New York: Pantheon Fairy Tale and Folklore Library.

Estrada, Alvaro. 1981. *Maria Sabina: Her Life and Chants.* Santa Barbara: Ross-Erickson Publishers. English translation.

Fergusson, Erna. 1988. *Dancing Gods: Indian Ceremonials of New Mexico and Arizona.* Albuquerque: University of New Mexico Press.

Galeano, Eduardo. 1985. *Memory of Fire: Genesis.* New York: Pantheon.

Girard, Raphael. 1979. *Esotericism of the Popul Vuh: The Sacred History of the Quiché Maya.* Pasadena: Theosophical University Press.

Gunn, John M. [1917] 1977. *Schat-Chen: History, Traditions, and Narratives of the Queres Indians of Laguna and Acoma.* Albuquerque: Albright and Anderson; reprint, New York: AMS.

———. "The Trail of the Sumerian Cushites, or The Ancient History of the Queres Pueblo Indians [of] Laguna and Acoma." Unpublished manuscript.

Haile, Father Bernard, O.F.M. 1978. *Love-Magic and Butterfly People: The Slim Curly Version of the Ajilee and Mothway Myths.* Flagstaff: Museum of Northern Arizona Press. Distributed by University of Nebraska Press.

———. 1981. *Upward Moving and Emergence Way.* Volume 7 of *American Tribal Religions.* Lincoln: University of Nebraska Press.

Keen, Sam. 1989. "Original Blessing, Not Original Sin." *Psychology Today* (June).

Kilpatrick, Jack F. 1966. "The Wahnenauhi Manuscript: Historical Sketches of the Superstitions." *Bureau of American Ethnology Bulletin* 196, no. 77: 175–213.

Kilpatrick, Jack F., and Anna G. Kilpatrick. 1964. *Friends of Thunder: Folktales of the Oklahoma Cherokees.* Dallas: Southern Methodist University Press.

———. 1966. "Eastern Cherokee Folktales Reconstructed from the Field Notes of Frans M. Olbrects." *Bureau of American Ethnology Bulletin* 196, no. 90: 379–447.

Kroeber, A. L. 1976. *Yurok Myths.* Berkeley: University of California Press.

Kroeber, A. L., and E. W. Gifford. 1980. *Karok Myths.* Edited by Grace Buzalijko. Berkeley: University of California Press.

————. 1976. *Handbook of the Indians of California.* Reprint. New York: Dover Publications.

Kurzweil, Edith. 1980. *The Age of Structuralism: Lévi-Strauss to Foucault.* New York: Columbia University Press.

Lame Deer, John (Fire), and Richard Erdoes. 1972. *Lame Deer: Seeker of Visions.* New York: Simon and Schuster, Touchstone Books.

Landes, Ruth. [1938] 1977. *Objiway Woman.* New York: Columbia University Press.

LaPointe, James. 1976. *Legends of the Lakota.* San Francisco: Indian Historian Press.

LePlongeon, Augustus. 1973. *Maya/Atlantis: Queen Móo and the Egyptian Sphinx.* Blauvelt, New York: Rudolph Steiner Publications.

————. 1973. *Sacred Mysteries among the Mayas and the Quiches 11,500 Years Ago: Their Relation to the Sacred Mysteries of Egypt, Greece, Chaldea, and India.* Minneapolis: Wizards Bookshelf Secret Doctrine Reference Series.

Lévi-Strauss, Claude. 1963. *Structural Anthropology.* New York: Basic Books.

Linderman, Frank B. 1972. *Pretty Shield: Medicine Woman of the Crows.* Lincoln: University of Nebraska Press.

Marriott, Alice. 1945. *The Ten Grandmothers.* Norman: University of Oklahoma Press.

Moon, Sheila. 1984. *Changing Woman and Her Sisters: Feminine Aspects of Selves and Deities.* San Francisco: Guild for Psychological Studies Publishing House.

Mooney, James. 1982. *Myths of the Cherokee and Sacred Formulas of the Cherokees.* Nashville: Charles and Randy Elder–Booksellers.

Morley, Sylvanus Griswold. 1946. *The Ancient Maya.* Stanford: Stanford University Press.

Morley, Sylvanus Griswold, and Delia Goetz. 1950. *Popul Vuh: The Sacred Book of the Ancient Quiché Maya.* From the translation of Adrian Recinos. Norman: University of Oklahoma Press.

Mullett, G. M. 1979. *Spider Woman Stories: Legends of the Hopi Indians.* Tucson: University of Arizona Press.

Murray, Henry A., ed. 1960. *Myth and Mythmakers.* New York: George Braziller.

Purley, Anthony. 1974. "Keres Pueblo Concepts of Deity." *American Indian Culture and Research Journal* 1, no. 1: 29–32.

Reichard, Gladys A. 1950. *Navajo Religion: A Study in Symbolism.* Bollingen Series 18. Princeton: Princeton University Press.

Sanders, Thomas E., and Walter W. Peek, eds. 1973. *Literature of the American Indian.* New York: Glencoe Press.

Silko, Leslie Marmon. 1978. *Ceremony.* New York: Viking Press.

Skeat, Walter W. 1978. *An Etymological Dictionary of the English Language.* 4th revised edition. Oxford: Oxford University Press.

Tedlock, Dennis, trans. 1985. *Popul Vuh: The Mayan Book of the Dawn of Life.* New York: Simon and Schuster, Touchstone Books.

Tyler, Hamilton A. 1964. *Pueblo Gods and Myths.* Norman: University of Oklahoma Press.

Ugvwiyuhi. 1977. *Journey to Sunrise: Myths and Legends of the Cherokee.* Claremore, Oklahoma: Egi Press (P.O. 1397, Claremore, Oklahoma 74017).

Vecsey, Christopher. 1988. *Imagine Ourselves Richly: Mythic Narratives of North American Indians.* New York: Crossroad Publishing Company.

Walker, James R. 1983. *Lakota Myth.* Edited by Elaine Jahner. Lincoln: University of Nebraska Press.

Waters, Frank. 1963. *The Book of the Hopi.* New York: Ballantine Books.

Wyman, Leland C. 1970. *Blessingway.* Tucson: University of Arizona Press.

Zolbrod, Paul G. 1984. *Diné Bahané: The Navajo Creation Story.* Albuquerque: University of New Mexico Press.